NATURAL RESOURCE MANAGEMENT

Volume 6

The Rural Economy and the British Countryside

T0347528

Full list of titles in the set
Natural Resource Management

The Rural Economy and the British Countryside

Edited by Paul Allanson and Martin Whitby

from Routledge

THE RURAL ECONOMY
AND THE BRITISH COUNTRYSIDE

THE
RURAL ECONOMY
AND THE BRITISH
COUNTRYSIDE

Edited by

Paul Allanson and Martin Whitby

from Routledge

First published by Earthscan in the UK and USA in 1996

This edition published 2013 by Earthscan

For a full list of publications please contact:
Earthscan
2 Park Square, Milton Park, Abingdon, Oxfordshire OX14 4RN
Simultaneously published in the USA and Canada by Earthscan
711 Third Avenue, New York, NY 10017

First issued in paperback 2014

Earthscan is an imprint of the Taylor & Francis Group, an informa business

A catalogue record for this book is available from the British Library

ISBN: 978-1-85383-366-3 (hbk)
ISBN: 978-0-415-85045-2 (pbk)

Typesetting and page design by BookEns Ltd, Royston, Herts.

Cover design by Andrew Corbett
Cover photograph courtesy of Mary Whitby

Contents

Contributors

Paul Allanson
Lecturer in Economics at the University of Dundee. Former Lord Richard Percy Research Fellow in the Centre for Rural Economy, Newcastle (1993 to 1995).

Guy Garrod
Senior Research Associate in the Environmental Appraisal Research Group, Department of Town and Country Planning, Newcastle upon Tyne; and formerly a Research Associate in the Centre for Rural Economy, Newcastle.

David Harvey
Head of the Agricultural Economics and Food Marketing Department, University of Newcastle upon Tyne since 1992 and also an Associate Director of the Centre for Rural Economy, Newcastle.

Sharron Kuzniesof
Research Associate in the Department of Agricultural Economics and Food Marketing, University of Newcastle upon Tyne.

Philip Lowe
Director of the Centre for Rural Economy, Newcastle, since its inception in 1992. Formerly Reader in Environmental Planning at University College London.

Jonathan Murdoch
Lecturer in Sociology, Department of Town and Country Planning, the University of Wales at Cardiff. Former Runciman Research Fellow in the Centre for Rural Economy, Newcastle (1992 to 1995).

Christopher Ray
Research Associate in the Centre for Rural Economy, Newcastle, on an EU project on the effects of stewardship policies.

Christopher Ritson
Professor of Agricultural Marketing and Dean of the Faculty of Agriculture and Biological Sciences at the University of Newcastle upon Tyne.

Neil Ward
Lecturer in the Department of Geography at the University of Newcastle upon Tyne, formerly a Research Associate in the Centre for Rural Economy, Newcastle.

Martin Whitby
Associate Director of the Centre for Rural Economy, Newcastle, and Professor of Countryside Management at the University of Newcastle upon Tyne since 1992.

Ben White
Lecturer in the Agricultural Economics and Food Marketing Department of the University of Newcastle upon Tyne.

List of Figures

List of Tables

Preface

In the late 1980s there was a resurgence of interest in the changing countryside and rural economy. This led the Economic and Social Research Council (ESRC) to launch a four-year research initiative on Countryside Change. After intense competition two teams were selected to undertake this research: one based at Newcastle, focusing on the application of economic analysis to countryside issues; and the other in London, where the emphasis was on the sociology and political science of rural change.

Further research was also commissioned jointly between the ESRC, the Natural Environment Research Council (NERC) and the Agricultural and Food Research Council (AFRC), establishing a series of programmes, many combining natural and social sciences. The Joint Agricultural and Environment Research Programme (JAEP) supported several projects in a number of centres whilst another, the NERC/ESRC Land Use Programme, was established at the University of Newcastle upon Tyne and ran for several years, successfully developing multidisciplinary land use models of the Tyne and other catchments.

The result of this flow of research funding has been reported in many academic journals, working papers and books emanating from individuals and teams. So far, few of them have attempted to produce an overview of the state of the countryside and the rural economy, incorporating more than one disciplinary perspective. Such an attempt would be avoided by most academics who advance their careers on the basis of the esteem of their disciplinary peers. However, the work reported is funded by the public who are entitled to expect some feedback in an accessible form to account for the funds applied and justify the expenditure.

It was in that spirit that this volume was put together. The material has been assembled within the Centre for Rural Economy (CRE) which was set up within the Department of Agricultural Economics and Food

Marketing at Newcastle in 1992 with staff from both the London and the Newcastle Countryside Change Centres. The list of contributors, though, includes participants from all of the major funded research programmes mentioned above. The resulting volume therefore reflects and draws on a uniquely productive period in British rural research, which, like the CRE, is multidisciplinary in focus and attempts to reach a broad readership.

The editing of this volume has benefited immensely from the patience and support of many colleagues, not all of whom appear in the list of contributors. We have also relied on the valuable skills of Eileen Curry in putting together the consolidated bibliography and of Richard Hill and Julia Curry in assisting with the editorial work. The remaining participant in this exercise is, of course, the reader who we hope will find the result stimulating.

Paul Allanson and Martin Whitby
June 1996

List of Acronyms and Abbreviations

ADAS	Agricultural Development and Advisory Service
AFRC	Agricultural and Food Research Council
AONB	Area of Outstanding Natural Beauty
ARC	Agricultural Research Council
CAP	Common Agricultural Policy
CARE	conservation, amenity and rural environment (goods)
CART	conservation, amenity and recreation trust
CBA	cost-benefit analysis
CEC	Commission of European Communities
CPRE	Council for the Protection of Rural England
CRE	Centre for Rural Economy (Newcastle)
CVM	contingent valuation method
DoE	Department of the Environment
EC	European Community (now the European Union)
ESA	Environmentally Sensitive Area
ESRC	Economic and Social Research Council
EU	European Union
HPM	hedonic price method
ICM	integrated crop management
IFS	integrated farming systems
JAEP	Joint Agricultural and Environment Research Programme
LEADER	Liaisons Entre Actions de Developpement de l'Economie Rurale
LEAF	Linking Environment and Farming
LIFE	Less Intensive Farming and Environment
MAFF	Ministry of Agriculture, Fisheries and Food
MMB	Milk Marketing Board

NAAS	National Agricultural Advisory Service
NERC	Natural Environment Research Council
NRA	National Rivers Authority
NSA	Nitrate Sensitive Areas
SSSI	Site of Special Scientific Interest
PDO	Potentially Damaging Operation
PDR	processing, distribution and retailing
PPG7	Planning and Policy Guidance (Note) 7 (DoE)
R&D	research and development
RDA	Rural Development Areas
RDC	Rural Development Commission
SPARC	South-West Pembrokeshire Action with Rural Communities
TEV	total economic value
TCM	travel-cost method
WTP	willingness to pay

Prologue: Rural Policy and the British Countryside

Paul Allanson and Martin Whitby

The countryside evokes popular images of rural idyll. However, this romantic vision no longer provides an accurate picture of the state of rural areas, if indeed it ever did. For rural Britain has always been subject to change – from the prehistoric clearances of the native woodlands, through the parliamentary enclosures to the introduction of modern agricultural practices in this century. But the changes of the post-war years have been perhaps the most far reaching of our history in terms of their nature and scale. The declining importance of farming as a source of income and employment in recent years has undermined the simple equation between the rural economy and the agricultural sector. The social composition of many villages has been transformed by incomers who commute to nearby towns and cities for their work. And European Union (EU) policy is playing an increasingly important role in both the regulation of the countryside, through environmental and other directives, and the promotion of rural development through structural assistance and other programmes.

This introduction takes preliminary stock of the changing nature of rural Britain by examining the broad pattern of development in the countryside since the Second World War in the light of the growing recognition that the post-war policy framework with regard to rural areas is no longer sustainable in its own terms or appropriate to emerging realities (see Newby, 1991). The account is framed historically by two government statements, produced more than 50 years apart, on the future of the countryside. First, the Scott Report (Ministry of Works and Planning, 1942), written during the war, provided a vision of the countryside that informed much of the post-war legislation on agriculture, town and country planning, countryside recreation and nature conservation, and thereby shaped the post-war evolution of rural areas. Secondly, the recent set of White Papers on rural England (Department of the Environment/Ministry of Agriculture, Fisheries and Food (DoE/MAFF), 1995), Wales (Welsh Office, 1996) and Scotland (Scottish Office, 1995) look to draw together a diverse range of policy strands into integrated rural policies informed by a commitment to sustainable development. The introduction closes with an overview of the structure and content of the remainder of the book.

THE POST-WAR POLICY FRAMEWORK

The philosophy and objectives which have guided public policy with regard to rural areas since the Second World War were laid out in their essentials by the official Committee on Land Utilisation in Rural Areas, appointed in October 1941 under the chairmanship of Lord Justice Scott. The fundamental thesis of the Scott Report (Ministry of Works and Planning, 1942) was that a prosperous farming industry would preserve both the rural landscape and rural communities. The major threat to rural areas, apart from government neglect, was seen to arise from building and industrial pressures which, it was argued, threatened to mar the countryside, take land out of farming and entice labour away from agriculture. The report was optimistic that, if these pressures could be resisted, farm incomes boosted and modern services provided in villages, then the amenities of the countryside would be preserved for the nation and traditional rural life revived.

These assumptions were embedded in the three fundamental legislative acts which established the post-war public policy framework for rural areas: the Agriculture Act of 1947, the Town and Country Planning Act of 1947 and the National Parks and Access to the Countryside Act of 1949. The first of these, with its overriding concern with food production, sought to maintain the predominance of agriculture in the countryside; the second, with its paramount concern for urban containment, sought to protect agricultural land from encroachment; and the third, with its vision of the countryside as the heritage of the whole nation, sought to ensure both landscape and nature conservation, and recreational access. However, the consequences of this legislative framework were to have profound and largely unanticipated social, economic and environmental impacts.

The Scott Report assumed that with the benefit of state support there would be 'a continuance of the essentially mixed and varied but inter-related character of British farming' (p 46). Future changes would be:

> of the nature of simplification of farm boundaries, field shapes and sizes, of gradual reorganisation according to the needs of increasing mechanisation or of improved methods of husbandry or in response to changing demands, rather than a complete change to entirely new types of farming. (p 46).

The report thus significantly underestimated the extent of what Mingay (1990) describes as the only true 'agricultural revolution' in British history, marked by the contemporaneous processes of farm rationalisation, mechanisation, intensification and specialisation promoted by agricultural policies. Accordingly, the commitment made in the Agriculture Act of 1947 to a:

> stable and efficient [agricultural] industry capable of producing such part of the nation's food and other agricultural produce as in the national interest it is desirable to produce in the United Kingdom

has not led to the preservation of the countryside and the maintenance of rural communities in the manner envisaged.

On the one hand, the assumption that farming stewardship of the land would ensure the preservation of rural amenities has been compromised as agricultural modernisation has placed increasing pressure on the environment. The Scott Report considered the beauty and pattern of the countryside to be the direct result of the cultivation of the soil and thus foresaw no antagonism between use and beauty. In keeping with this view, agricultural operations and uses were specifically excluded from development controls in the Town and Country Planning Act of 1947 and, even in the National Parks where conservation and public access were intended to be priorities, restrictions on farming were minimal. However, the environmental impact of the specialisation and intensification of farming practices has been far from benign.

First, the traditional pattern of mixed farming has been largely superseded, with increasing specialisation both within individual farm businesses and between regions. Land-use specialisation has led to the concentration of cash cropping on the best farmland in the lowlands and of permanent pasture elsewhere, and to the polarisation of regional cropping patterns between the predominantly arable South and East and the largely pastoral North and West (Allanson and Moxey, 1996). Examination of the effects of these changes on lowland landscapes (Westmacott and Worthington, 1984) found the erosion of local character in seven study areas due to the disappearance of features such as hedgerows and farmland trees, and the erection of non-traditional farm buildings. Over the period 1947 to 1983, estimated losses of hedgerows ranged between 10 and 60 per cent, and of farmland trees between 35 and 90 per cent. More recent evidence provided by the Countryside Surveys of 1984 and 1990 and the Hedgerow Survey of 1993 indicate the continuing loss of these countryside features (see Department of the Environment (DoE), 1996).

The post-war development of agriculture has also been associated with the conversion of land from semi-natural habitats into intensive agricultural use, with the 'improvement' of species-rich hay meadows, drainage of grazing marshes and other wetland areas, and the ploughing of moorland fringes. Between 1947 and 1980, approximately 50 per cent of unimproved grassland, 75 per cent of lowland semi-natural vegetation and 20 per cent of upland semi-natural vegetation in England and Wales was converted into either crop and grass production or woodland (see Whitby, 1991). These losses have threatened the character and beauty of the relatively wild landscapes found particularly in National Parks and Areas of Outstanding Natural Beauty (AONBs). The resultant loss of habitats has also endangered the success of nature conservation policies as the integrity of many protected sites depends upon the biodiversity of the wider countryside rather than just of the land designated as being of particular importance for wildlife (Adams, 1996).

Finally, the intensification of agricultural production has raised a number of issues of environmental pollution, human health and animal welfare. In particular, the increasing adoption and use of fertilisers and other agrochemicals has been associated with the eutrophication of watercourses, damage to ecosystems and the contamination of drinking water and foodstuffs. The intensification of livestock production has also led to: pollution incidents as a result of discharges of slurry and silage effluent; a number of food safety 'scares', of which bovine spongiform encephalopathy (BSE or 'mad cow disease') in cattle has been the most serious; concerns about the welfare of farm animals, such as battery hens and veal calves; and protests about the transport of live animals. More generally, the sustainability of current agricultural practices has been called into question by the increasing demands placed on the environment.

On the other hand, the simple equation between agricultural and rural communities has been undermined by the continuing decline in the agricultural workforce (Table 0.1). In the post-war period, this fall is primarily associated with capital investment in machinery to substitute for labour in many traditional farming tasks, encouraged by the stability and prosperity afforded by agricultural support policies and facilitated by the rationalisation of farm structures to enable exploitation of the resultant economies of scale in production. Between the population censuses of 1951 and 1991, the size of the agricultural workforce in England and Wales declined from 920,000 to 380,000 or from 4.6 to 1.8 per cent of the total workforce, with the number of farmers falling from 327,000 to 178,000 as farm growth led to an increase in mean size from 43 to 66 hectares (Allanson, 1992).

However, the drift from the land has not led to further overall decline in the rural population (Table 0.2), as was the case before the war, but rather to changes in the social and occupational composition of many rural areas (Newby, 1979). In this transformation the planning system has played an important role by effectively constraining the extent of non-agricultural development in rural areas and by channelling such development as was permitted into selected and concentrated locations. Thus, as labour was shed from agriculture, there were limited alternative employment opportunities for the rural working class to prevent further out-migration and community disintegration. Yet, the decline in the farming population was more than matched, particularly in the areas surrounding major cities, by the movement of middle-class commuters, retirees and owners of second homes into the countryside. Counter-urbanisation has been the dominant geographical trend in Great Britain since the 1960s with the dispersal of both population and economic activity leading to

Table 0.1 Agricultural employment in England and Wales, 1851–1991

Year	Number of farmers[a] (thousands)	Agricultural workforce (thousands)	Total workforce (thousands)	Percentage of workforce in agriculture
1851	249	1,725	8,065	21.4
1871	250	1,462	10,219	14.3
1891	224	1,225	12,899	9.5
1911	229	1,211	16,284	7.4
1931	248	1,026	18,853	5.4
1951	327	921	19,940	4.6
1961	306	697	21,122	3.3
1971	234	521	21,565	2.4
1981	206	425	20,810	2.0
1991	178	379	21,378	1.8

[a] Farmers includes horticulturists from 1951 onwards
Sources: Taylor (1955), Bellerby (1958) and Office of Population Censuses and Surveys

Table 0.2 Trends in the rural population of England and Wales, 1851–1991

Year	Total population (thousands)	Population in rural districts (thousands)	%	Population in 'remoter mainly rural districts' (thousands)	%
1851	17,928	8,928	49.8	–	–
1871	22,712	8,676	38.2	–	–
1891	29,003	8,121	28.0	–	–
1911	36,070	7,899	21.9	–	–
1931	39,952	7,990	20.0	–	–
1951	43,758	8,193	18.7	–	–
1961	46,105	8,954	19.4	4,142	9.0
1971	48,750	10,568	21.7	4,545	9.3
1981	49,017	11,320	23.1	5,013	10.2
1991	48,969	–	–	5,422	11.1

Sources: Saville (1957, p 62) and Office of Population Censuses and Surveys

growth rates in rural areas consistently above the national average (see Champion, 1994).

The net effect of these changes has been to leave a rural population which is less rooted in the countryside, increasingly free of farming as a source of either income or employment. However the pattern of migration has not been uniform, leading to considerable diversity in the economic and social complexion of rural localities (Marsden et al, 1993). Thus, throughout most of Southern England, the middle classes are now dominant and have enshrined anti-development objectives into local planning. In other parts of the countryside, for example in the West of England and Wales, which lie outside the main commuter catchments and which may be of no particular scenic merit, developmental interests are often politically influential, and development proposals typically provoke less opposition, especially if they avoid middle-class enclaves. Finally, in areas such as the North of England and parts of Scotland, the rural economy remains dominated by large landowners who are relatively unhindered by middle-class preservationism. These landowners can often act with considerable autonomy in initiating and achieving (agricultural and non-agricultural) development projects.

Furthermore, at a sub-regional level, change has been spatially moulded by the inherited settlement pattern which the planning system has been dedicated to retain (Cloke, 1983). In so doing, policies have been pursued to concentrate residential and other forms of development in order to protect agricultural land, to preserve selected villages, to economise in the provision of public services and to underpin the viability of employment and service centres. Thus the concept of a hierarchical settlement pattern containing 'natural' service centres and hinterland rural areas, became instilled in British rural settlement planning. Villages and towns were differentiated between those where development was to be restricted and those where it was to be encouraged. In this way, distinct development trajectories for different rural places became enshrined within development plans.

Those places which were earmarked for preservation and tight restrictions on growth became increasingly attractive to members of the middle class, while the poorer members of rural society were forced to gravitate towards those settlements where public housing and services were provided. Moreover, the operation of the planning system has in turn served to reinforce the selective effect of people's private means, as those who had settled in the countryside sought to use the preservationist procedures of the planning system to safeguard their own residential amenity. Conversely, less affluent and deprived groups in the countryside did not compete in the struggle over development (Blowers, 1980; Cloke, 1983) and thus received less and less benefit from the planning process as employment opportunities were constrained, the supply of affordable housing restricted, and other local services and amenities withdrawn.

In summary, the post-war policy framework has ensured that agriculture remains the dominant land use, if no longer the major economic activity, in rural areas. The traditional pattern of mixed farming has been superseded by the spread of modern agricultural production techniques leading to the degradation of landscapes and natural habitats. Concurrently, the traditional village community which the Scott Report sought to preserve has been submerged by an incoming population which is not dependent on farming as a source of either income or employment, but places increasing demands on the countryside for conservation, amenity and recreation. Finally, the very success of agricultural policy in creating the conditions for the modernisation of agriculture has brought its own problems in terms of the increasing economic costs of supporting the resultant levels of agricultural production.

THE EVOLUTION OF POLICY

The broad framework of rural policy has remained largely unchanged since the war, though specific policies have undergone considerable modification. As such, the process of policy change has been incremental, with the evolution of individual policies characterised as much by a series of piecemeal reactions to immediate pressures as by a considered response to longer-term developments in the rural economy and environment. In particular, agricultural policies, the main mechanism to deliver benefits to rural areas, have been subject to successive changes as a result of recurrent budgetary crises stemming from the rising level of agricultural production induced by high support prices. Even so, a growing recognition that the post-war assumptions, philosophy and objectives of public policy for rural areas are no longer either sustainable in their own terms or appropriate to emerging realities, is increasingly apparent in more recent policy initiatives.

Pressures for the reform of agricultural policy became evident within a decade of the Agriculture Act of 1947 which set up a system of deficiency payments to bridge the gap between guaranteed farm prices and world prices for selected agricultural commodities. The open-ended nature of this commitment was soon exposed by the expansion of domestic production and the liberalisation of world commodity markets, which resulted in both the escalation of and fluctuations in the budgetary costs of agricultural policy. There followed various attempts to contain government expenditures through the imposition of guaranteed quantities and the introduction of minimum import prices and quotas for certain products, before the UK joined the European Community (EC) in 1973 and thereby entered into the Common Agricultural Policy (CAP).

The basic CAP commodity regime at the time consisted of an intervention system to provide internal price support and a combination of variable import levies and export subsidies to provide external protection. However, the seemingly inexorable growth of farm output has over time forced a succession of reforms to contain the resultant budgetary crises and external relations problems. For example, milk quotas were imposed in 1984, price restraint was institutionalised through the stabiliser mechanism in 1988 and, most recently, direct payments were introduced on a limited area/headage basis in the MacSharry reform package of 1992.

But the sense of continuing crisis has also led to a growing recognition that the CAP is not sustainable even on its own terms, prompting moves to recast agricultural policy in terms of broader environmental and rural development goals (see for example, Commission of the European Communities (CEC), 1985, 1991). The motivation behind this shift in emphasis is open to question and there is certainly some inconsistency (if not downright incoherence) in the fact that agricultural support policies which promote further agricultural rationalisation and intensification are still being pursued at the same time as measures have been introduced to preserve the social and environmental fabric of rural areas. Nevertheless, the reorientation does represent the first steps to align agricultural policy within a broader rural economy agenda.

First, in terms of the rural environment, agricultural policy has increasingly sought to pay farmers for managing the countryside rather than for the production of agricultural commodities per se. The original vehicle for this agri-environment policy was Regulation 797/85 of 1985 on farm structures, Article 19 of which authorised member states to introduce 'special national schemes in environmentally sensitive areas' where the continuation of the use of traditional farming methods would protect rare ecosystems. This was an essentially British concept, arising out of a long tradition of designation of areas for particular policy purposes. The new Environmentally Sensitive Area (ESA) designation was incorporated in British legislation in the Agriculture Act of 1986 (which also assigned to the Ministry of Agriculture, Fisheries and Food the obligation to have regard for the environment in pursuing its policies). Although hailed at the time as a cynical recognition of the environment (Bowers, 1991), this move could also be seen as a (too rare) genuine and positive contribution to European policy-making from Britain.

Partly because they particularly suited British policy experience, particularly in regard to the designation of areas of land for policy purposes, ESAs have been taken up with enthusiasm in Britain (Whitby, 1994; 1996). At the time of writing (early 1996) there are some 10,000 ESA agreements operating in Britain and they are the single most numerous form of management agreement which farmers may make with the government. The second most popular in terms of numbers is the Countryside Stewardship Scheme with 5000 agreements in England, developed initially by the Countryside Commission and recently taken over by the Ministry of Agriculture, Fisheries and Food (MAFF), which is also supported with EU funding under the same regulation. These are the two main instruments of agri-environment policy, though there are also a number of other payment, grant and tax relief schemes which offer economic incentives to farmers to manage their land in ways which deliver environmental benefits (Whitby and Ray, 1996).

Countryside Stewardship and ESAs both offer agreements with comparatively few strings attached and no sanctions available to the government if they are refused by farmers. This voluntary approach differs from earlier legislation which does incorporate the possibility of compulsion and thereby reassigns the rights of property owners by constraining their use of land in particular circumstances. The most sweeping such constraint was introduced in the Town and Country

Planning Act of 1947 which required landowners to obtain permission to develop their land without any general entitlement to compensation for the loss of development rights if permission was refused. A much smaller change was introduced in the Wildlife and Countryside Act of 1981 whereby those farming within Sites of Special Scientific Interest (SSSIs) may not undertake specified Potentially Damaging Operations (PDOs) without prior notification and those subsequently dissuaded from carrying them out may be compensated through an individually negotiated management agreement. Mechanisms of compulsion, such as compulsory purchase, access and conservation orders, also exist and, although rarely used, may form an important part of the armoury of officials engaged in negotiations to limit environmental damage.

Second, in terms of rural development, the principal policy theme to emerge during the 1980s has been that of diversification. This applies at the farm level, where it refers to the extent to which farm families are dependent on traditional agricultural enterprises for their livelihood, and at the sub-regional level, with reference to the extent that the rural economy is dependent on one or more traditional industries.

At the farm level, pluriactivity (multiple job-holding) is a phenomenon of long standing and has provided the means for the establishment and social reproduction of many farms, as well as keeping them going as businesses through times of agricultural recession. The introduction of the Farm Diversification Grants Scheme by MAFF in 1988 lent official support to this process in spite of the inequity of farmers being given assistance to enter non-agricultural business activities, for which other individuals within society would not receive similar support. Diversification has proved a popular strategy with farmers and a national survey by McInerny and Turner (1991) shows that a substantial proportion of farms undertake some form of diversified activity, with contracting and tourism being the two most favoured activities. However, the dominant trend on part-time farms is for farmers and other farm family members to take paid employment off the farm, in occupations unrelated to agriculture, which then constitute the main source of income (see Gasson, 1988). The general promotion of rural employment opportunities may therefore prove a more appropriate policy goal than farm diversification per se.

At a sub-regional level, economic diversification has also emerged as an important objective of public policy with regard to rural areas. One aim of rural diversification is to open up wider and more varied employment opportunities for local people, but the overall impact of rural development policies may also be enhanced when new economic activities use locally produced inputs or sell to other businesses in the area. Such multiplier effects tend to be small in rural areas (see Rayment, 1995) given that the size of multipliers tends to be larger the more diverse the economy, and diversity typically increases with the size of the economy. Even so, appropriate diversification may offer the prospect of increased policy benefits in terms of the additional impact on employment, income and output of a given cash injection into a rural economy.

In England, the Rural Development Commission (RDC) has a principal goal of diversifying and strengthening the rural economy in priority Rural Development Areas which currently cover some 35 per cent of the country. Within the constraints of a very limited budget (less than £40m in 1993/94), the RDC has sought to promote development in these areas through a number of instruments including the provision of workspace for rent, the subsidised conversion of redundant farm buildings to other uses and, more recently, the Rural Challenge programme. In Wales and Scotland, the Welsh Development Agencies and Scottish Enterprise respectively have the primary responsibility for the (national) promotion of economic development, with the particular problems of remote regions addressed by the Development Board for Rural Wales and Highland and Islands Enterprise. The programmes pursued by these agencies concentrated initially on the promotion of employment, especially through the provision of factory space for rent, but now encompass a broader range of services supporting rural development.

The planning system has also been brought to bear directly on problems of rural development with the publication of Planning and Policy Guidance Note 7 (DoE, 1988; 1992a). Elson et al. (1995) record that PPG7 was informed by a range of rural concerns including: the loss of jobs from agriculture, declining rural accessibility and the erosion of service provision in rural areas, the quest for alternative enterprises by farmers, growth in the size of the rural-based population and increasing development pressures on the countryside. PPG7 argues in favour of the economic diversification of rural areas in order to adjust to such changes, but recognises that a balance must be struck between conservation and development. Thus redundant agricultural buildings are seen to provide an opportunity for re-development but controls over new development in the open countryside are retained, with particular application in the National Parks and AONBs which, together with green belts, cover about 40 per cent of rural England and Wales.

In addition to these national policies, the EU has provided rural development assistance through Objective 1 and Objective 5b of the European Structural Funds since 1989. In particular, Objective 5b applies to designated rural areas with below average levels of economic development, high levels of dependence on agricultural employment and low levels of agricultural income, though problems of peripherality, depopulation and vulnerability to CAP reform may also be taken into account. EU funding is provided to support up to 50 per cent of the costs of projects within an agreed five-year integrated development programme to reduce the weakness of the rural economy of the area, and looks set to become increasingly important within a British context following the extension of the areas eligible for support in 1993 (with £415m available between 1994 and 1999 in England and Wales alone).

THE WAY AHEAD

The post-war philosophy and objectives of public policy with regard to rural areas have become increasingly untenable, leading the Government to reconsider the future development of rural areas in a recent set of White Papers on Rural England (DoE/MAFF, 1995), Wales (Welsh Office, 1996) and Scotland (Scottish Office, 1995). Thus, the White Paper on Rural England, jointly produced by DoE and MAFF, seeks to provide a new rural policy framework informed by a commitment to sustainable development. This is taken to imply:

> meeting the economic and social needs of the people who live and work in rural areas ... [while] conserving the character of the countryside – its landscape, wildlife, agricultural, recreational and natural resource value – for the benefit of present and future generations. (pp 9–10).

Moreover, within this overall objective, the twin goals of an attractive rural environment and a healthy rural economy are seen to reinforce each other.

The concerns of the 1995 White Paper are thus similar to those of the Scott Report, published some fifty years before, but the previous emphasis on the prosperity of farming is replaced by a broader perception of the vitality of the rural economy, society and environment. Economic diversification is welcomed as a means of strengthening the economic base of rural areas and making rural jobs less vulnerable to structural economic change. 'Active', 'living' communities are encouraged which have 'a reasonable mix of age, income and occupation, and which offer jobs, affordable housing and other opportunities' (p 14). And the rural environment is to be conserved and enhanced 'for the benefit of local people and as a national resource' (p 15).

However, the White Paper does not present an overall strategy to achieve the protection of the character of the countryside and continued rural prosperity, but argues instead that:

> the reality of life in the countryside is that many small scale changes which respect the real differences in local circumstances are what are most likely to succeed. (p 6)

Policies must recognise the economic and social diversity of the countryside and target programmes on areas of greatest need. But the future health of rural England does not lie primarily in the hands of government, since local people are generally best placed to identify their own needs and the best ways to meet them. 'Shared responsibility for the quality of life in the countryside involves a combination of responsive national polices and local discretion' (p 26).

True to this vision, the White Paper claims merely to set the scene for a wider debate about the future of rural England, but that future is increasingly being shaped within a European policy framework. The European basis of the Common Agricultural Policy is apparent, but roughly 80 per cent of environmental legislation is now decided collectively in Brussels and the majority of public funds for rural development are provided through the structural programmes of the European Union (House of Commons Environment Committee, 1996).

The European Commission's approach to rural development is set out in *The Future of Rural Society* (CEC, 1988a). This envisages a shift from a sectoral concept of agricultural policy towards a wider integrated concept of rural development in response to the continuing decline in the importance of the agricultural sector in rural areas and the unavoidable adjustment of farming in Europe to actual circumstances on the markets. However, rural policies must be tailored to the particular economic and social circumstances of specific localities.

The Future of Rural Society recognises this diversity of rural conditions within the European Community and identifies three types of area and the standard problems associated with them:

1 Rural areas, usually near to conurbations (eg South-East England) or coastal regions (eg Southern England), that are suffering from the pressures of modern development such that strengthened protection of the rural environment is a priority.
2 Rural areas in decline (eg much of rural Wales and Scotland but also, perhaps, some of the less populated areas of England granted Objective 5b status in 1993) which would benefit from economic diversification within an integrated rural development programme.
3 Marginal and usually very remote areas (eg parts of the Scottish Highlands and Islands) which are vulnerable to desertification or abandonment in the absence of high and continuing levels of assistance to the existing population.

But *The Future of Rural Society* also argues that this very regional diversity in rural conditions requires action by the Community to ensure economic and social cohesion as called for in the Single European Act of 1985. The impoverishment of rural areas outside the mainstream of national and Community life is not to be tolerated given that roughly half the population of Europe lives and/or works in the countryside. Britain's membership of the European Union thus looks set to ensure the continuation of a more active rural policy in this country than would appear from a reading of the rural White Paper alone.

OUTLINE OF THE BOOK

The remainder of this book is divided into two parts, the first dealing with Rural Resources and the second with broader issues of the Rural Economy. In the first part, Chapter 1, by David Harvey, provides an overview of rural resource issues which considers the way in which the structure of property rights shapes the multiple uses to which land is put. The failure of markets to incorporate environmental values into allocation decisions is identified as the key factor in explaining the threat to the countryside from the intensification of agriculture. The following two chapters then examine these issues in relation to the management of specific resource systems. Chapter 2, by Neil Ward, explores the problem of water pollution which has arisen from the widespread adoption and use of agricultural pesticides and draws conclusions on the requirements for the emergence of sustainable agricultural practices. Chapter 3, by Ben White, examines the conservation and use of heather moorland as a resource for both sheep grazing and grouse shooting, employing bio-economic models to identify the optimal mixture of land uses. Chapter 4, by Guy Garrod, then provides an introduction to the environmental valuation techniques which have been used to put a 'price' on the unmarketed attributes of the countryside. Empirical results from these techniques are presented and an indication given of their possible role in the decision-making process. The final chapter in this part, by Christopher Ritson and Sharron Kuznesof, considers the extent to which the intangible qualities of the countryside might be exploited through the marketing process. Three case studies are used to show how rural food products may earn a premium through appropriate marketing.

The second part of the book deals with broader themes in the rural economy. Chapter 6, by Paul Allanson, seeks to define the nature of the rural economy as a complex, open system and explores the implications of an evolutionary perspective for the design of sustainable rural development policies. Chapter 7, by Jonathan Murdoch, reviews the changing role ascribed to rural areas within the British nation state, and how this has been reflected in agricultural and planning policies which have variously treated the countryside as vital national resource and priceless natural heritage. Chapter 8, by Christopher Ray, considers the concept of community and examines how the European Community's LEADER programme has sought to promote a 'bottom up' rural development strategy in preference to traditional 'top down' approaches. Chapter 9, by Martin Whitby, presents a reconsideration of rural economic policies in terms of the distribution of their benefits rather than their efficiency outcomes, and shows how these distributional effects tend to reinforce existing inequalities in society. Finally, the volume ends with a chapter by Philip Lowe which provides a critique of the recent rural White Papers and presents a blueprint for the design of future rural policies.

PART I

Rural Resources

CHAPTER 1

The Role of Markets in the Rural Economy

David Harvey

INTRODUCTION

Adam Smith's 'Invisible Hand' and subsequent theories stemming from this proposition suggest that, under certain rather specific and possibly unrealistic conditions, the freely competitive marketplace can achieve an economically efficient allocation of resources – the so-called 'social optimum'. This theoretical case for the market economy is often linked with socio-political and philosophical theories supporting libertarianism and the freedom of the individual. When and how might the market fail the rural economy?

This chapter focuses on the role played by markets and market mechanisms in sustainable policies for the rural economy. The principal illustrations are drawn from agricultural and environmental policies. The chapter begins with an abbreviated sketch of the market mechanism's effects on the development of the rural economy. The second section illustrates the primary importance of property rights. Thirdly, the story is advanced by concentrating on the conflicts which arise over the use of the countryside – the key feature distinguishing rural from urban areas. This examination lays the groundwork for a consideration of the nature and role of government within the market paradigm. The final section of the chapter draws out the major implications for the future development of rural economies and sustainable use of rural environments.

THE MARKET MECHANISM AND THE RURAL ECONOMY

Economic development tends to become centred on urban areas, attracting people and wealth (capital) and leading to further development – encouraged by early economies of scale in the provision of services (both public and private) in the form of schools, shops, entertainment, banks, post offices, etc. Denser populations make the initial provision of these cheaper, and they are thus encouraged. Typically, these urban centres are at natural transportation nodes, in the lowlands, close to rivers or the coast, and often on Grade 1 farming land. 'Modern' growth and economic development thus appears naturally centred on urban rather than rural areas.[1]

The development process also involves a reduction in the time and effort devoted to food and shelter. This leads to a relative, though not necessarily absolute, decline in agriculture, and thus to the economic activity which surrounds agriculture, often located in rural areas. However, development also leads to an increasing demand for food off the farm so that the development process leads to the commercialisation of farming and a growth in its interactions with the wider economy through both the input supply industries ('upstream') and the food-processing, distribution and retailing sectors ('PDR' or 'downstream').

Furthermore, as incomes grow, a smaller share of total income is spent on raw food products, and more is spent on other things. The inevitable result of economic growth is that fewer people can earn a full-time living from agriculture. People are encouraged to leave farming for other occupations, typically located in urban areas. However, expansion of population and industrial growth creates a strong demand for food (and much motive power) from the farm sector, which has to compete with the urban and industrial sectors for both labour and capital. This competition helps maintain returns to both labour and capital on the farm (and thus in rural areas) relative to those in the rest of the economy.

When national economic development is coupled with both technological change and an open international trading policy, as has been the case in the UK, the domestic farm sector becomes subject to global competition. The industry declines, well exemplified by the great agricultural depression of the last part of the last century, mirrored in the decline of rural areas and their economies. By 1911, 80 per cent of the British lived in towns. The farm labour force (especially of women) had been declining since the 1850s, and the early contribution of the rural industrial and commercial sectors had given way to the concentration of both population, commerce and industry in predominantly urban areas (see, for example, Mingay, 1987, chapter 1). This tendency has been reinforced by technological development which has historically substituted capital (plant, machinery and purchased inputs) for labour and land – more agricultural inputs come from the urban, commercial and industrial areas of the country, and thus more spending on food returns to the urban areas rather than staying in the countryside.

Rural areas have thus been subject to a net out-migration as the development process occurs, and have become more sparsely populated. Those rural dwellers with prospects (and command of higher salaries and wages because of their skills) leave the countryside and migrate to the towns. Consequent increases in costs of providing services for the remaining population (leading to closure of village schools and shops, etc) lead to the emergence of the rural 'transport poor' problem, exacerbated by market incentives tending to attract the more able and better-skilled away from the countryside.

Subsequent wealth accumulation in the cities, however, leads (at least in Britain) to capital flows back to the countryside as country estates become stores and signs of wealth, and also playgrounds and gardens for the better-off. But this capital inflow is concentrated in blocks mostly controlled by single individuals and locked up in land and property, rather than in development ventures. Hence the market mechanism leads to middle-class, prosperous, mobile and 'countryside conscious' incomers to the countryside, taking over and protecting their 'positional goods'[2] (houses, estates and rural quality of life) whose values are absolutely dependent on limited numbers of people having access to them.

The appeal of the country retreat depends on it being qualitatively different from the town. Since the market power resides among the wealthy, they can control not only their own (non-) development of the countryside, but also enforce these values on the rest of the rural vicinity. The countryside becomes the playground of the rich and the workhouse of the disadvantaged and resource-poor, who cannot find the opportunity to leave and better themselves, and whose public and private services and amenities are continually reduced. In caricature, rural areas become the land of the feudal (and capitalist) lord and the peasant.[3]

However, market forces do not stop here. As the economic development process proceeds, growth tends to happen in services at the expense of manufacturing. This is accurately reflected in the proportion of incomes spent on services rather than manufactured products. So manufacturing tends to decline and service activity (media, entertainment, food processing, etc) grows in importance.[4]

Continuing technological change, often associated with public spending to improve transport and communication links, brings the countryside closer to the town. The 'comparative advantage' of rural areas begins to change as transport and communication costs fall. Industries and activities are no longer tied to urban areas to be competitive; they can move, though why should they? Part of the answer lies in the 'diseconomies' of towns and conurbations, and consequent desires to move to the countryside, not only to live, but also where possible to work. The attractions of minimum commuting and a greater quality of life leads to reverse migration as people move out of towns and back into the countryside, a trend which has been evident in the population surveys of the UK for some considerable time.

Furthermore, economic development appears to be associated with a growing emphasis on 'footloose' industries (those which do not 'mind' where they are, since they do not depend on raw materials and resources and don't involve major transport problems for either their inputs or their products) and even to specifically rural industries (crafts, tourism, up-market products with a green or craft image). The greater variety of industry and commerce admits more variety in products, (potentially opening niches for smaller companies), all of which experience relative growth potential in a growing modern economy. The countryside now revives as the development process proceeds, but markets are paying more attention to rural areas as a bank of environmental capital, elsewhere termed the 'reservoir of natural resources and values', as playgrounds, gardens and living/working spaces rather than directly as the means of providing a living.

The land of the feudal lord and the peasant has now become a potential battleground between the farmers (representing, also, quarriers and commercial foresters) trying to make a living and the 'incomers' trying to have a life in the countryside – between those trying to live off and those trying to live in the countryside. How do markets resolve this battle?

The short answer is through property rights. There has always been a potential conflict between those who want to live on and those who want to make a living from the same resource (land and the natural environment). In the 'old' days, this was simply solved through the (typically rich) landowner claiming property rights over large areas of land and dictating the use of it towards his/her own ends – highland clearances, access to Kinder Scout, 'model' and landscaped estates and so forth. Once property rights are established,[5] the owners of the property determine how the property will be used, either for consumption or production or a judicious though personal mix of the two. Furthermore, landowners are typically powerful enough to sustain these rights in the face of considerable opposition. Nevertheless, the question of whether this pattern is considered socially just or justified raises the further query about the social sustainability of these rights, and hence raises the possibility of political changes to these rights.

PROPERTY RIGHTS OVER THE USE OF THE COUNTRYSIDE

The Analytical Framework

The focus is clearly on property rights over the natural environment and land use – since these features most clearly identify the distinction between the rural economy and its urban neighbour. This focus highlights the role of agricultural policy, as both a major influence on land use and as the principal vehicle through which governments have sought (to date) to influence the specific dimensions of the rural economy. There are, of course, other government policies which affect rural economies, but these do so through their particular application in rural areas rather than being specifically designed for rural economies (Hill and Young, 1989).

Traill (1988) presents an economic picture of the trade-offs and possible conflicts between various elements of the rural environment by concentrating on the issue of the intensity of land use (Figure 1.1). In

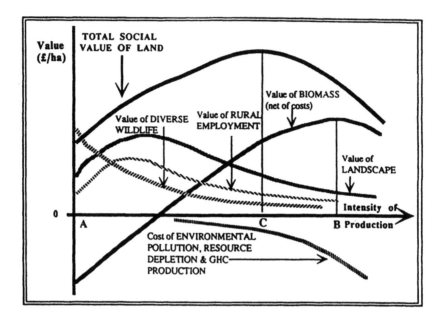

Figure 1.1: Value of land-using activity as intensity of production increases
Source: modified after Traill, 1988

this figure, intensity is measured as quantity of inputs per hectare. The net value of marketable goods from the land base (food, wood, fibre, etc) reaches a peak at point B – the typical private profit-maximising level of intensity. The other curves represent hypothetical relationships between intensity and other more or less intangible aspects of the rural environment, which have been christened Conservation, Amenity, and Rural Environment (CARE) goods (McInerney, 1986). In addition to these CARE goods, a further curve reflects a possible relationship between intensity of land use and rural employment, as one measure of socio-economic concern, here assuming that greater intensity tends to be associated with a shift in employment associated with land use (at least in terms of producing biomass) away from rural areas and towards the industrial and urban areas, or even offshore. In principle, separate curves could be added to represent contributions to reducing greenhouse gases and net costs of depleting non-renewable resources, here included in the general pollution curve.

This representation of the rural environment emphasises three

critical components of analysis of land-use and countryside management. First, it is necessary to understand the socio-economics of land-
use decisions and management practice. From an economist's
perspective, this understanding emphasises responses to market and
policy conditions given peoples' motivations and circumstances.
Second, the physical consequences of particular land-use decisions
and practices for the rural environment need to be identified. The
combination of these two elements provide the definition of the several
curves in Figure 1.1 in physical terms and the likely position on the
horizontal axis chosen by land users. The third element concerns
identification of the social valuations of the several goods and services
provided through the interaction of land use and the rural environment.

Given that these three components can be identified, then it is
possible to conceive a socially optimal intensity of production at point
C, defined as the maximum of the vertical sum of each of the
component valuations. Typically this would imply a reduction in
intensity from present levels, at least in the majority of circumstances in
which the social valuations of the intangible aspects of rural land use
are not reflected to the land users, who thus have no incentive other
than altruism to respect such values in their private decisions. Thus,
although there is a reluctance to 'price' intangible aspects of the rural
environment on the part of non-economists, this representation
emphasises that all public and private land-use decisions imply such
a societal valuation. In turn, this representation casts the debate and
controversy over the rural environment as arguments about the
behaviour of land users, the physical relationships between land use
and the environment and the social values of the various outputs and
consequences (goods and services in economic terms) from the rural
environmental system.

Apart from environmental designations such as Environmentally
Sensitive Areas (ESAs), Sites of Special Scientific Interest (SSSIs),
Nitrate Sensitive Areas (NSAs), National Parks, Areas of Outstanding
Natural Beauty (AONBs) and Stewardship Schemes, and with the
exception of specific pollution controls and regulations, the social value
of wildlife and environmental assets is seldom reflected back to farmers
and land users in the form of incentives or penalties for particular land
use practices. Thus the major relationship determining land use is the
biomass net profit function (curve). Furthermore, notwithstanding the

1992 reforms, the Common Agricultural Policy still supports market prices and producer returns to biomass production, which artificially inflates the biomass net profit curve, tending to shift the actual intensity of use of land substantially to the right of point C (that is, has shifted point B to the right of where it would be in the absence of support and intervention). Strictly speaking, increasing the biomass net profit through farm price support simply shifts the curve upwards. However, the feedback consequences of this increased profitability can also be expected to encourage its shift to the right as well, through encouraging investment in production-increasing technologies.

Thus, the twin focus of sustainable policies from this perspective becomes:

1 get the price of biomass 'right' (without distorting and supporting it as under the CAP, which shifts the biomass curve upwards and to the right);
2 'properly' reflect the public or social values of the CARE goods (including pollution) back to the landowners and users.

Only when this is done can we expect market forces to encourage land users to operate at the socially optimal level of intensity at point C. Notice, however, that even this prescription relies on an assumption that the majority of land users are at least constrained by, if not actually driven by, the need to make normal profits and thus earn an acceptable living from their land, rather than treating their land-use activities as consumption or lifestyle practice.

Three important characteristics of land use are worthy of emphasis in concluding this brief outline of the framework. First, both social valuations and the underlying technical relationships will vary between different regions and locations depending on their circumstances and conditions – no one hectare is identical with the next, if for no other reason than its exact location and spatial relationship with adjacent land. This makes the spatial representation of this framework a critical feature of the analysis and also means that appropriate policy prescriptions are likely to be highly regionally and locationally specific – as already reflected in ESA and NSA policy design and implementation.

Second, responses of land users to both the physical production possibilities and to market incentives and policy signals/constraints are likely to vary depending on individual and social circumstances, and on their motives. Responses to similar market and policy conditions in similar regions are likely to be heterogeneous simply because people do different things for different reasons. Even the economist's assumption that individual behaviour is 'economically rational' – driven by profit/income on the production side and rational choice leading to increased satisfaction on the consumption side – allows for different responses depending on whether land use is seen predominantly as a production or consumption activity. In practice, people are more complex than is conceived of in the economic model, and their responses will be more diverse than is envisaged in a rigorous mathematical application of this framework, though not more diverse than is catered for in the marketplace.

Third, different policy options, technological possibilities and market conditions will encourage different production techniques which will shift and alter these curves. At the same time, changing incomes, prices and preferences (possibly associated with better or more information) among the general population will change social valuations associated with the goods and services. Thus, the picture is but a snapshot, and is subject to substantial and not always very predictable change over time. The dynamics of land-use relationships are deliberately ignored in Figure 1.1, but cannot be forgotten in the use of the framework for the identification of appropriate policies. In practice, the picture which emerges is dramatically heterogeneous and variegated: there is no simple picture or analysis which can be relied upon to provide a 'sustainably' satisfactory answer to the question of whether or not any social system is sufficient.

The Major Implications

This framework has seven important implications for the design of agricultural and environmental policies. First, sustainability in this framework is dependent on social valuations of environmental assets. Any private or public decision to encourage, regulate or compensate for production practices in favour of the environment implies some notional valuation of the environment, at a minimum that the environmental gain is worth at least the foregone production plus any additional effort required to produce the environmental gain. Such decisions involve choices about the allocation of resources (including effort), and these choices imply relative valuations of the outcomes, regardless of whether or not the market mechanism is used. Not only is valuation of environmental assets possible, it is inevitably implicit in any decision as to whether to preserve or conserve such assets.

Second, the importance of social valuations means that public decisions require mechanisms to establish and legitimise these values. Even presupposing that agreement is reached on appropriate physical measures of environmental assets and their quality (Parris, 1994), if these mechanisms are less than transparent (as is typically the case), the political process is likely to be subject to 'interest group capture' and political failure. Both information on revealed social preferences and understanding of environmental issues are thus critical for the development of sensible and sustainable agricultural, trade and environmental policies. That is, in terms of Figure 2.1, the *process* of defining the social values of the wildlife, landscape, pollution and employment aspects of rural land use is critical to the definition of the optimal level of intensity (point C).

Third, however, dependence on social valuations is *not* equivalent to arguing that the only way to approach the socially optimal land-use pattern ('C') is to use the market mechanism. It may be more socially efficient on occasions to make use of direct regulations on land-use practices, or a judicious combination of both approaches. This will depend on a number of factors, the most important being: the certainty about the relationships between intensity and environment; the costs of policing the regulation alternative; the transactions and information costs of the market-based and regulation alternatives; the assignment and enforcement of property rights; ultimately, the capacity of both market and the political systems for 'failure' (see below).

Fourth, *both* the physical/technical relationships between intensity and environmental assets *and* their social valuations are likely to vary substantially between localities and regions (as already noted). Hence appropriate price or regulation signals for the development of 'sustainable' agriculture and land use will vary substantially between localities and regions, notwithstanding the global nature of some environmental concerns. In turn, this variation may well militate against both common European payment/penalty systems and against conventional market mechanisms (price signals) because of the increased transaction and information costs, as opposed to regulations or combinations of regulations and price signals. Subsidiarity, in this case, involves a presumption in favour of local decision and action within national and international frameworks of property rights and compensation mechanisms. Furthermore, wide differences in family and business circumstances, and in motivations and constraints between farms and land users mean that responses to policy and market signals will vary considerably between users even within the same region or locality. Diversity and heterogeneity thus mitigate against central planning, though they may also contribute to environmental sustainability.

Fifth, following this point, attempts to define 'level playing fields' in terms of common definitions of environmentally friendly practices (either within countries or, a fortiori, between them) is also in violation of the very concept of sustainability as advanced here. The 'level playing field' concept does not mean that trading nations (or regions) should have identical environmental conditions or identical social valuations (and hence opportunity costs) of environmental assets, any more than it means that they should have identical costs of land, labour or capital. In fact, it is regional and national differences in these resource endowments, capabilities and social valuations which provide the very basis for economic gains from trade.

Sixth, 'getting prices right' is critical for the development of sustainable systems of resource allocation. If farm product prices are over-valued, then this framework implies that the system cannot be sustainable (either environmentally or socio-economically). The only viable definition of 'appropriate' value of marketable goods from the land-using sector is the 'free-trade' world price. Any other price level requires a direct social valuation of agricultural output which is different from private market valuations, and, as such, requires both that the domestic product be identifiably different from its inter-regional or international competitors and that the social valuation of this difference is demonstrably not manifest in private market valuations of the differentiated products. Differences in the environmental conditions of their production can and should be identified at the point of sale, on which information consumers should be relied upon to take action as they see fit.

A final implication of this analysis is that support of farm (or rural) incomes over and above those provided by a proper reflection of all social valuations of outputs and environmental asset maintenance is unjustified, other than from purely distributional and equity arguments, typically and sensibly handled through social security and general taxation policies. However, having said this, it is important to realise (at least on the superficial evidence of previous policies and political concerns) that distribution issues include an important component of both geographical and sectoral distribution of economic activity. Thus there appears to be a powerful set of constituencies in favour of a more equitable distribution of economic activity between favoured and less favoured areas than would necessarily be achieved through the unhindered operation of market forces. There has also been in the past a clear presumption in favour of a larger agricultural sector than would be the consequence of an unfettered marketplace.

It may be that the last presumption is simply a reflection of the socio-political concern over the security of food supplies. Since this is now of largely historical interest, it is the geographical distribution which is of major concern as far as farm policy is concerned. In this case, conventional economic analysis strongly suggests that policy concerns ought to be about the provision of an adequate infrastructure of communication and transport links, and of a pattern of communal and social services, sufficient to support sustainable local rural economies. In addition, concern ought to be about the economies and dis-economies of different sizes and concentrations of market-based commercial activity.

However, it is plausible that there is a concern over an 'optimal' structure of agriculture – in terms of farm sizes and types in particular regions, both as this contributes to a socially acceptable and desirable landscape as well as the (arguable) contribution to the pattern of rural employment, activity and social structure. Encouragement of such an ill-defined (and possibly undefinable) optimal structure (loosely characterised as the preservation of the 'traditional family farm') may also be an effective force in favour of more or less traditional forms of farm support, even if barely justified on rational or logical grounds.

THE NATURE AND ROLE OF GOVERNMENT IN THE MARKET PLACE

As mentioned at the beginning of this chapter, the economic theory of welfare optimisation stems from Adam Smith, and although variously extended and developed, still provides the foundation for economic policy analysis (Just et al, 1985). In essence, the theory holds that a system of perfectly competitive markets (in which there is freedom of entry and exit in all markets, all actors are price-takers and for whom private costs and benefits are identical with social costs and benefits) is capable of generating a socially optimal allocation of resources to the production of goods and services for the population, such that no one person can be made better off without making at least one other person worse off (the Pareto welfare criterion). While the elementary versions of this theory assume perfect information, more sophisticated developments allow that information can never be perfect and that information-gathering, decision-making and associated risk-taking themselves are resource-using activities, and subject to optimisation within the economic welfare calculus.

In this simple model of the world, there are four major functions for government (see for example, Grant (1975)):

1 *The policeman*: to establish and maintain the legal and judicial framework within which the market will operate, both at the national and the international level, including the important role of establishing and policing property rights. The free market involves a massive number of transactions, each of which can be viewed as a contract between buyer and seller. The efficient working of this system requires that both sides of the market have confidence in the security and probity of these transactions. The costs of ensuring this are typically assumed away in elementary analyses, but are not insignificant, especially in atomistic markets (with a great many individual buyers and/or sellers) characterised by long-term decisions and associated difficulties of uncertainty and risk, such as in the agricultural or housing sectors. Solid and well-policed laws of contract are necessary (but not always sufficient) conditions for the efficient operation of the free market. In short, at the door of every auction room there stands a policeman, and the long arm of the law is necessarily attached to Adam Smith's invisible hand.

2 *The doctor/engineer*: to correct 'market failures' including at least the organisation of the provision of public goods (defence, government itself, etc) and the correction of the free enterprise system for externalities, imperfect competition and monopoly, all of which prevent the free market from attaining the social optimum. The key problems with public goods are: a) that these goods are non-rival in

consumption, meaning that one person's use or consumption of the good (or service) does not deny another person use of that same (unit of) good; and b) that prevention of people (such as non-payers) from consuming or using the good is either impossible or impossibly expensive – the so-called non-exclusion characteristic. In other words, once a public good is supplied to one, it is supplied freely to all, a market condition in which private entrepreneurs cannot survive. Hence the pure free market would not be expected to provide any of these goods.[6]

Externalities (pollution is the traditional example, pretty land-scapes, pleasant housing estates or the converse, dilapidated estates, are others) exhibit a similar problem in that rational market transactions cannot account properly for their production or consumption. They arise as more or less unintended by-products of either consumption or production, and once produced are difficult or impossible to price, often since they have public good characteristics, as in the above examples. However, since they are directly associated with normal market transactions, textbook solutions of adjusting the price of the marketable good through taxes or subsidies can theoretically correct the market signals for these goods.

3 *The pharmacist/mechanic*: to encourage and foster economic effi-ciency, both in static terms – the need for which can be seen as resulting from the public good characteristics of information – and in dynamic terms to assist in adjustment to changing circumstances, which might be associated with externalities of progress and growth and with the public good aspects of technological change. This function can also be seen as operating at both the macro and micro levels in the economy.

4 *The judge*: to redistribute income and wealth in the interests of equity, since welfare optimisation theory takes the initial resource endowment distribution between people as given, while (eg Rawls, 1971) there is every reason to suppose that societies regard equitable (not necessarily equal) distributions of endowments (wealth, income, good and service provision and entitlement, and spatial patterns of economic activity) as desirable.

In addition to these four well-recognised functions of government in a market economy, a fifth function should also be added: *The priest* – as

Table 1.1: Countryside functions and potential for market failure

Function	Rival?	Excludable?	Public good?	Externalities:
Factory floor	√	√	×	P/P; C/P
Private garden	√	√	×	C/C
Real estate	√	√	×	none
Playground	√	√	×	C/C
Museum/art gallery	?	?	?	C/C
Nature reserve	?	√	?	P/C
Wilderness retreat	√	?	?	none
Landscape	×	×	√	C/P; C/C
Option reservoir	×	×	√	C/P; C/C
Existence value	×	×	√	C/P; C/C

P production
C consumption

the guardian of public morals and ethics, requiring additional roles to those envisaged by the clinical calculus of neoclassical economics for the policeman and the judge.

At the risk of gross simplification, but in the interests of systematic analysis, Table 1.1 identifies the principal functions fulfilled by the countryside, and the potential reasons for government intervention associated with each function. The countryside is a multiple-activity, joint-product complex. The question is: if markets worked perfectly, with public goods properly supplied, does the fact that many goods and services of the countryside which are both jointly produced and consumed cause any insurmountable problems for the market mechanism's potential achievement of social optimality? For example: the consumers' regard for the methods of production as well as the quantities and qualities of product; the interactions between agricultural production practices and the provision of wildlife and landscape; the potential consumer regard for other peoples' enjoyment/benefit of the natural environment (both now and in the future); and the potential rival consumption of a non-excludable (or non-excluded) good – crowding of wilderness areas or natural habitats – all constitute *prima facie* examples of externalities which potentially destroy the social optimality of the market. As the obverse of the same argument, it is an economic necessity that those people supplying the various elements of the countryside package receive sufficient income to persuade them to continue supplying the package. 'Unadulterated' market prices may not provide sufficient income.

Even in the event that all goods and services could be provided through the appropriately governed (regulated) marketplace (accounting perfectly for all externalities and jointness through appropriately modified prices using the subsidy/tax adjustments), it may be that it would be less expensive (more efficient) to provide at least some of the countryside attributes through the public sector given the resources necessary to establish, implement and police appropriate policies. In other words, inclusion of the costs of information, decision making, policing and implementation may result in sufficient economies of scale in organisation to make the conventional competitive market inefficient. In this case, public provision/organisation of part of the countryside portfolio of goods/services might be justified on efficiency grounds, requiring at least extensive public regulation if not public operation. These arguments parallel those regarding the efficiency of the Coasian tax/subsidy solution to externalities versus regulation (see, eg, Pearce and Turner, 1990).

Even given all these arguments, there remains the fact that the market system results in a distribution of goods and services amongst consumers on the basis of ability to pay. Although in abstract any objections to this could be overcome through appropriate re-distribution of income and wealth, the difficulties of designing (as opposed to defining) the necessary resource-neutral transfers means that distributional objectives have a legitimate place in determining the question of who should pay for the countryside.

As a final point, the above arguments have been outlined in terms of the Pareto criterion for maximising social welfare.[7] However, other criteria may well provide strong arguments in favour of public provision of some countryside goods.

There is some evidence that the Lindahl/Samuelson negotiation solution to part of the 'public good problem' (non-rival consumption) can be achieved in practice (eg, van den Doel, 1979). This solution involves one person (or group) acting as the contractor for the provision of the good for many, negotiating with the contractor on the amount to be paid for a given quantity of the good. This can be shown to result in a Pareto optimal production/consumption of the non-rival good so long as consumers are willing to reveal their preferences and so long as there is no problem with free-riders – ie the good is more or less excludable. RSPB bird sanctuaries are an example of this solution in practice, where members grant the society the right to negotiate with landowners on their behalf. This idea could be more widespread as argued in Hodge's suggestion for CARTs (Conservation, Amenity and Recreation Trusts – Hodge, 1988).

Such solutions can be regarded as a 'market adaptation' to the potentially damaging behaviour of unrestricted and narrow self-interest. In this sense, to anticipate discussion below, they can be viewed as the 'natural' extension of market forces into the 'political' or collective choice arena. However, there are clearly limits to the countryside attributes which can be provided through such negotiated solutions. Provision of the last three functions of the countryside in Table 1.1 at socially acceptable levels seem likely to require some public or government assistance to voluntary negotiations, contracts or contributions.

Typically, economic policy analysis finds it impossible to reconcile these potential functions of government with the observed character-istics of the policy. Such analysis is limited to providing estimates of the 'social welfare cost' of existing policy compared with the benchmark of an 'unregulated' though policed, well-engineered and maintained healthy economy. It is obliged to conclude that the re-distributive effects of the policy must be the reason for its existence. The apparent fact that many policies actually transfer income and resources from the poor to the rich rather than *vice versa* compounds the embarrassment of neoclassical economics in explaining and understanding farm policy. 'Clearly agricultural support has been neither in the national interest nor justified by widely held perceptions of social justice' (Wilson, 1977) or 'the political system exists to legitimise the protection of vested interests at the expense of unsatisfied or badly expressed and represented interests' (Josling, 1974).

The neoclassical economic model, however, contains within it the seeds of its own destruction. Consider the implications of profit-seeking firms and utility-seeking consumers combined (as theory admits it must be) with a government whose major function is the redistribution of income and wealth. The workings of the competitive market mean that this redistribution, even if entirely resource-neutral, will need to be continuous. Even in the absence of market imperfections and failures, the market model includes a government continually engaged in economic activity, taking and redistributing income.

The existence of such a government provides entrepreneurs, consumers and tax payers with the means to influence their economic environment, including government, to their own ends. Add to this model the evident gains to be made from collective action (especially but not only in the labour market) and the pressures in favour of the maintenance of workable competition are now turned in favour of winning control over the government, as well as over the marketplace.

Consider the effect of high support prices for the products of agriculture (see, for example, Harvey, 1991). More money accrues to the agricultural sector than would otherwise be the case as a result of supported product prices. Increased revenues (with the politically assured prospect of these revenues being sustained in the future) means increased incomes (at first) for those in farming. People who previously did not consider farming returns sufficiently attractive to stay in (or join) the business now re-asses their decisions. More people now seek to earn a living from farming (either directly or through selling farmers more inputs and lending them money). The business of farming is stimulated (this being a point of the support system). But the land base on which this sector is fundamentally based is more or less fixed. The inevitable consequence is that the land is used more intensively, and earns more than without support. Rents and land prices increase, as the opposite side of the coin of increased intensity of production.

Put as simply as possible, wheat at £150/tonne pays for more fertilizers, chemicals, and tractors, equipment and drivers to apply them, than does wheat at £90/tonne. The result is both increased output and an increased intensity of production, as well as greater capital and labour use than would otherwise be the case. Harvey (1990) estimates that the agricultural value of land in England and Wales has been inflated by about 40 per cent as a consequence of the European Union farm support system. This increase in land values, in turn, accounts for some 55 per cent of the total support, implying that the remaining 45 per cent of support is dissipated in increased returns to other owners of fixed factors (labour and capital) associated with farming, including the suppliers of farm inputs and capital equipment.

Farmers' incomes, however, are not necessarily increased by this process. Farmers' demands for more land, labour, capital and other inputs tends to drive these prices up, so net returns (farm incomes) do not increase. The end result of the market system faced with such 'interventionist' policies is that more people earn a full-time living from farming (and thus earn less from doing other things). Meanwhile, the artificial security of the 'controlled' marketplace lends support to increased investment in agriculture, encouraging the pace of capital-intensive technological change, and aggravating farm expansion and land intensification (removal of hedgerows, enlargement of fields, development of monocultures).

Farm policy creates vested interests (including bureaucrats) with clear advantage in continuation of the system. Costs (to both taxpayer and consumer) are more widely distributed and cause less individual pain, so weakening political opposition. There is an inbuilt tendency towards the status quo. MacLaren (1992) discusses this tendency, referring to the concept of a 'conservative social welfare function' under which the political process tends to do as little as possible as late as possible. Thus, in terms of the evolutionary perspective developed in Chapter 6, once a particular policy trajectory has been established (as under the original development of the Common Agricultural Policy), an interaction/feedback system is established which heavily conditions the future development of the policy, potentially transforming 'market-improving' policies into those which frustrate and subvert the more socially desirable aspects of the market mechanism, leading to policy failure. See, for example, Allanson (et al (1994)). Rausser (1982) also explores (from a more conventionally economic base) the notion that socially desirable policies can 'deteriorate' into socially unjustified policies. For an evolutionary perspective on the future development of the CAP, see Harvey (1995).

CONCLUSIONS AND IMPLICATIONS: RECONCILIATION OF MARKET AND STATE

The future represents a genuine watershed for many rural areas – how to protect the good and encourage development without destroying the very attributes which make these regions attractive for development in the first place. The only sustainable resolution to the battle between those seeking to live *off* and those seeking to live *in* the countryside is one which enables us all to live *with* the countryside.

The central message of this chapter is that markets are *not* independent of government – markets assume government is there, market theory has to take account of the fact that governments (at least in democracies) are made of the same people who operate the marketplace – it would be both naive and inconsistent to assume otherwise. In addition, if it is assumed that markets operate to take advantage of profitable opportunities, it should also be assumed that the same people will act in similar ways when arguing for (or against) government policies. Hence political failure comes from market failure and *vice versa*.

The artificial distinction between the state and the (private) market is no longer useful or productive. Civil institutions and procedures including a wide variety of quasi-state and quasi-market systems are already evolving to deal with conflicts and competition for limited resources. From this perspective, politics is the system used to moderate and regulate individualistic behaviour to minimise social ill-fare and maximise social welfare, and can be viewed as a 'marketplace' within which social opinions are discussed, collected and balanced to produce a consensus, coalition or compromise in support of social or public decisions and choices. To divorce this 'market' from the commercial or private market can only be an analytical fiction, whose convenience is now fundamentally obsolete.

The conclusion is that both 'smart markets' (individual action with appropriate recognition and integration of both the limits and effects of individual actions) *and* 'sympathetic states' (collective action which recognises and incorporates the value and power of individual actions) are required for a genuinely sustainable future. The combination might be termed 'smarsets'.[8] The opposite might well be 'mastate': more market mistakes, more political failures, more unbridled selfishness or more mis-guided patronage.

Notes

1 This modern pattern of geographic development did not manifest itself seriously until the major industrial substitution of fossil fuel, especially coal, for wood and associated transition from animal to mechanical power. By 1750, Britain was 'already distinguished by the variety and prosperity of its industries ... but much industrial organisation, including that of some of the most important industries in the country, took a rural form, as it had done for centuries since the sharp distinction between town and country of the high Middle Ages had broken down' (Court, 1967, p 43). Court also

notes (chapter 3) the congruence of substantial changes in industrial organisation (leading to the concentration of previous cottage industries into large-scale factories), new technologies associated with the Industrial Revolution and the rapid decline in forests.

2 Those which attract value not because of their absolute scarcity but because of their 'distributional' scarcity — in that their wide availability and use detracts from their appeal, either through congestion and decline in quality, or through their erosion as indicators of wealth and success.

3 Of course, there are other things going on in rural areas than farming and field sports, and other people living and working there than those in farming and those living in the manor house.

4 Thus, although the decline in manufacturing is frequently decried as indicating economic regression, it is more realistically seen as a natural reflection of consumer demand and economic progress.

5 Typically, this involves a radical re-assignment of rights, resulting in enclosure of village and traditional common land, thus sweeping away the previous socio-economic structures and populations (Dahlman, 1980)

6 A moment's reflection will provide real-life examples which contradict this proposition: public service television in the US for instance, which relies on voluntary subscriptions from those with a social conscience, or the Trinity House lighthouse system. In fact, more sophisticated analysis, attributable to Lindahl and Samuelson (see, eg van den Doel, 1979) shows the possibility of negotiations between people co-operating to ensure provision of such goods, while the simple theory does not deny the possibility that one or two rich people might choose to 'buy' such goods for themselves and thus also provide them for others. Nevertheless, traditional economic theory driven by self-interested rationality finds it difficult to explain private (non-government) provision of public goods to the extent observed.

7 The Pareto principle employs the simplistic criterion that no policy (or market) change can be judged a social improvement unless at least one person is made better off while no-one else is made worse off. More applied analysis of real-world choices modifies this criterion to allow those made better off to compensate any losers before deciding if the change constitutes an improvement, though this modification clearly requires inter-personal comparisons of welfare, which are not without considerable difficulty.

8 The author hereby claims intellectual property rights over this term!

CHAPTER 2

Pesticides, Pollution and Sustainability

Neil Ward

INTRODUCTION

Of the modern agricultural technologies introduced since the Second World War, none has been more important (both in terms of transforming farming practices and in attracting controversy) than the pesticide. Controversy arises in part because pesticides are dangerous chemicals by their very nature. They are designed as biocides specifically to kill living things – be they insect pests, fungi or weeds. In recent years, controversy has focused in Britain and elsewhere in Europe upon the presence of pesticides in the water environment in general and in drinking water supplies in particular. This chapter examines the emergence of a water pollution problem in Britain associated with pesticides used in agriculture. It addresses the question of how pesticides have become such an important part of arable farming practice; how the problem of pesticide pollution has emerged; and how meeting new 'sustainable development' policy objectives might affect the regulation of pesticide use in the future. Survey evidence from the River Ouse catchment in Bedfordshire and Buckinghamshire is also presented to shed light on how farmers decide to use pesticides and how they understand the associated environmental risks.

In Britain, the first widespread concerns about the environmental impacts of pesticide use were aroused in the early 1960s following the publication of Rachel Carson's book *Silent Spring* (Carson, 1962). The American biologist's concerns drew international attention to the persistence of pesticides in ecosystems and the accumulation of organochlorine compounds in food chains. It was, however, only as recently as the late 1980s that the problem of pesticide contamination of watercourses and the threat to drinking water has come to light as an issue of public and political concern in Britain. The previous lack of concern can be explained by a lack of systematic monitoring to check levels of pesticides in the water environment. As a result, little evidence of any pollution problem existed. The lack of data, and thus of public concern, meant an absence of pressure on policy makers and closed a vicious circle ensuring that pesticides in water remained a 'non-problem' (Figure 2.1). For example, the Royal Commission on Environmental Pollution, in its 1979 study of agricultural pollution, devoted over a quarter of its report to discussing pesticides but the threat of water pollution was not specifically dealt with.

The European Community's Drinking Water Directive (80/778/EEC) profoundly changed this situation. The Directive, which was agreed by the Member States in 1980 and became law in 1985, required that water suppliers systematically monitor drinking water supplied at customers' taps for a range of pollutants including

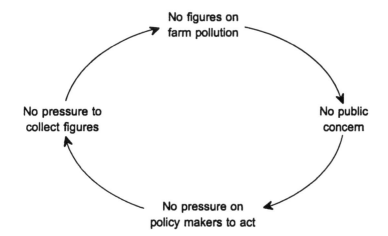

Figure 2.1 Pesticide pollution in the 1970s: the vicious circle of a 'non-problem'
Source: Ward, 1994

pesticides. This requirement enabled Friends of the Earth in Britain to analyse the results of monitoring and provide the first comprehensive account of the spread and levels of pesticide contamination of water. The Directive set a Maximum Admissible Concentration – a legal standard – of 0.1µg/l (or 1 part per billion) for any individual pesticide in any sample of drinking water. Friends of the Earth found that between 1985 and 1987 the standard was exceeded in almost 300 water supply zones (Friends of the Earth, 1988). The data also highlighted the geographical distribution of contamination (Figure 2.2). The worst affected areas were, and continue to be, the East Anglia and Thames regions – the regions most dominated by arable farming, and particularly by cereal production. Using the data that water companies are now obliged to supply to the Government's Drinking Water Inspectorate, Friends of the Earth have calculated that in 1992 approximately 14.5 million people in England and Wales lived in zones supplied with drinking water in which pesticide levels breached the European standard (Friends of the Earth, 1993). The most commonly detected contaminants are herbicides (accounting for 98 per cent of breaches), particularly pre-emergent cereal herbicides which are sprayed directly on to, and linger in, the soil, killing weeds as they emerge.

Since implementation of the Drinking Water Directive brought the issue of pesticide pollution to light, it has become increasingly recognised that pesticides can enter ground and surface waters not only through accidental or deliberate spillages but also as a result of routine and legitimate crop spraying complying with the statutory recommendations laid down on product labels. In other words, the 'normal' use of pesticides can still leave them vulnerable to being leached through the soil or being washed into streams and rivers. Therefore, in exploring the causes of pesticide pollution, the sets of processes that have encouraged their increasing use require some consideration.

THE GROWTH OF PESTICIDE USE

As new technologies spread through social and economic systems, the implicit assumptions held about technological change often go unrecognised. When we think of the rapid computerisation of everyday

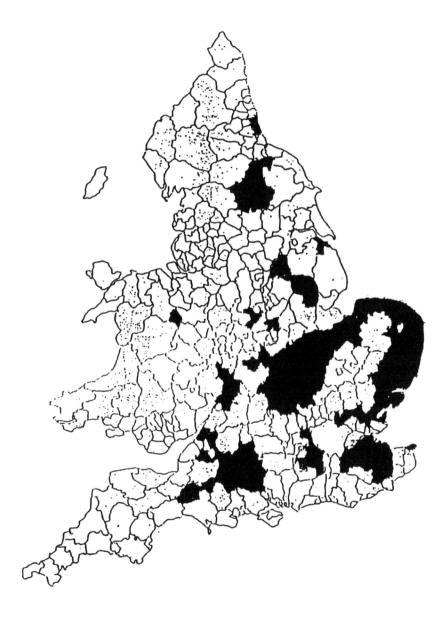

Figure 2.2 Areas where water supplies breach the European standard, 1988
Source: Friends of the Earth, 1988

life, the development of new and improved gadgetry for our cars, kitchens and hi-fi's, it is always tempting to see these changes as something inevitable – as part of the 'natural progress' of things. Indeed, the belief in technological modernisation as a unilinear process leading to a better future for us all has prevailed amongst societies and governments for much of the period since the agricultural and industrial revolutions. Technological determinism, or the idea that technological change is somehow separate from social processes, has been cited as 'the single most influential theory of the relationship between technology and society' (Mackenzie and Wajcman, 1985, p 4). It assumes that while technologies shape and change society, they are not reciprocally influenced; new technologies are simply produced by the impartial efforts of disinterested science in the pursuit of human advance and development.

The dominance of this belief has led social scientists to tend to concentrate their research on the impacts that new technologies have on societies, rather than on the ways that societies influence how technological change proceeds. Following from this dominant view, the task becomes for societies to continually strive to adapt to technological change, with technology being the determining factor and often the ultimate determinant of our future existence. However, we can also view the process of technological change and its environmental consequences from the opposite direction. This chapter therefore attempts to understand how the pesticide pollution problem has arisen by first understanding how social factors have influenced rising pesticide use. Such an approach fits well with a more evolutionary conceptualisation of rural change, as outlined in Chapter 6. The emergence of the pesticide pollution problem shows the co-evolution of technology, society, policy, farming practice and the environment – all interlocking and intermeshing. From such a co-evolutionary perspective, it is not sufficient to understand rising pesticide use simply by examining what farmers do on farms. We also need to understand how pesticides came to arrive in the farmers' hands in the first place.

A brief look at how the use of pesticides has spread throughout Britain during the post-war period sheds light on this process. Because it is herbicides that are most widely used and that currently pose the greatest threats to water, this chapter concentrates in particular on their growing use. Particular attention is paid to the cereals sector, because it is cereal herbicides that cause the most frequent pollution problems.

Sixty years ago, herbicides were hardly used in Britain. The search for chemicals to control weeds in agricultural crops began in earnest in the 1930s and the Second World War provided a major impetus to research efforts, not least because of the concern to increase domestic self-sufficiency in food production and to find ways of destroying the enemy's crops. At the end of the war, MCPA was launched in the UK as the first 'scientifically produced' selective herbicide. Although no data exist on the area treated or the volume of pesticides applied in the early post-war period, the number of spraying machines in use provides a good indicator of the growing use of pesticides at this time. Between 1942 and 1946, the number of ground crop sprayers in use in England and Wales more than doubled from 1600 to 3455 and the immediate aftermath of the 1947 Agriculture Act saw almost a three-fold increase to 9330 sprayers by 1952, with a further five-fold increase to 49,075, by 1959 (Laverton, 1962, p 38). Of the chemicals used at the time, it was herbicides that had the most profound implications for cereal production, expanding the areas of Britain where profitable cereal cropping could take place and reducing the need for rotations. By the late 1960s, not much more than twenty years after the introduction of herbicides, 65 per cent of the UK's cereal acreage was treated with them, a figure that rose to 94 per cent by 1975 (Grigg, 1989).

While farming practices are the obvious immediate cause of most pesticide pollution, the underlying causes of the problem spread much wider than just the farmers' actions. Given this, how might the process of pesticide pollution be conceptualised? The relations surrounding pesticide use and pollution can be shown as a network (Figure 2.3). While the farmer's role is central and the farm is a compulsory location in the story of pesticide pollution, the processes that foster pesticide use and lead to pollution involve many other types of people. We should be sensitive to the farmer's position among this assemblage of other actors.

Figure 2.3 illustrates how pesticide technologies have been produced by scientists in the public and private research and development (R&D) sectors of the agro-food system. New products enter the technology transfer system where they are subject to regulatory control prior to their clearance. Once authorised for the market, they can be used on farms. Adoption of particular pesticides will be influenced by

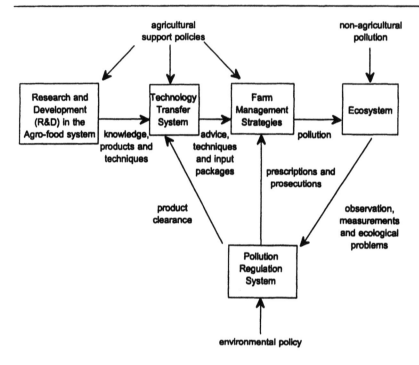

Figure 2.3 The pesticide 'pollution production process'
Source: developed from Lowe et al, 1990.

the advice farmers receive and the marketing strategies of the companies that sell them pesticides.

The use of pesticides within farm management strategies causes pollution. Farm strategies are subject to three main sets of external influences – agricultural policies, technology transfer, and the regulatory system (which sets maximum pesticide dose rates and prosecutes farmers for pollution incidents). Pollution regulation can be affected in turn by wider environmental policy objectives, such as, for example, the implementation of the polluter pays principle or the meeting of European environmental standards. Another important influence is the information gathered on environmental change, as observations and measurements of pollution in the environment are used to inform regulatory strategies.

If we turn to think about what this network looked like in the early post-war period when herbicide use was first becoming widespread, we can begin to see the dynamics of how the network has evolved. The introduction of the new herbicides after the war helped revolutionise weed control in cereal cropping, allowing farmers to abandon the use of wide rows and horse hoeing, which until then had been the only means of keeping weeds in cereals under control. However, for widespread adoption to take place, much more was required than simply the development of new chemicals. Farmers had to be encouraged to adopt new technologies and practices, and to achieve this a new framework for British agricultural policy was required. The cornerstone of the policy was the 1947 Agriculture Act which encouraged agricultural expansion through a system of guaranteed prices. In order to limit the costs of agricultural support to the exchequer, farmers were encouraged to improve their efficiency through the adoption of new technologies. In addition, new public institutions were put in place to promote the technological revolution, and research and technical education in agriculture were expanded. The Agricultural Research Council (ARC) directed research in the agricultural sciences, and the National Agricultural Advisory Service (NAAS), the predecessor of the Agricultural Development and Advisory Service (ADAS), was established as a state advisory service to encourage the adoption of new practices. There was a strong sense of the public sector orchestrating the flow of technologies from scientific laboratories onto the farm, and nowhere was this more so than in the diffusion of weed-control technologies. The 1947 Act contained a section on pest control to encourage (and even 'enforce') 'good farming practice' which included the elimination of weeds. The ARC set up a Unit of Experimental Agronomy at Oxford in 1950 which, in 1960, became the Weed Research Organisation, and the NAAS stationed a senior advisor there permanently to keep abreast of changes and help the flow of new techniques onto farms (McCann, 1989, p 55).

The rising costs of agricultural support in the 1950s led to a greater emphasis on promoting agricultural efficiency. After 1951, the annual additions to guaranteed prices paid to farmers were typically less than the annual increase in their costs of production, and were sometimes negative (Bowers, 1985), meaning that the only way farm incomes could be maintained or improved was through increased efficiency. This 'cost–price squeeze' intensified the search for improvements in efficiency at the same time as adopting pesticides became increasingly economically attractive to farmers.

During the 1950s the promise of global agricultural expansion put the agrochemical industry on a sound footing and the rate of innovation increased. Around 140 new agrochemical products were introduced in that decade (Acilladelis et al, 1987). The variety of compositions of herbicides increased and by the 1960s they had become the most important of the crop protection chemicals in terms of both the number of innovations and the value of total sales. This 'demand' did not materialise from thin air, however, and cannot be used on its own to provide an 'explanation' of rising pesticide use. Rather, demand was continually created and stimulated. The cost–price squeeze provided a push factor, but in addition, agrochemical companies targeted 'lead' farmers considered to be local opinion-formers and provided them with pesticides at greatly reduced prices, or even free of charge, in order to encourage their use (Tait, 1976). At the same time, a greater understanding of pesticide efficacy, falling unit costs of pesticide production and the developing infrastructure around pesticide usage fostered 'increasing returns to adoption', making these new technologies increasingly attractive to farmers as active profit-seekers (Allanson et al, 1995, pp 1807–8).

The 30 years from 1950 to 1980 thus saw a chemical revolution in British agriculture. Farming practices were transformed, and herbicides, in particular, became the mainstay of crop protection. A whole technological system came into being with its own dominant paradigm. Central to this paradigm was the view that it was through chemical treatment that pest problems in arable farming could best be tackled, and so scientists were most concerned with continually improving the efficacy of pesticide use in this context. A network of people had a common interest in maintaining the technological system. This network included: the state – which wanted to contain the costs of price support by encouraging improvements in agricultural efficiency; the agricultural scientists of both the public and private sectors – whose role it was to produce the new chemicals and the optimal means of applying them; and agro-industrial interests – including those farmers prepared to adopt, modernise and grow, and the manufacturers of agrochemicals and spraying machinery who saw their markets expand.

Total sales of pesticides in the UK rose from £70 million to £542 million between 1948 and 1982 (both at 1982 prices), almost an eight-fold increase in real terms, and the number of different products rose from 216 to 700 over the same period (Department of the Environment, 1983, p 3). By 1982 over 31 000 tonnes of pesticide active ingredient were being applied to over 3.8 million hectares. Yields rose as a result, and between the late 1940s and the mid-1970s, the average yield of winter wheat, for example, rose from just over 2 tonnes/ha to approximately 4.5 tonnes/ha.

Applications of pesticide, and especially herbicides, became routine and prophylactic as farmers simplified and standardised crop management strategies. This was aided by the availability since the 1960s of pre-emergent herbicides sprayed onto the soil to kill weeds as they emerge. The growing importance of herbicides in crop production signalled an important turning point in farming practice, and provided a significant trigger to further intensification in the arable sector. Before the availability of herbicides, weed populations were kept down by means of crop rotations and cultivations so that no one weed species could benefit from a consistently favourable environment. Until the 1950s, the emphasis had been on incorporating herbicides into existing husbandry systems that were basically unchanged. Their use merely replaced the hoe, harrow and sickle. However, during the 1960s, herbicides began to be used as part of a far more fundamental change in crop husbandry. This change arose from their unique ability to kill off vegetation on a large scale without relying on cultivations, enabling farmers to grow a succession of cereal crops without recourse to the plough. In other words, the farming system became oriented around the herbicide. Until the 1950s it 'continued to be regarded as bad farming to grow more than two straw crops in succession' (Elliott, 1980, p 288) because of the increased risk of weed infestation. The use of herbicides, however, meant that, by the late 1960s 'rotation was considered an old fashioned word' (p 288).

As a result of the favourable economics of pesticide use, the chemical option has become standard practice for pest control. Other factors have helped close off non-chemical options such as the use of cultivations and rotations. First is the increasing reliance among farmers upon the crop protection advice of technical advisors. Second, the routinisation of spraying programmes and the reliability of many sprays makes for a much less complicated pest control strategy with less risk of subsequent problems in the crop. The preventative use of pesticides as an 'insurance' against the risk of pest problems arising has saved farmers having to modify crop husbandry strategies in a more reactive sense after problems have appeared.

The availability and competitiveness of pre-emergent cereal

herbicides also made the switch to winter cereals technically feasible and economically viable, but at the same time increased pollution risks. The area of land in England and Wales sown to winter cereals has increased by a factor of three since 1969, and research by Evans (1990) found that this land has been the most susceptible to soil erosion caused by run-off. More erosive rain falls in October and November when poorly covered ground is vulnerable to run-off and herbicides have been recently applied and are more likely to be washed into surrounding watercourses. Indeed, studies have detected pre-emergent cereal herbicides in run-off water from such land at up to 500 times the EC limit for drinking water following autumn spraying (ENDS, 1992a).

FARMERS AND PESTICIDE POLLUTION

A farm survey was conducted in 1991 to examine the ways that farmers understood pesticide pollution concerns and the way the 'pollution production process' was operating (see Ward, 1995). Cereal producers were interviewed in the catchment of the Bedford Ouse which straddles Bedfordshire and Buckinghamshire, an area pointed to by regulatory officials in the water industry as a possible future target for restrictions on pesticide use.

The survey highlighted farmers' dependence upon advice from technical advisors when deciding both what types of pesticide to apply and at what dose rates (Ward and Munton, 1992; Ward, 1995). The most common source of advice amongst the surveyed farmers was the representatives of agrochemical merchants, whose role it is to sell pesticides. Commercial interests often provide 'free' advice as part of their service, while farmers have to pay for technical advice from independent consultants or ADAS. While it is difficult to be sure that merchants' advisors routinely encourage the greater use of pesticides, a majority of farmers interviewed acknowledged the potential for such advice linked to the commercial sales of pesticides to be 'biased', either because higher dose rates or more profitable chemicals are recommended by sales staff. Several farmers, however, seemed to suggest that their own advisor was quite exceptional and was even giving them special favours.

Interviews also revealed how farmers were extremely reluctant to do other than what their advisor told them. Almost 90 per cent said that they already undercut pesticide dose rates recommended on the product labels, but usually did so *only on the recommendation of their advisor*. When asked if they ever undercut the dose rates recommended by their advisor, fewer than 40 per cent of farmers said they did so, in spite of the fact that many recognised that commercial advice potentially encouraged a greater use of pesticides. They acknowledged that merchants had an interest in selling pesticides, but felt that their own advisor, with whom they had often struck up a close working relationship, was not biased. Farmers justified their reluctance to overrule technical advice by arguing that they did not have the necessary technical expertise themselves to take such risks. If the pesticide failed, the farmers' negotiating position with the merchant would be undermined and their opportunity to claim compensation for failure would be jeopardised. (This Catch 22 situation has been recognised by the Labour Party (1994) which has pledged, as part of its environmental policy, to reform the compensation arrangements to help farmers cut pesticide dose rates further). The minority of farmers prepared to apply pesticides at dose rates lower than those recommended by their advisors stressed the preconditions for such action. It was not something that they would do as a matter of course, but 'occasionally', or after 'some convincing', or 'under ideal weather conditions', they may decide to take a chance.

The survey interviews also revealed the low profile of pesticide pollution issues when farmers think about their farming practices and the associated environmental risks. Ideas of resource management and conservation are not new to farming, particularly with regards to the productive capacity of the soil. Indeed, a central part of the ethos of 'family farming' has been to make a living out of the family's asset (the farm) but also to pass it on to the next generation in sound working order. Conserving some of the resources of the farm environment (such as the productive capacity of the soil) is often also strongly linked to ideas of family continuity and succession. In order to explore such ideas, the surveyed farmers were asked about this notion of 'improving' their farms. The question was worded; 'farmers often say that they would like to pass on their farm to the next generation in a better condition than when they took it on themselves. What does the phrase "in a better condition" mean to you?'

Many farmers tended to talk about the land being 'in good heart', and for most, this implied that the soil be fertile and capable of sustaining high yields. But it also implied a responsibility to the land. There was broad agreement that a good farmer 'should not take more out of the soil than gets put back in'. The soil should not be 'robbed' of its nutrients.

It is within the context of this idea of farm 'improvement' that farmers' attitudes to environmental change in the countryside must be set. The survey suggested that farmers have, in the main, become sensitised to environmental issues. Almost two-thirds of the farmers interviewed acknowledged that modern agricultural practices can have an adverse effect on the environment, for example. However, the types of environmental problem these farmers went on to talk about varied. Just under a quarter mentioned problems with 'the overuse of sprays', but when questioned further, most were more specifically concerned about the effects of insecticides on friendly predator species like ladybirds. The threat to water quality from leaching and run-off was hardly mentioned. While some general unease about heavy usage of pesticides was expressed, the pesticide threat to water was not an issue that loomed large in the minds of the farmers interviewed.

Unsurprisingly perhaps, production-enhancing values held strong currency amongst farmers, although notions of good husbandry were also important. (Two-thirds of farmers acknowledged that environmental concerns had begun to influence the way that they farmed and several cited the management of environmental features on their farms). The improvement of yields was an important goal of agricultural policy throughout the productivist period and was the central feature in farmers' strategies. However, since the 1980s the national and European goals have been radically altered. By means of co-responsibility levies and compulsory set-aside, agricultural policy has sought to reduce over-production at the aggregate level. However, at the level of the individual farm, efforts to increase yields are an important legacy of the productivist era and powerful economic motives remain. This is despite the increasing promotion of strategies which seek to encourage the maximisation of margins through improving the efficiency of input use as the most financially sound strategy for maintaining farm incomes.

Linked to the preoccupation with yields among the farmers was their concern with weeds. The farmers were asked whether they compared how they were doing with their neighbours, and found that weeds provided a useful gauge of farming 'success'. Half the farmers said that they looked over the hedge to see whether neighbours were winning the battle against weeds, and many expressed strong aesthetic concerns about 'clean', weed-free fields. The survey suggested that utilitarian notions of clean (weed-free), tidy farm environments continue to dominate farming culture. The majority of farmers interviewed saw their contributions to rural environmental management as essentially having two strands. First, they could plant trees in field corners or on unproductive parcels of land, dig ponds and manage footpaths, thus helping to create 'pockets' of nature and facilitate access for walkers to enjoy them. Second, however, they could ensure that the farmed environment was kept clean and tidy without scrubby, unkempt land where 'rubbish' was growing.

On the heavy soils of the Ouse catchment, where forty years ago, cereal cropping would not have been viable, farmers see the presence of weeds as one of the biggest threats to their farming. Uniformly coloured fields with as few blemishes of weeds as possible and with the crop drilled in straight lines symbolise their success in the battle against nature's constraints on production. Moreover, these deeply felt convictions and the clear understanding about the role of weeds contrasted with doubts and uncertainties about some of the environmental impacts of agrochemical use. Because impacts might be unapparent in the short and medium term, farmers find it difficult to imagine that their efforts against weeds are problematic. In addition, they argue that they would surely not be allowed to use any chemicals that pose real threats. Their faith in the justice of fighting weeds is mirrored by a faith in the inherent safety of the chemical weapons they use. So, in the trade-off between the profitable production of cereal crops and the threats posed to surface and ground-waters, the interests of agronomy tend to transcend those of the water environment because of the relative strengths of these two convictions within the farmers' ways of thinking. Weeds are an easily identifiable economic threat, whose presence goes against the farmers' strong convictions in favour of rationalised, clean fields. However, there are no such strong convictions about the environmental impacts of agrochemicals, and pollution threats seem doubtful, long-term, distant and unproved, and this is coupled with a relatively strong faith in the registration and approval of chemicals that have been properly and 'scientifically' tested.

REGULATING PESTICIDE POLLUTION

As suggested above, it was the implementation of the EC's Drinking Water Directive that first highlighted the problem of pesticide pollution of water in Britain. Indeed, a breach of the Directive's standard has tended to be used in Britain as the very definition of what counts as pollution. When traces of pesticides are found in drinking water at concentrations even lower than the already very strict European standard, they are not registered as a 'breach' and are not recorded in official statistics. Although the standard is used to define what counts as pollution, it has provoked controversy amongst scientists and policy makers who argue about whether it is too strict or not strict enough. Scientific knowledge about the movement of pesticides in the environment is far from complete, and little is known about the impact of very small but frequent doses on public health. These scientific uncertainties have left the framing of the pollution issue open to contestation between different groups. Two broad bodies of opinion can be identified.

The first view is held by the European Commission and several Northern European Member States who argue that pesticides have no place in water. It was as a result of this 'precautionary approach' to environmental protection that the drinking water standard was first devised as a surrogate zero. Friends of the Earth, consumer groups and the governments of Denmark, the Netherlands and Germany all share this view. They also argue that there is uncertainty over the precise nature of the health risks involved. Moreover, toxicological standards do not exist for many of the active ingredients in use in Britain and the synergistic effects of consuming water containing a mix of several pesticides – a sort of pesticide cocktail – even at low levels, have hardly been investigated.

A second view is put forward by the manufacturers of pesticides and some farming groups who argue that the standard is 'unscientific' because it does not relate to the toxicologically derived health risks associated with the ingestion of different pesticides. In Britain, this argument has won the support of the government which has pressed for a review of the operation of the Drinking Water Directive and a relaxation of the standard. Among this group, pollution is seen as an inevitable consequence of pesticide use, but the minute quantities detected reflect an unforeseen technical irritant rather than a fundamental problem with the organisation of agricultural production. The dominance of this view amongst policy-makers has resulted in regulatory action to reduce pesticides in drinking water without hampering agriculture.

Instead of preventing pollution happening in the first place, the British response to the pesticide pollution problem has been to clean up drinking water at water works. The water companies in England and Wales have estimated that installing equipment at water works to remove pesticides from drinking water will cost £800 million in capital equipment and a further £80 million per year in running costs (ENDS, 1992b). Given the arrangements under which the water industry was privatised in 1989, water companies are able to pass these costs on to water consumers. This, in effect, turns the polluter pays principle on its head – consumers rather than polluters of water have to bear the costs of the pollution. The prospect of rapidly rising water bills has prompted Ofwat, the water watchdog, to press the Government to 'renegotiate' (for which we might read 'relax') the European standards (Ofwat, 1993). This the Government has sought to do and the European Commission in 1992 agreed to a review of all water quality directives, especially in the light of new World Health Organisation standards for pesticides in water. A new draft Drinking Water Directive is being circulated by the Commission at the time of writing. The new draft directive leaves the 0.1µg/l uniform limit for pesticides in drinking water unchanged, but a footnote does provide for the Commission to set varying standards for individual pesticides in the future.

The two different views about the appropriateness of the standards sketched out above also reflect wider perspectives on the use of pesticides in agriculture. Those in favour of maintaining the strict standards argue that pesticide pollution should be prevented irrespective of any health risks, and the onus of proof should not fall on those seeking to prove that there is a health risk. According to Friends of the Earth, for example, the mere presence of unwanted pesticides in drinking water ought to prompt greater controls over their use to prevent pollution happening in the first place. On the other hand, those who have been pressing for the standards to be relaxed see pesticide use as essential to efficient and competitive agriculture. Any controls on their use which do not arise from any proven public health risks associated with pesticide pollution will only serve to put British farmers at a competitive disadvantage in global markets. The

Government in Britain (UK Government, 1991) tends towards this latter view and a deep reluctance to regulate farmers – unless public and political pressures become unbearable – currently prevails.

It continues to be politically difficult, however, for water quality standards to be relaxed at the European level, particularly given the influence of environmental politics upon Germany's coalition government. Relaxing the pesticide standard could be problematic in Britain too. The strength of public concern and the extent of scepticism about scientific assessments of health risks have been highlighted by a recent opinion poll. When asked 'would you accept more pesticides in your drinking water if you were told that the levels were not dangerous and water charges were lower as a result?', 77 per cent of respondents said 'No' (Clover, 1993). However, the nature of the current debate surrounding the pesticide standard for *drinking* water has tended to frame discussions in public health terms. This, combined with a shortage of scientific information about the movements and impacts of pesticides in the wider water environment, has meant that the implications of pesticide pollution for aquatic environments and ecosystems have hardly been considered. In other words, we still know very little about what persistent low-level pesticide contamination does to aquatic ecosystems.

It seems likely that the European standard for pesticides in water will remain for the foreseeable future. This will leave the use of pesticides in European agriculture open to increased regulation in order that the standards be met. In Britain, the Secretary of State for the Environment has, since 1974, had powers to designate water protection zones in which land use practices can be controlled for the sake of protecting surface and ground-waters, although these powers have not been used. However, the National Rivers Authority (NRA) has begun to discuss how the regulation of pesticide use might operate (ENDS, 1990; NRA, 1995).

But what might greater restrictions on polluting pesticides cost British farmers? Some indication is provided by the case of Isoproturon – a pre-emergent cereal herbicide which, in the Anglian region in 1993, for example, accounted for more than 70 per cent of those breaches of the drinking water standard attributable to agricultural pesticides. Isoproturon is a cheap and reliable herbicide in the fight against grass weeds like blackgrass and wild oats. If it had been banned in 1991 – the year of the farm survey reported above – the total cost to all British farmers of using the nearest non-polluting alternative – a more expensive herbicide called Cheetah – would have been around £14 million (Ward et al, 1993). This compares with the £800 million capital costs and £80 million a year running costs of removing pesticides at water-works after the pollution has happened. In any case, in 1991 Cheetah was a brand new chemical, and several farmers explained during the survey that with time, and a little experimentation, they could probably cut the dose rates at which they apply Cheetah, making it an even less costly alternative. One farmer had already achieved comparable levels of weed control with Cheetah at low dose rates which made it competitive with Isoproturon. (In other words, a ban on the use of Isoproturon would have cost him nothing). As seems to be happening in Denmark, Holland and elsewhere, increased regulation, rather than stifling innovation, can actually encourage the search for more 'environmentally friendly' methods. These simple calculations suggest it might make good economic sense to address the pesticide pollution problem at source – ie at the level of pesticide use – rather than cleaning up the pollution after it has happened.

The Ministry of Agriculture, Fisheries and Food (MAFF) has recently begun taking the first tentative steps to control pesticide use in order to improve compliance with the Drinking Water Directive. First MAFF banned the non-agricultural use of two major pesticide pollutants, Atrazine and Simazine in 1992. Both were widely used by local authorities and British Rail for weed control. Although the ban has not involved restrictions on farmers, it is viewed as a precedent because it is the first substantial regulatory decision to be influenced directly by the need to comply with the Drinking Water Directive's standards rather than by conventional toxicological considerations (ENDS, 1992c). In July 1995 MAFF also placed restrictions on the use of Isoproturon following a review by the Advisory Committee on Pesticides and because of its record in contaminating water supplies. The restrictions include the withdrawal of registration for pre-emergence uses on wheat and barley and the requirement that product labels carry advice against use where soils are cracked. The NRA (1995, p 46), however, 'does not believe that these restrictions will be sufficient to reduce pesticide contamination of water'.

A recent development in Europe ought also to lead to greater pressure for controls on polluting pesticides. In June 1994, after two years of negotiations, the Agriculture Council agreed the annex to a directive (91/414) laying down uniform principles for the authorisation of pesticides. Originally a harmonisation measure to standardise product clearance procedures across the Community, the European Commission had proposed that a pesticide's active ingredient should not be authorised for use if its concentration in groundwater was likely to exceed the standard laid down in the Drinking Water Directive. This idea was defended by Denmark and the Netherlands against the pesticide manufacturers as a valuable precautionary measure. The compromise has been that individual Member States will only be able to approve the use of such polluting pesticides conditionally for five years, subject to extensive monitoring and efforts to reduce contamination to below the standard, and these products will not be able to circulate freely in other Member States. These changes mark an important shift in European policy from the regulation of environmental outcomes (ie drinking water quality) to the application of environmental standards in product regulation (Ward, 1994b), and have major implications for the relationship between innovation (in the form of pesticide R&D) and environmental protection. British laxity is again likely to be challenged by rules agreed at the European level.

PESTICIDE POLLUTION AND SUSTAINABLE DEVELOPMENT

The theme of this book is the 'sustainable rural economy'. Of course, just what the term 'sustainability' might mean is open to contest by different groups. The most commonly quoted definition of sustainable development – 'development that meets the needs of the present without compromising the ability of future generations to meet their own needs' (World Commission on Environment and Development, 1987, p 43) – is suitably vague, especially in terms if defining 'needs', to ensure widespread endorsement. But while politicians may talk of sustainability in distinctly narrow terms (how many times have we heard the phrase 'a sustainable economic recovery'?), it seems clear that to most people sustainable development means bringing economic activities more firmly within the constraints of the natural environment. With respect to pesticides in water, while we might not be able to define what a sustainable end-state might be, particularly given our lack of understanding of the long-term impacts of pesticide pollution on human health and aquatic ecosystems, we could probably agree that it would be more sustainable to have less pollution (and vice versa). In particular, the contamination of groundwaters which are especially difficult to clean up, ought to be avoided, although the evidence currently suggests rising levels of contamination of groundwaters by pesticides across Europe.

The new emphasis on sustainable development has led to a range of recent policy initiatives at the European level which begin to address the problem of pesticide pollution from an environmentally led, rather than an agriculturally dominated, perspective. For example, the European Commission has made a commitment in its Fifth Environmental Action Programme, published in 1992, to integrate sustainable development objectives in every area of European policy (Commission of the European Communities, 1992). Agriculture has been selected as a target sector in the Action Programme and the registration and control of the sales and use of pesticides is highlighted as a key area of regulatory action. In the Action Programme, the EU also aims to achieve by 2000 'a significant reduction of pesticide use per unit of land under production' (Commission of the European Communities, 1992a, p 37; see also ENDS, 1994).

In the UK, the Government's *Strategy for Sustainable Development*, (Department of the Environment, 1994) also restates its aim to 'minimize the use of pesticides', an objective first explicitly stated in 1983 (Department of the Environment, 1983). So far, however, there have been no specific policy measures to achieve this aim, except for those voluntary schemes inside Environmentally Sensitive Areas. This voluntary – almost 'do nothing' – approach can be contrasted with those of other places. Denmark, the Netherlands, Sweden, Norway and Ontario in Canada all have pesticide use reduction programmes in place and are progressing towards their targets by the end of the decade. The Dutch aim to cut the quantity of pesticide active ingredient applied to half of its 1990 level by the year 2000. The Danish plan, introduced in 1986 has aimed for a 50 per cent reduction by 1997. Crucially, these use-reduction programmes have provided an important spur to the development of new, non-chemical crop protection methods – and have been backed up by massive state-funded research programmes.

But what sort of crop protection techniques are available as alternatives to the use of pesticides? Several recent initiatives in the UK and elsewhere have sought to promote pesticide minimisation and reduction through the greater use of non-chemical pest-control practices. For example, some British schemes espouse the adoption of Integrated Farming Systems (IFS) which rely as much as possible on cultural and biological methods of crop protection with chemicals as integrated supplements. These systems imply a much more holistic approach to land use, combining concerns for efficient and viable farm business management with efforts to minimise detrimental environmental impacts.

One such scheme has been the Less Intensive Farming and Environment (LIFE) project administered since 1989 from the Institute for Arable Crop Research at Long Ashton near Bristol. Since 1993, two commercial pilot farms have converted to IFS, and monitoring of the financial and environmental implications of such schemes ought to shed light on the opportunities for, and constraints upon, their reproducibility. A second initiative has been the Linking Environment and Farming (LEAF) scheme administered from the National Agricultural Centre at Stoneleigh. This scheme involves 18 demonstration farms which employ Integrated Crop Management (ICM) techniques and are aimed at encouraging the adoption of such techniques in agriculture more generally. Specific ICM techniques include the rotation of crops to minimise their susceptibility to pest infestation and the construction of 'beetle banks' across fields which provide homes to predator species such as beetles which then counter pest infestations.

Crucially, however, schemes such as LIFE and LEAF remain at the research or demonstration phase. They, like many similar schemes, are couched in the rhetoric of 'sustainable agriculture' yet tend to represent incremental rather than large-scale and systemic reform (along, for example, the lines of the reforms to farming systems that took place during and immediately after the Second World War). More importantly, the adoption of IFS/ICM or other pesticide-minimisation techniques remains entirely voluntary and there is nothing stopping the vast majority of British farmers carrying on with 'business as usual'. Nonetheless, with respect to pesticide use and pollution, IFS/ICM practices do represent perhaps the most significant challenge to the chemically oriented paradigm of the productivist era.

Moving away from the current level of dependence upon chemical crop protection in Britain requires that the momentum generated by previous rounds of technological change be recognised. Reducing pollution from pesticides in order to move towards more sustainable systems is much more than a simple technical issue. It also involves the reorientation of a social and occupational community bred on an ethos of agricultural productivism and chemical crop protection. The early evidence from those European countries with pesticide reduction programmes in place suggest that such new strategic policies can generate open debate about the role of, and dependence upon, the use of pesticides in contemporary agriculture and stimulate the search for innovative alternative crop protection techniques (Agricultural Economics Research Institute, 1995). Reduction policies would also help shift the focus of debate away from defining what precisely 'sustainable agriculture' as an end-state might involve and what levels of pesticide contamination might be compatible with 'sustainability', and towards a set of concerns about the direction set by present courses of action.

SUMMARY

To conclude, in the early post-war period, the needs of public policy – coupled with a great faith in new scientific technologies – helped stimulate the pesticide revolution in Britain over a very short period. In the story of rising pesticide use, however, it is important to recognise that farmers operate within a complex technological system, and one which can be shaped and influenced by government and public policy. There is no reason to take current pesticide use as some inevitable, given factor, simply the contemporary outcome of the inexorable march of technological 'progress', and something over which we have little public or regulatory control. With respect to pesticides, pollution and sustainability in the British context, the task now is to learn from the strategies and experiences of some of our more forward-looking neighbours, encourage farmers to minimise the use of more-polluting pesticides, and to stimulate more actively the search for more sustainable crop protection practices.

CHAPTER 3

Natural Resource Management: the Case of Heather Moorland

Ben White

INTRODUCTION

The conservation of agricultural habitats has become an integral part of agricultural policy within both the EC and the UK. Payments to farmers for following environmental guidelines are in the form of management agreements associated with Sites of Special Scientific Interest (SSSI), Environmentally Sensitive Areas (ESAs), The Moorland Scheme and Countryside Stewardship and many other schemes. These payments are justified on the grounds that: the public values ecosystems which are associated with low-intensity grazing systems; farmers have property rights over land to the extent that they can modify the ecology; and modern agriculture has increased the rarity of some ecosystems to a level where their marginal public value is greater than their marginal conservation cost.

The alternative payment mechanisms for delivering conserved ecosystems have been extensively analysed by environmental and agricultural economists, notably, Colman (1994), Whitby and Lowe (1994), Frazer (1995) and Hodge (1995). The consensus is that where a range of policies are identified, these policies are characterised as involving varying degrees of property right transfer from the landowner to the regulator: compulsory purchase is at one extreme, while cross-compliance is at another extreme where access to other subsidies is based upon farmers accepting environmental constraints. Schemes also vary in terms of the bargaining mechanisms they use and the associated administrative costs: Some management agreements are individually negotiated, while those in ESAs are offered on a voluntary basis at a fixed rate to all farmers within the designated area. Other attributes of contracts concern the length of commitment to the contract and the intensity of monitoring. We argue that the scheme chosen should reflect all market and non-market benefits and costs associated with conserving a particular class of agricultural ecosystem. The Organisation for Economic Co-operation and Development (OECD) generalise the various payment vehicles as a provider gets principle which is a direct analogue of the polluter pays principle in pollution control (Hanley et al, 1996).

Despite the extensive analysis of SSSIs, ESAs and the like there is little evidence that new economic models are emerging which are able to reflect the ecological complexity of the issues surrounding land conservation. In particular, policy for land conservation must take into account the spatial juxtaposition of different land parcels and it must also account for the stochastic nature of ecological processes and their long gestation periods. These issues affect the costs and benefits of providing conserved agricultural ecosystems. Ecologists have been increasingly concerned with interactions that occur within a broader landscape, and with the stability of ecosystems, (Holling, 1973). Some economists, notably Common and Perrings (1992), Moxey et al, (1995) have noted the problems of linking economic activity to ecology. Generally we have a poor understanding of ecological processes of habitat regeneration and preservation. Thus, as was noted by the House of Lords Environmental Committee (1991), there is a lack of a co-ordinated policy for the agricultural environment: such a policy would include national targets for the area and spatial distribution of 'valued' habitats such as heather moorland.

Heather moorland exemplifies issues which surround the preservation of biodiversity and landscape in the UK. For many people it is an attractive characteristic of the 'wilder' areas of Northern England and Scotland. Ecologically it is valued first because *Calluna vulgaris* heath is virtually confined to the UK and the heath is an important habitat for European populations of merlin, red grouse and hen harriers. Despite the apparent 'naturalness' of heather moorland it is in fact a man-made habitat created through time by practices associated with sheep production and grouse shooting. In ecological terms, *Calluna vulgaris* heath does not represent a climax vegetation community: without the necessary management inputs of controlled sheep grazing and burning, heather moorland would disappear and would be replaced, eventually, by grassland, woodland or mire communities (Rodwell, 1991).

The problems of conserving heather moorland are similar to those encountered in preserving most of the ecologically valued agricultural grasslands, including chalk downland and northern hay meadows. These ecosystems are sustained by extensive systems of grazing livestock management and are lost through both agricultural abandonment and agricultural intensification.

In most environments these ecosystems are the product of older systems of agricultural production and have been gradually replaced by ecosystems associated with intensive agriculture. Incentives exist, through market prices and production subsidies, for farmers to produce at levels of intensity which have reduced the extent and viability of the upland heath ecosystem. Public concern over the loss of such habitats has led to policies such as ESAs which have primarily been established to conserve low-intensity traditional grazing systems. The policy problem is one of equating the perceived public benefits of conservation with the costs of compensating farmers to forgo profit opportunities. There are many facets of this problem. First, what area should be preserved and how should it be regionally distributed? Second, who should manage it? And, third how should a scheme be designed to ensure that the ecosystem is preserved efficiently?

The appropriate contract depends upon the value of the habitat and the cost of monitoring and negotiation. Costs include the loss of social value due to habitat degradation, genuine opportunity costs incurred by producers; and information costs, due to asymmetric information between producers and regulators, which are manifested as negotiation, monitoring costs and overpaying producers for their opportunity cost. In the case of a highly valued habitat which requires a sophisticated management system, such as large areas of wetlands, public ownership may well be the most efficient option. For small areas of valued habitat, then an SSSI-type designation is appropriate, so long as it is relatively cheap to monitor compliance with management agreements. Finally, for large-scale landscape features which depend upon extensive agriculture, voluntary participation in binding long-term contracts may be sufficient. Table 3.1 considers conservation contracts as regulatory instruments which can be used to ensure the production of a

Table 3.1 Characteristics of selected regulatory mechanisms employed in agri-environmental schemes

Regulatory mechanism	ESA	SSSI	Moorland Scheme
Monitor compliance	Yes (30% sample)	Yes	Yes
Individual negotiation	No	Yes	Yes but limited
Audit costs ex-post	No	Ex-ante not ex-post	No
Commitment	Fixed term interim review	Finite with reviews (20 years the norm)	Fixed term
Payment rate	Flat rate	Individual contract	Flat rate
Designated region	Yes	Yes	No
Participation	Voluntary	Compulsory	Voluntary
Variable payments based on constraints accepted	Yes (tiers)	Negotiated	No
Compulsory purchase	No	Yes (last resort)	No
Property right implications	Constrained inputs	Constrained actions & inputs	Constrained inputs

quantity of an environmental good of a particular quality. Unfortunately in terms of regulation (see Laffont and Tirole (1993)), regulating agriculture to provide environmental goods efficiently has proved to be a particularly difficult policy problem. The reasons for this rest with the large number of firms involved, their heterogeneity, the requirement for long-term commitment to a particular scheme and the complexity of the goods involved.

Heather moorland, in most locations, is adequately managed by private landowners and their tenants, who have expertise in sheep and heather management. Indeed it must be managed by farmers, as a grazing input is essential. The area is extensive and is estimated for 1980 as 509,800 hectares in England and Wales (Bradbury et al, 1989).* As a habitat it is under threat but not, as yet, on the list of very rare or endangered habitats. However, it should be noted that a smaller

---

* Three methods have been employed to estimate the area of heather moorland: air photographs, satellite imagery (Landsat TM) and survey estimates. These all give markedly different results. To allow for a comparison between earlier years the Monitoring Land Use Change estimates based on air photographs are cited here.

area, 353,851 hectares, on the basis of Landsat estimates, is dominant or managed for grouse shooting. Thus a voluntary scheme, such as the Moorland Scheme may prove to be an efficient means of conservation.

EVIDENCE OF DECLINE

This section reviews the evidence of a decline in the area and quality of heather moorland over the post-war period. In common with monitoring of other extensive vegetation features, monitoring changes in the extent and viability of heath ecosystems is problematic. First, it is only possible to undertake a field assessment for a relatively small proportion of the areas containing heather. Second, more appropriate aggregate measures of heather cover require either satellite imagery or air photographs. Table 3.2, based on air photographs, shows that the most rapid losses in heather occurred between 1947 and 1969. The slow-down in the rate of loss between 1969 and 1980 was mainly attributable to the regeneration of heather in Northern England.

Table 3.2 Area of upland heath in England and Wales (dominant and managed) (thousand hectares)

	1947	1969	1980
England	501.4	387.7	393.2
Wales	130.0	124.5	116.6
Total	631.4	512.2	509.8

Source: Hunting Surveys and Consultants Ltd (1986)

The land covers to which heather is converted are given in Table 3.3. This shows that by far the largest percentage of the heather moorland lost is converted to upland grasses which include Bent grass and Matt grass communities. Afforestation is next in the list, with bracken infestation also an important weed problem on heather moorland.

However, the absolute loss of heather does not give the whole story, there is also concern over the sustainability of the remaining area of heather moorland. To highlight this the Nature Conservancy Council (now English Nature) gives an estimate of the state of the remaining stock of heather in England and Wales based upon the implied stocking rates in Table 3.4. This indicates at least half of the heather

Table 3.3 Distribution of cover on land converted from heather moorland in England and Wales, 1947–80

Land cover	Area	Percentage
Upland grasses	81.2	66.6
Conifer plantation	15.4	12.6
Bracken	15.2	12.5
Improved grass and crops	5.0	4.1
Mixed plantation	2.6	2.1
Blanket bog	2.5	2.1
Total	121.9	100

Source: Nature Conservancy Council (1990)

Table 3.4 State of heather moorland in England and Wales, 1986 (thousand hectares)

Heather condition	Ewes/ha	Moorland area	Heather area
Good	<2	425.5	300.0
Poor	2–3	464.0	225.0
Suppressed	3–4	246.5	98.9
Absent	>4	319.0	–
Total		1455.0	623.9

1986: Based on the June Agricultural Census, excludes common land and non-agricultural heather moorland. Nature Conservancy Council (1990)

area is in a 'poor' or 'suppressed' condition due to overgrazing. Thus there is considerable evidence that both the quantity and quality of heather moorland has declined due to an increase in sheep stocking rates and a decline in grouse shooting.

THE DETERMINANTS OF HEATHER MOORLAND DECLINE

Heather moorland is an example of a complex form of natural capital which provides both a private production input and a public good with a non-market, existence and use value. As a productive resource it is unusual in that, in some locations, the grouse-shooting enterprise provides the incentives for its preservation. The area of managed heather moorland was estimated at 117,200 hectares in 1984 for England and Wales (Bradbury et al, 1989). Other examples of this sort of ecosystem include the preservation of broadleaved woods for pheasant shooting, Scottish moorlands for deer stalking and, on a larger scale, African savannah for hunting game parks. Commercial hunting places a market value on an ecosystem which would otherwise have none. Ironically, hunting may partly satisfy the objectives of conservationists, who may not entirely agree with the methods of habitat management, but would prefer an ecosystem to be managed for hunting rather than being irreversibly lost. It is notable that conservation agencies and organisations such as English Nature (Nature Conservancy Council, 1990) and the RSPB tend to encourage the sensitive management of heather moorland for grouse shooting.

In evaluating reasons for the decline in the area of heather moorland it is important to appreciate its place as a vegetation community and the economic factors which lead either to its destruction or enhancement. Figure 3.1 is based on the National Vegetation Classification (NVC) (Rodwell, 1991). Heather moorland is represented by the heath

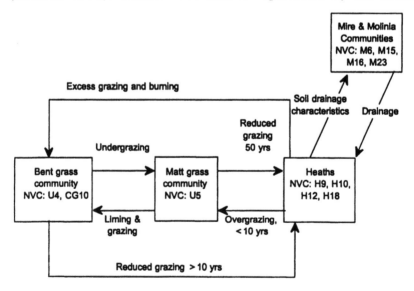

Figure 3.1 Upland grass moor and mire communities

communities. Three important patterns of vegetation change have been observed in response to the management of heather moorland. First, overgrazing heather leads to a matt grass community which is a persistent state; once established, it would require a long period to rehabilitate as heather. In addition, the matt grass community is of little ecological interest and is unproductive for sheep production. A bent grass community is another potential outcome of overgrazing combined with large-scale burning. This is agriculturally productive and is more amenable to being converted back to heather moorland than matt grass. Finally, where soil drainage is impeded, heather moorland could gradually convert to the mire communities, which have low agricultural productivity, but are of considerable ecological value due to their rarity.

The loss of heather is effectively an irreversible process. There has been limited experience in re-establishing heather moorland, but the evidence is that it may require 50 years or more to re-establish, especially from hill areas dominated by matt grass. This long period of re-establishment is characteristic of most valued agricultural ecosystems.

ECONOMIC FACTORS IN THE DECLINE OF HEATHER MOORLAND

Heather moorland represents an equilibrium between the vegetation, grazing and burning management. Ideally it should be grazed extensively and burnt on a once-in-eight-years rotation in small patches. The incentives for pursuing a relatively labour intensive approach to vegetation management derive from the profit from grouse shooting. The inter-linkages are illustrated in Figure 3.2. The heather vegetation mosaic is managed by burning and grazing, and its status determines how many grouse territories are available and the stocking rate that can be carried. The state of this heather mosaic is critical to the sustainability of heather moorland, it is described in terms of the age distribution of heather and the invasion of encroaching species such as bracken and the grasses.

Sheep grazing has a variable effect. Heather remains palatable to sheep during the winter, and thus heather is prone to most damage at this time of year. Further, sheep prefer shoots from young heather plants, and so young plants tend to incur a disproportionate amount of damage. Established plants can sustain a 30 per cent utilisation rate and

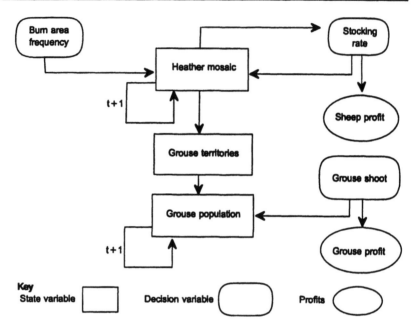

Figure 3.2 Linkages between heather, sheep and grouse

remain undamaged (Grant, 1971; Grant and Armstrong, 1993). Thus, defining the effective stocking rate depends on numerous factors: including the flock's access to alternative sources of forage and the intensity of shepherding activity which, by distributing the flock across the hill, can reduce damage.

The competition between the sheep and the grouse enterprise is through the heather mosaic. Managing heather entirely for sheep involves burning large patches of heather at a time, possibly encouraging the invasion of favourable grass species and stocking at relatively high levels (above two ewes per hectare). Managing for grouse shooting requires small-patch burning and low stocking rates, of between one and two ewes per hectare. This management regime increases the number of available grouse territories. Red grouse are territorial birds which define territories to include older heather for nesting and younger heather for food. If these resources are not available close together then the size of territories must expand to cover a larger area. The state of the heather mosaic determines the potential number of territories available. However, due to disease cycles, the grouse population is prone to marked fluctuations from season to season (Hudson, 1986). The population is also affected by the shooting rate which in turn determines the profitability of the grouse enterprise.

The equilibrium on any moor depends upon its environmental characteristics, the relative profitability of sheep and grouse and the distribution of property rights. This last point concerns situations where the right to graze the moor and the right to shoot grouse may be held by different firms. The possible outcomes on the moor are illustrated in Figure 3.3. The profitability of the moor is expressed as a function of sheep numbers which stand as a proxy for the state of the heather mosaic: at high stocking rates, the moor requires large-area burning and a decline in the dominance of heather whilst, at low stocking rates, small-patch burning is acceptable. Consider first the marginal sheep profit: as sheep numbers increase, this declines to zero at a stocking rate s_3. At this stocking rate, the profit from sheep (the area under the sheep marginal profit curve) is maximised. This outcome is likely to occur where the heather is managed by a sheep farmer on common land, who takes no account of grouse profits Grouse profits are increased by a reduction in sheep numbers from s_3 and are maximised at a stocking rate of s_1. This outcome would occur where the moor is owned by a firm primarily interested in grouse

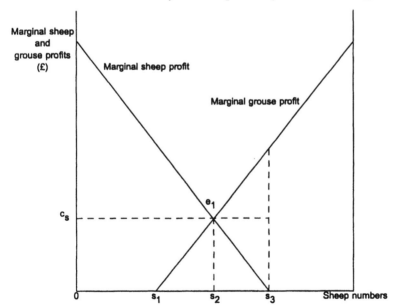

Figure 3.3 Static economic equilibrium for a heather moor

shooting, which rents out the grazing rights for a restricted number of sheep. If grazing and shooting rights are jointly owned, as is typically the case in Scotland (Hooper and Whitby, 1988), then the owner would maximise profit by equating the marginal profit from sheep with the marginal profit from grouse shooting. One further outcome is possible. If the moor is owned by the sheep-grazing firm, then an incentive exists for the shooting firm to compensate the grazing firm at a rate cs per head for a reduction in sheep numbers. Both the sheep firm and the shooting firm benefit from this agreement, which is an example of Coasian bargaining (Coase, 1960). This type of agreement is more difficult to negotiate where a large number of graziers control the moor, as is the case on common land, and their stints (grazing rights) far exceed the carrying capacity of the moor. (Topham, 1985). Common-land management typically involves two forms of externality: those imposed on one grazing firm by another and those imposed upon the shooting firms by the grazing firms. In such situations it may not be possible to reach a negotiated settlement which satisfies all the firms.

The equilibrium is also affected by agricultural policies, in particular headage payments and ewe quotas. Ewe headage payments are subsidies on the livestock capital employed in lamb and wool production. Their predicted effect is illustrated by a modified version of Figure 3.3. From Figure 3.4 we note that the headage payment has shifted the marginal sheep profit curve up vertically by the amount of the headage payment. The equilibrium under sole-ownership by the sheep firm has shifted to a higher stocking rate. This is generally detrimental to the grouse firm and to the sustainability of heather. Ewe quotas may be environmentally beneficial only if they constrain producers to stocking rates which relate specifically to particular environmental conditions.

A CASE STUDY

As an illustration of these principles, White and Wadsworth (1994) analysed a dynamic model of heather management and grouse shooting for a hypothetical 1000 hectare moor in North Yorkshire at 1994 prices. This region has a large proportion of commercial heather moorland and the environment is favourable for grouse shooting.

The results are for a comparative dynamic analysis but to simplify

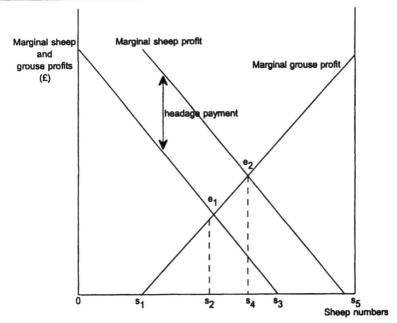

Figure 3.4 The effect of sheep headage payments on the heather moor economic equilibrium

the account they are presented as annual averages. From Figures 3.5 and 3.6 it is notable that where headage payments are paid to sheep producers the profitability of the sheep enterprise on the moor dominates the contribution of grouse shooting, and the optimal stocking rate is 2.5 ewes per hectare which would effectively preclude a viable grouse-shooting enterprise. When the headage payment is removed the optimal sheep stocking rate is between 1 and 1.5 ewes per hectare which includes an active shooting enterprise and small-area burning policy. With headage payments, there is limited scope for Coasian bargaining when the property rights rest with the grazing firm as the grouse enterprise does not generate sufficient profit to justify compensating the sheep producer.

The other potential determinant of decline is the relative uncertainty of the income from grouse shooting. By its nature the grouse population is known to fluctuate from season to season due, it is believed, to parasitic threadworms (Hudson, 1986). Thus the available shooting days and the income from a moor can vary markedly from year to year. While such fluctuations in income may be acceptable to a large estate where risk can be diversified among a number of different

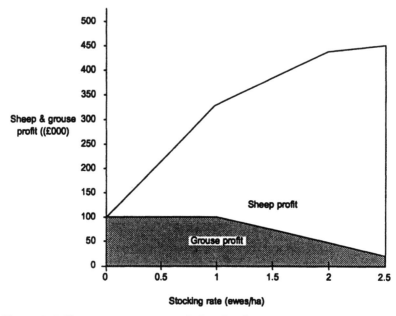

Figure 3.5 Sheep gross margin including headage payment

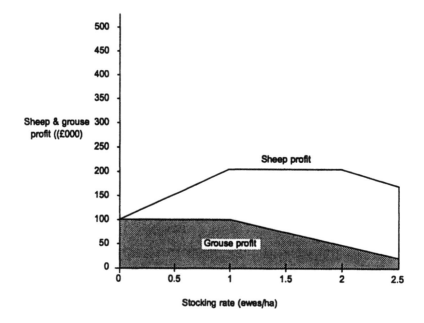

Figure 3.6 Sheep gross margin without headage payment

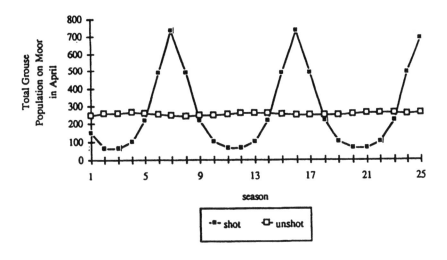

Figure 3.7 Grouse population on a moor managed for grouse
Note: this is assuming 0.5 ewes/ha, and small-patch burning (100 × 50 m) every 8 years

enterprises, a highly risky income is not acceptable to a family farmer who would tend to favour the relatively reliable returns from sheep production over uncertain returns from grouse shooting. This point is illustrated in Figure 3.7 for a moor intensively managed for grouse shooting.

THE NON-MARKET VALUE OF HEATHER

Contingent Valuation Estimates

Some evidence was presented above which indicates that the heather area of England and Wales is declining and that a significant proportion of the remaining heather is threatened either through improper management or deliberate intensification. Heather can be viewed as a form of natural capital which has a non-market value in addition to its value as a productive resource. This non-market value derives from its use, existence and option value (see Garrod, this volume). In the absence of this non-market value there would be no need for policy intervention.

Valuing heather moorland as a landscape entity and determining the socially optimal area of heather moorland is probably beyond current methods of non-market valuation. It may be possible to value the non-market benefits of a project which marginally increases the area of heather. However, the fundamental difficulty of valuing heather moorland is that peoples' perceptions of it and attraction to a heather landscape are not readily separable from other aspects of the landscape. In fact, the social optimum may involve a diverse landscape which includes heather as a significant component along with woodland and grassland. Further, respondents would find it difficult to value a hypothetical situation where they are asked to place a marginal value on heather when there is a substantially increased or reduced area compared with the current area: by definition, marginal values are only appropriate where a marginal change in the area conserved is assessed.

On the basis of the National Vegetation Survey which recognises 19 main communities as upland heather moorland habitats, five of these are confined to Britain and a further six are well-developed in Britain. In other words, heather moorland is important in a global context as a source of biodiversity. Heather moorland supports substantial proportions of the European populations of merlin, red grouse, golden plover and dunlin. Ground-nesting birds benefit from the control of predators, especially foxes and crows, which is associated with grouse shooting. However some raptors, most notably the hen harrier, have been controlled, sometimes illegally, by gamekeepers. The 'ecological' value of heather should be considered in the context of heather as a vegetation community in transition: some of the mire communities, which may be replaced by heather after drainage, are of greater rarity value. A value, in terms of ecological rarity, diversity and scientific interest does not necessarily imply an economic value which depends on other attributes including the aesthetic value of the resource and the value placed upon its use in recreation.

The evidence on the economic value of heather moorland is less complete. In the first of two studies by Garrod and Willis (Garrod and Willis, 1993), survey respondents were asked whether they would like to see an increase in particular attributes of the Yorkshire Dales landscape. The results, presented in Table 3.5, indicate that a clear

Table 3.5 Recreation and non-use value of heather

Vegetation type		Quality preferred (%)		
		Less	Same	More
Heather moorland	Visitors	2.6	63.9	33.4
	Resident	3.7	69.2	27.1
Wild flowers	Visitors	0.3	32.1	67.5
	Resident	0.3	23.7	75.9
Conifer woodland	Visitors	37.0	45.2	17.7
	Resident	45.1	48.5	6.4
Broadleaved woodland	Visitors	0.3	44.3	45.8
	Resident	6.4	55.4	53.9

Source: Garrod and Willis (1993) (September 1990, 300 visitors and 300 resident households Craven District North Yorkshire)

majority of both visitors and residents would like to see more of the same area of heather moorland. This should, however, be taken in context with the responses for broadleaved woodland and wild flowers where respondents were more clearly in favour of an increase in the present area.

In another study (Garrod and Willis, 1994), administered to members of the Northumberland Wildlife Trust, respondents were asked to allocate to each 'valued' habitat found in Trust reserves a share of 100 points (not all habitats are given here, thus scores do not sum to 100). Table 3.6 shows that heather moorland scores quite highly in terms both of the personal preferences of members and the number of visits per annum, but poorly in terms of the additional subscription that the members were willing to pay. This may, however, be a regional phenomenon: heather moorland is relatively extensive in Northumberland and Durham, while other preferred habitats, broadleaved woodland and hay meadows are relatively rare and inaccessible.

There is evidence that heather moorland represents a globally rare vegetation habitat, which supports a number of rare bird species. However, 'ecological value' does not necessarily imply an economic value, although it is a component of it: individuals may place an existence value on biodiversity and enjoy bird-watching as a leisure activity. The evidence from economic surveys is that both the general public and members of a wildlife trust place both use and existence value on heather moorland. The fact that this value is not accounted for directly by a market may lead to market failure where the area of heather moorland is reduced below its socially optimal level.

Table 3.6 Ranking visits and valuation of heather moorland

	Mean preference (score out of 100)	Mean number of visits per annum	Mean additional payment (£/annum)
Heather moorland	12.3	6.2	0.67
Peat bog	4.0	1.0	0.79
Broadleaved woodland	19.5	11.5	2.32
Conifer forest	3.1	4.5	0.29
Hay meadows	10.2	2.6	1.44

Source: Garrod and Willis (1994) (227 members of Northumberland Wildlife Trust, surveyed by postal questionnaire, administered in 1992).

Quasi-Option Value

In the previous section the elements are outlined for either a cost-benefit analysis or, at least, a cost-effectiveness analysis of heather moorland. A form of cost-effectiveness analysis is reported by Hanley et al (1996) where there is a measure of the cost of reducing stocking rates to a carrying capacity which will ensure the long-term survival of heather moorland on The Shetlands. A cost-benefit analysis would require a measure of the benefits as well as the costs of reduced agricultural output and, as discussed above, this is very difficult to estimate.

The observation that re-establishing damaged heather may take up to 50 years and that uncertainty remains over the current and future value of heather represents a case where the quasi-option value of preservation is likely to be an important factor. Quasi-option value is an additional value associated with delaying an irreversible environmental change when uncertainty surrounds either the costs or benefits of that decision. In this example this is interpreted as a value of preservation which involves maintaining the area of heather until uncertainty over the social value of heather has been resolved (see Arrow and Fisher, 1974; Graham-Tomasi, 1995).

The notion of a quasi-option value can be illustrated with a simple example. Consider the decision to preserve heather or to convert it to grassland. To make the example concrete, suppose the current estimate of the marginal social value of a hectare of heather is either £100 or

£20 per annum with equal probability as a result of two contingent valuation surveys. It is anticipated that this uncertainty will resolve when a more comprehensive survey is completed in a year's time. The value of conversion is £70 per annum with certainty in terms of additional sheep output. The social discount rate is 5 per cent. The expected monetary value of this project if the decision must be taken immediately is £70/0.05 = £1400, that is an income of £70 in perpetuity, as the conversion option is more profitable than preservation which has an expected value of 0.5(£100/0.05)+ 0.5(£20/0.05 = £1200). However, if the project can be delayed and the uncertainty resolves the payoff is:

$$£1,666.67 = 0.5 \frac{1}{(1.05)(0.05)} £70 + 0.5 \frac{£100}{0.05}$$

Note that the additional delay allows the best decision to be taken under both states of nature. However, the benefits from development are delayed for a year and must be discounted by one year. The expected value of delaying the project is thus £1,666.67 − £1400 = £266.67, which is the quasi-option value.

The implication of this analysis is that there exists a value to preserving heather moorland which is due first to the irreversibility of its loss and second to uncertainty surrounding its value. In practice this may lead to a series of policies, such as the Moorland Scheme, which reduce the rate of heather lost to allow time for a clearer understanding of its social value to emerge.

THE POLICY RESPONSE

Policy instruments directed to conserve heather moorland must reflect the non-market economic value of heather on the one hand and the variability of heather moorland as an ecosystem on the other. Present policies for conserving significant areas of heather include the North and South Peak District ESA (Froud, 1994) and the recently introduced Moorland Scheme (MAFF, 1995). The nature of ESA policy is that farmers are paid to accept input constraints, but this does not guarantee that heather moorland will be preserved or reinstated as it is typically difficult to specify the restrictions closely enough to reflect local conditions. The Moorland Scheme is specifically designed to regenerate heather; eligible moorland areas must contain at least 25 per cent heather and participating farmers must agree to reduce stocking rates to specified limits in return for a headage payment of £30 per ewe removed. The fact that there is scope for varying the specified stocking limit implies that this scheme can be adapted to reflect local conditions.

An alternative approach to these schemes would be to pay farmers a fixed fee for entering a scheme, and bonuses based on the improvement of the state of heather moorland under their control relative to a base period. Such contracts would ideally have to be over a very long period given the time-scales associated with reinstating heather moorland, and may take the form of restrictions which apply indefinitely to certain areas of land. Arguably, the weakness in the current ESA scheme is that producers have an incentive to enter into the agreement for the first five years and then leave.

The issue of the extent of heather moorland which should be conserved is a difficult issue and is not readily addressed by current methods of environmental valuation. In particular, respondents would need to answer questions which concern their current valuation of the marginal area of heather and their valuation as the area of heather either increased or decreased substantially. Conceptually the socially optimal area of heather is represented in Figure 3.8. Costs and benefits are a function of the proportion of a fixed land area devoted to heather or, conversely, grass. The marginal social cost (MC_G) is initially a negative function of the proportion of heather area. This indicates that in the least suitable regions for upland grasses there is a cost, relative to heather, of maintaining any grassland in terms of labour and capital. As the proportion of heather increases then costs increase as the heather area is moved to less suitable land. Marginal benefits are of two types: marginal private benefits (MPB_H) from grouse shooting and sheep grazing and marginal public benefits (MGB_H) in terms of use and non-use values. If only private benefits are considered, then the area of heather is H_1; if both private and public benefits are taken into account it is H_2.

The implication of quasi-option value arises where the current area of heather is greater than the expected social optimum H_2. Uncertainty over the location of the marginal public benefits MGB_H implies a greater area should be retained than is expected to be optimal, because this decision may later be regretted if the true social value is greater than expected when uncertainty over MGB_H is resolved. This is a

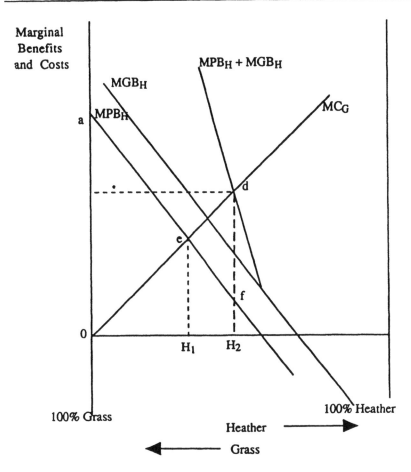

Figure 3.8 Representation of the 'optimal' heather area

complex issue. It is a gross simplification to suggest that uncertainty resolves. Ideally, the statistical distribution of the value of the marginal hectare of heather will become narrower as repeated contingent valuation studies are undertaken and their methods and values converge to a stable mean and variance. In practice, this may not occur, the variance of contingent valuation estimates may actually increase in which case there remains a permanent quasi-option value.

CONCLUSIONS

Heather moorland represents a case where a valued ecological system is under threat from agricultural intensification and neglect. Grouse shooting provides an incentive for preserving the heather, but this incentive depends upon the profitability of grouse relative to the profitability of sheep, the clear definition of property rights between the grazing firm and the shooting firm and the willingness of the owner of shooting rights to accept wide fluctuations in profitability from season to season.

The evidence of contingent valuation studies indicates that heather has a social value in addition to its private economic value as a factor of production. This social value may be increased by a quasi-option value which arises due to the effective irreversibility of heather destruction and uncertainty over its current social value.

Heather moorland provides an attractive feature of the rural landscape, and grouse shooting provides a source of rural employment, diversifies landowners away from declining agricultural production and attracts visitors to rural areas. Conserving heather moorland may contribute towards the sustainability of rural areas from both an ecological and an economic perspective.

CHAPTER 4

Valuing Environmental Goods in the Countryside

Guy Garrod

INTRODUCTION

A principal concern of environmental economics is the analysis of human interactions with environmental goods and services such as landscape, recreational amenity, clean air and water. Each of these is an example of a positive externality, that is an unintentional by-product of traditional land uses in the countryside which itself provides benefits to certain individuals (there may also be less desirable side-effects of traditional land uses like agriculture, in the form of negative externalities such as pollution).

Even when their benefits are substantial, environmental externalities are seldom traded in the marketplace like normal goods and so do not have a conventional market value attached to them. Generally speaking, the consumption of these non-market goods is non-excludable, that is no one can prevent anyone else from consuming them; they are also non-rival in consumption, which means that their enjoyment by one individual cannot affect the amount consumed by any other individual. These public-good characteristics have, in the past, meant that the economic value of positive environmental externalities has been largely ignored. Such an omission can lead to an inefficient allocation of resources in the countryside and today, with the British countryside subject to a larger number of competing land uses than ever before, the efficient allocation of scarce resources has become a serious problem for decision makers.

Economists have endeavoured to alleviate this problem by proposing that for any policy or project likely to lead to changes in the quality of environmental goods and services, the effects of these changes should be evaluated in economic terms in order to ensure commensurability with monetary revenues and costs (Pearce and Markandya, 1989). This requires the investigation of public preferences for improvements in environmental goods and services, or in cases of damage or degradation the measurement of the resultant loss of public well-being. For convenience, this process is referred to as environmental valuation, and the resulting estimates as environmental values. These measures are often conveniently expressed in monetary terms. Thus, researchers may seek to estimate how much members of the public would be willing to pay for a given improvement in the level of environmental quality, or alternatively the amount of compensation that they would require to make up for a given level of environmental damage.

In this chapter the notion of environmental value is discussed, introducing a typology of values for environmental goods and services. Following this, a number of case examples introduce three of the techniques most commonly used to estimate the benefits of environmental goods in the countryside. The validity and reliability of such estimates are then briefly discussed before a final examination of the usefulness of environmental values to project and policy appraisal.

WHAT ARE ENVIRONMENTAL VALUES?

In a practical context, environmental valuation conventionally requires the estimation of the monetary value of a given externality, be it negative (a cost) or positive (a benefit). This monetary value can reflect part or all of the total economic value of the environmental externality being studied, depending on which aspects of its value have been enumerated. Thus, the total economic value of an environmental good or service is the sum of all use values derived from it, plus any non-use values which it may generate. Use values are benefits arising either directly or indirectly from an environmental good, while non-use values are generated by the consumption of the flow of information about the good which is consumed as a preservation benefit, ie a value arising from the knowledge that an environmental good will persist (see Box 4.1).

Box 4.1 Definition of secondary environmental values

Use Values

Direct Use Value: goods and services that can be directly consumed by users, eg food crops, fisheries, tourism, recreation, medicines, education, research

Indirect Use Value: indirect benefits arising from environmental systems, eg drainage, coastal protection, support to other biological systems, carbon fixing

Non-Use Values

Option Value: the value individuals place on expected future use and indirect use of the components of environmental systems

Quasi-Option Value: the value arising from expected new information which will arise from the conservation of environmental systems for future use (see Arrow and Fisher, 1974)
   Existence Value: a range of values arising from some or all of the following motives:
   Bequest Motives: the value of preserving environmental systems for future generations
   Stewardship Motives: the idea of preserving environmental systems for their own sake
   Altruism: the value of preserving environmental systems so that they are available to benefit other people
   Q-Altruism: the belief that non-human resources have rights and should be left unmolested where possible

---

Some economists and ecologists favour a broader definition of value than is to be found in neoclassical economics, particularly in the case of the environmental or ecological systems that are instrumental in the generation of environmental goods. The total economic value concept focuses on the benefits that human systems derive from environmental goods, and is based very much on the perception that economic value is the same as market price. However, broader ecological systems perform a major role in sustaining life on this planet, and this function may be regarded as having value regardless of whether human beings have preferences for it or not.

This 'prior value' is part of what has been termed the primary value of ecological systems. Primary values reflect the notion that there is a value inherent in the existence of the underlying system, a value so fundamental that it cannot be measured in terms of human preferences (eg see Hargrove, 1992). Primary values are independent of the so-called use and non-use values (collectively termed secondary values) that are dependent upon externalities generated by the interactions of human beings with environmental systems.

The total economic value (TEV) of an environmental good may thus be defined as the sum of its secondary values, and this value can be placed in the context of the total value of the environmental systems that underpin it. Given the existence of primary value, the TEV of a set of environmental goods may be less than the total value of the framework of environmental systems that they exist within. It is, however, impossible to enumerate primary values and express them in the sort of economic frameworks within which decisions are typically made. This has led to a concentration on secondary values in economic appraisal and this may in the long term have important implications for the determination of sustainable combinations of economic and ecological systems.

ESTIMATING THE BENEFITS OF ENVIRONMENTAL GOODS

Having identified the values which may be associated with positive environmental externalities, there remains the question of how these may be estimated in a meaningful way. Normally, economists rely on observing market behaviour to determine value; however, because there is usually no market for environmental goods and services, other means have to be found to value them.

Environmental valuation methodologies fall into two broad categories. In the first category are techniques which are based solely on costs: these may capture only part of the total economic value of an environmental change, but are useful in cases where benefits are either hard to quantify, or where the intention is to achieve a given level of benefits at least cost. These methodologies have been described in detail elsewhere (eg Dixon and Hufschmidt, 1986) and it is the purpose of this chapter to illustrate some of the methodologies which fall into the second category. These attempt to quantify the benefits which result from environmental externalities. This may be done by examining the preferences of the general public, either as expressed through a questionnaire survey or as revealed through their behaviour.

Each of the methods outlined below is based on economic measures of human welfare, such as utility: economists define utility as the satisfaction or pleasure that individuals derive from the consumption of a good or service. The change in the level of welfare for an individual resulting from an environmental change is estimated as the amount of income necessary to maintain a constant level of utility before, and after, the change of provision.

The first method to be considered is contingent valuation. This is by far the most widely used technique for valuing the benefits of environmental goods, and has been used since the early 1960s in studies of recreation and the environment. The contingent valuation method (CVM) is the most versatile of valuation methods, and uses a questionnaire approach to elicit directly individuals' preferences for a wide variety of goods and scenarios. CVM offers considerable scope for the estimation of both the use and the non-use benefits which arise from environmental improvements.

In general, the use of CVM must be restricted to those environmental goods (such as landscape) that are within the experience of respondents and relevant to them. Any attempt to elicit an individual's willingness to pay (WTP) for an environmental change, the major consequences of which are poorly understood by the respondent, may generate an estimate of WTP that is biased by the lack of requisite information. For example, although it may be appropriate to use CVMs to evaluate projects and policies that will have both a reversible effect on the environment and a considerable impact on the amenity and recreational value of the general public, it may be unwise to apply it in situations where the effects on the environment could be both irreversible and detrimental.

CVM has been used to value reversible changes to agricultural landscapes: such changes will often impact on the recreational and visual amenity of the general public. A study of this nature was conducted in the Yorkshire Dales National Park in the summer of

1991. Here, samples of visitors and residents were interviewed on-site about their recreational activities in the Park and their preferences for a number of its features. Following this, respondents were shown pictures of eight hypothetical future Dales landscapes and asked to list the three which they liked best (Willis and Garrod, 1993a). These landscapes were depicted using artist's impressions and included a representation of the most common Dales landscape (labelled as today's landscape), together with a sporting landscape, a wild landscape, an abandoned landscape, two more agriculturally intensive landscapes, and two landscapes where planning directives or environmental policies had led to the conservation or enhancement of traditional Dales landscape features such as stone walls and barns and flower-rich hay meadows. Over half of the residents and nearly half of the visitors questioned stated that today's landscape was the one they preferred. The next most popular first choice, attracting around 30 per cent of respondents, was a conserved landscape where many of the traditional Dales features had been enhanced.

Respondents were then asked how much they would be willing to pay, in terms of additional taxes, in order to help preserve their preferred landscape, and if that landscape was not today's landscape what their maximum WTP would be to prevent today's landscape reverting to an abandoned landscape as depicted in another of the illustrations.

The values generated showed a strong preference for preserving the Dales landscape in the preferred form and a similarly strong desire to prevent the sort of landscape that would arise from a collapse in agricultural support structures (see Table 4.1). When aggregated across the populations of residents and visitors annual WTP for first-preference landscapes totalled over £107 million (in 1990 prices): this could be divided into £87 million for landscapes resulting from public interventionist policies and £20 million for those landscapes that would not result from such policies (eg abandoned, sporting or managed wild landscapes).

Public preferences for landscape in the UK were also investigated in a study of the Ministry of Agriculture, Fisheries and Food's Environmentally Sensitive Areas (ESA) scheme (Garrod and Willis, 1995). The ESA scheme represents an attempt by government to offset the effects of more intensive agricultural practices in the countryside by seeking to support the contribution of more traditional

Table 4.1   Estimates of willingness to pay to preserve Dales landscapes (1990 prices) (figures in mean £/household/year)

	Visitors	Residents
To preserve most preferred landscape	27.08	25.09
To preserve today's landscape when most preferred	22.12	26.03
To preserve today's landscape compared to abandoned landscape (when today's landscape is not most preferred)	26.21	21.71
To preserve today's landscape whether most preferred or not	24.56	24.05

farming practices to the appearance of the landscape. This is achieved by offering farmers in areas designated as ESAs a range of per hectare payments to farm their land in more environmentally friendly ways.

As part of a questionnaire survey carried out in the South Downs in the summer of 1992, members of the public were shown how the ESA scheme would eventually change various landscape features in the area. Those respondents (over 90 per cent) who preferred the ESA landscape to a more intensive agricultural landscape were asked how much additional tax they were willing to contribute towards the scheme, first for the ten ESAs that had been designated in England by that time, and then for the South Downs ESA alone. Maximum WTP was elicited using a payment card which helped respondents decide how much they would be willing to pay by telling them what they currently contributed towards various items of public spending. Estimates of mean WTP for a sample of over 450 visitors and local residents are shown in Table 4.2.

The magnitude of public WTP for the South Downs ESA was comparable with that for the Yorkshire Dales National Park, with local residents willing to pay more than visitors for this particular ESA, though less for ESAs in general. Respondents' willingness to allocate a substantial portion of their WTP for the ten English ESAs towards a single ESA may be explained by the fact that they either lived in or adjacent to the South Downs, or that they were already demonstrating a preference for the area by visiting it. In a further survey of 746 households across England based on a similar questionnaire, respondents were found to be willing to pay only £36 per year on

Table 4.2 Estimates of willingness to pay for the South Downs ESA (1992 prices) (mean £/household/year)

	Visitors	Residents
For 10 English ESAs	94.29	67.46
For the South Downs ESA	19.47	27.52

average towards the ESA scheme in the 10 English ESAs. This sum decreased to only £21 if respondents had never visited an area currently designated as an English ESA. Benefits to non-users such as these were not required to justify the estimated annual net public expenditure cost of the South Downs ESA (£970,000), which was considerably less than the aggregate benefits of the ESA for visitors and local residents.

Although the methodology used in the studies described above may sound straightforward, any contingent valuation application must be subjected to intense scrutiny designed to detect any evidence of the presence of biases. Contingent valuation estimates are greatly influenced by questionnaire design, and failure of the questionnaire may lead to biased estimates of benefits. The amount and type of information with which researchers provide respondents is crucial, as is the way in which the valuation questions are phrased and the payment mechanism through which the valuation is elicited. For example, use of an existing payment mechanism which is controversial or unpopular may mean that many respondents either fail to answer a WTP question or answer it in a way that does not reflect their true WTP.

Another important problem is that of embedding. Psychologists have found that when asking people questions about a particular environmental good, their answers often take account of the set of all similar goods. A striking example of this phenomenon in contingent valuation literature can be found in Kahneman and Knetsch (1992). In a study of WTP to maintain fish stocks in the Ontario Lakes the responses of two samples of people were analysed. Respondents in the first sample were asked their maximum WTP to maintain fish stocks in all Ontario Lakes, while respondents in the second sample were asked their maximum WTP to maintain fish stocks in only a small part of the province. Mean WTP for maintaining fish stocks was very similar across both samples, suggesting that CVM could not distinguish between public preferences for a small proportion of lakes in Ontario and preferences for all of them.

Kahneman and Knetsch explained this effect by postulating that respondents were purchasing moral satisfaction which was itself not related to the level of provision of the environmental good: this is described as a 'warm glow' effect. Kahneman and Knetsch considered that the results of their study represented a serious criticism of contingent valuation methodology. However, other economists have suggested that the embedding effect in this case was a product of flawed questionnaire design, rather than the result of any particular limitation of the basic methodology. In particular, not enough information was provided to respondents about the consequences of different levels of provision, and the context within which the valuation exercise was framed was inadequate. A well designed CVM survey looking at this issue should not have come up with the same result.

The other two approaches to be examined in this chapter use human behaviour to estimate the change in welfare associated with increased access to environmental goods. Recreational demand studies have consistently shown that as the price of access to a site increases, then the visit rate to the site falls. Where a site has no entrance charge, then the price of access is equivalent to the cost of getting there, both in terms of the cost of travel and the opportunity cost of time – the latter concept reflects the notion that our leisure time is precious and that we may treat its use as a cost.

These ideas form the basis of the travel-cost method (TCM), which is widely used to measure the value of informal recreation from the costs incurred in gaining access to the site. Visitors are interviewed on site and asked for information about their visits, the activities they undertake during them, their preferences for outdoor recreation and the characteristics of their households.

In the UK the method has been applied to the valuation of forests, canals, country parks and various other attractions. Willis and Garrod (1991) investigated the benefits accruing to visitors from informal recreation at Forestry Commission sites in the UK. Using data from a 1988 questionnaire survey of individual household visits to six sites they used ordinary least-squares and maximum-likelihood techniques to model households' annual number of visits to a site as a function of the cost of visiting the site, the availability of substitute sites and the socio-economic characteristics and preferences of visitors. The resulting models were used to derive estimates of the consumer surplus for these unpriced recreational visits (see Table 4.3).

Table 4.3 Estimates of consumer surplus per visit to six British forests based on travel cost (1989 prices) (mean £/household/visit)

Forest	Consumer surplus based on individual household data	Consumer surplus based on zonal aggregate data
Brecon	1.40	2.60
Buchan	0.50	2.26
Cheshire	0.40	1.91
Lorne	1.53	1.44
New Forest	2.32	1.43
Ruthin	1.29	2.52

The study described above is an example of the TCM based on individual household data. An alternative approach is to model demand for recreation using aggregate data based on observed visits to a site across a number of zones defined at various distances away from the recreational site (see Clawson and Knetsch, 1966). This approach explains variation in zonal visit rates using aggregate zonal data on the costs of travel, availability of substitute sites and population socio-economic characteristics. Zonal travel-cost models of the demand for recreation were also used by Willis and Garrod to estimate the net benefits accruing from unpriced visits to Forestry Commission sites (see Table 4.3).

Inspection of Table 4.3 shows that the two techniques give quite different estimates of benefit. This is chiefly a product of the differences in the two techniques. The zonal model assumes that the cost of travel for all individuals travelling to a site from a given zone is the same, while the use of data based on individual visits allows travel cost to vary across all individuals. Furthermore, using zonal data to model demand for on-site recreation means that much of the richness of data available when using individual data is lost. However, modelling variation in individual visit rates is subject to a number of problems, such as the possible wide variation in travel costs for individuals making the same annual number of visits to a site and the difficulties in adjusting the model to take account of that part of the population that does not choose to visit the site and hence cannot be represented in the data set.

An issue that tests practitioners using both zonal or individual data is the appropriate measurement of travel cost. The estimates given above were based on the estimated full cost of transport to and from the forests (for households who travelled by car this included an element of full running costs as well as the cost of petrol) plus an additional amount to represent the opportunity cost of travel time. The incorporation of the time-cost element and its appropriate measurement has been the subject of much debate.

A second method based on individuals revealing their preferences through their behaviour is hedonic pricing (Rosen, 1974). The hedonic price method (HPM) is based on consumer theory (Lancaster, 1966) and relies on the premise that, in the absence of financial constraints, the amount which an individual is willing to pay for a particular good is dependent upon the individual attributes of that good. Thus, the amount which an individual would be willing to pay for a new house would depend to a great extent on its location, the type of neighbourhood, the number of rooms it has, its state of repair, whether it is detached, semi-detached or terraced, the central heating provided, the amount of garden area and the provision of garage space.

In this case, then, for otherwise identical houses, an improvement in the level of one characteristic of one house should raise the price of that house by an amount equal to the value which the purchaser places on that improvement. For example, consider two identical houses facing opposite each other in the same street, sharing the same services and identical neighbours. The back windows of one house command a view of a brick wall, while from the back windows of the other house a pleasant area of woodland can be seen. If both houses are auctioned simultaneously then any difference in price between them is attributable to the difference in view.

In the UK, hedonic pricing has been used to value the premium which proximity to woodland and water has on house prices. For example, Garrod and Willis (1992) used an hedonic price technique to estimate the value of a number of countryside characteristics. Their study was based on an analysis of over 2000 house purchases over a five-year period across an area of 4800 square kilometres of Central England and the Welsh Borders centred around Gloucestershire.

Data were available from a building society on the purchase price and the structural characteristics of each property in the sample. These data were supplemented with socio-economic information from the 1981 census and with map data indicating whether or not the property was located adjacent to a variety of features including woodland, rivers, wetlands, schools, shops, settlements and industrial sites. The completed data set was used to derive a mathematical model which revealed the relationship between the attributes of a property and its sale price. The resulting model was used to estimate the premium that an improvement in a particular housing characteristic added to mean house prices in the area.

Thus, the hedonic pricing approach allowed a value to be estimated for the amount by which an extra unit of a particular characteristic will on average raise or depress the sale price of a property. If the characteristic involved is discrete, that is if it is either present or absent in the good and there is no in-between position, then the method will simply derive the premium which the presence or absence of that characteristic will generate.

In practice it is difficult to determine the premiums which structural characteristics will add to house prices. This is because most of the structural features of a house are inter-dependent and their effects on house price cannot easily be separated. For example, detached houses will in general have greater amounts of other desirable attributes such as bedrooms or bathrooms so part of the premium for a house being detached will be due to these other features. This problem does not arise for many environmental attributes, and the premium they add to house value can often be estimated. In the above study, the location of a house in an area with at least a 20 per cent woodland cover raised prices by just over 7 per cent, while location close to a river or canal added a premium of 4.9 per cent to house prices.

One limitation common to each of the techniques discussed is that, unless they are applied with great care and with a full knowledge of the theoretical and practical considerations underlying them, they will almost certainly produce estimates which fail to reflect the 'true' levels of the values being sought. This issue is addressed in the next section.

THE VALIDITY OF ENVIRONMENTAL VALUES

Environmental values will only be useful if decision makers are confident about their validity and their ability to provide useful information not available elsewhere. Where there is a need to place a value on environmental goods and services, there are often few good alternatives to the values which environmental economists estimate. The most obvious alternative is expert judgement.

Studies based on expert opinion may produce widely different estimates of environmental value depending on which experts are asked to provide them (eg see Willis and Garrod, 1993b). Indeed, there are numerous examples of the fallibility of expert judgement, many originating in medical journals. Even though experts may sometimes get things right, are their estimates of environmental value any more likely to be valid than those based on the observed and expressed preferences of substantial samples of the general public? Indeed, as Hanemann (1994) points out, it is unclear how experts can estimate the value which the public places on an environmental improvement without resorting to some form of survey instrument. As notable economists including Arrow and Becker have argued, decisions about what people value should be based on their opinions – and it is the people rather than the faceless expert who are really the best advocates of public preferences for the environment.

If decision makers are to accept this, how can they be convinced that the environmental values generated by economists are to be trusted any more than those based on expert judgement? While experts can call on anecdotal evidence and their own experience, economists are armed with a battery of more objective techniques that can be used to test the robustness and reliability of their models. Using these, they can show how stable their values are over changes in data and modelling assumptions. They can also test with reasonable confidence whether or not the estimates of environmental value derived from their models are consistent with underlying economic theory, and whether they are compatible with values drawn from studies of similar environmental goods.

However, the models which economists build are only as good as the data from which they are derived. Inadequate or inaccurate data will lead to the development of inappropriate models which will in turn generate estimates which do not reflect society's underlying preferences. It is easy to generate estimates of value that are neither reasonable nor credible; however, as in all disciplines, the use of correct practice will eliminate the majority of systematic sources of error, generating estimates which can be confidently used by decision makers.

Monetary valuation does not seek to set a price on these things so that they can be purchased by the highest bidder, it merely allows individual members of society to express their preferences for them in a convenient way that can then be taken account of in the decision-making process. Indeed, this monetary expression of preference may be the most effective way of introducing an element of social choice into economic development decisions. The problem remains that for some people placing monetary values on environmental goods is morally unacceptable. For certain individuals no amount of money is sufficient to compensate them for a decrease in environmental quality. If individuals persist in holding such lexicographic preferences (Hanley, 1995) then conventional economic appraisal techniques generally fail to incorporate them into the decision-making process, thus disenfranchising the people who hold them. The effect that this will have overall cannot be judged until a better understanding is reached of how common such preferences are. However, if lexicographic preferences are taken seriously and given full weight in decision making then they will automatically outweigh all other weaker preferences, a situation which itself could lead to serious problems of equity and efficiency.

THE USE OF ENVIRONMENTAL VALUES IN PROJECT AND POLICY APPRAISAL

Prior to their implementation, many projects and policies that have significant impacts on the environment are assessed using cost-benefit analysis (CBA) or other environmental appraisal techniques. In CBA, as many of the impacts of a project as possible are expressed in terms of the monetary value placed on them by society. After adjustments are made for effects which occur at different times, the estimated net benefit – or cost – is then used by policy makers to inform decision making.

In order to make CBA more efficient it has been argued that environmental values should be included in the analysis along with the more conventional values. This follows because some notion of the monetary value of the benefits of environmental goods is necessary to offset the traditional economic bias towards the more conventional revenue-generating functions of the countryside. Without this, the benefits generated by outputs such as timber and agricultural products would automatically take precedence over non-marketed goods such as biodiversity and landscape which do not attract a price.

In common with other nations, the UK has increasingly recognised the need to incorporate environmental values into both project appraisal and policy appraisal (eg HM Treasury, 1991; DoE, 1991; 1994). As a result a number of government departments and statutory bodies regularly commission projects which are required to estimate the environmental costs and benefits of given projects and policies.

In the United States the process has gone a stage further, and legislation has been passed allowing contingent valuation to be used to help assess environmental damage liability, and CVM estimates are now being used in multimillion dollar litigation such as that surrounding the Exxon Valdez oil spill. The debate that arose from this case as a result of the high level of damages set using CVM (most of which accrued from non-use values) culminated in the National Oceanographic and Atmospheric Administration sponsoring the formation of a distinguished panel of economists who went on to make a series of important recommendations for the implementation of future CVM studies (see Arrow et al, 1993).

The preceding discussion has shown that environmental values can perform an important role in both the appraisal process and the generation of monetary estimates of environmental damage. At the same time efforts are being made to improve the reliability of these estimates and so increase their usefulness. However, while incorporating environmental values into CBA may provide better information for project and policy appraisal, this does not necessarily ensure that an ecologically desirable solution is reached. Some authors (eg Soderbaum, 1987; Common and Perrings, 1992) criticise economic estimates of environmental values on the grounds that their use may lead to sub-optimal policy decisions that could eventually have undesirable consequences for both economic and ecological systems. Briefly, these authors argue that environmental valuation represents an over-simplification and, by concentrating exclusively on the secondary values imparted by environmental goods, ignores the total value of broader environmental systems.

While these criticisms are to some extent valid as an argument against important decisions being made solely on the grounds of CBA undertaken within a partial equilibrium framework, they do not mean that environmental values cannot play an important part the appraisal process. Given a belief that the rural economy is a complex, open, dynamic system, it is not unreasonable to argue that any decision-making process within it that is based strictly on economic optimisation, while ignoring the complex relationships between economic and ecological systems, would not be effective. Like all economic estimates, environmental values should be used appropriately – in this context as part of a more holistic decision-making process. Indeed, decisions regarding environmental policy are rarely taken on the basis of economic appraisal alone, but are made as part of a political process that reflects the prevailing balance of interests; these are by no means all financial but reflect many other contemporary concerns including ecological ones.

While few economists would dispute the continuing need to enhance the methodologies used to estimate environmental values, perhaps a more pressing challenge is to improve our appreciation of how these values should be used most appropriately in project and policy appraisal. Environmental values are only part of the evidence that must be weighed in making these judgements, and should be considered along with all other relevant information in order to achieve an outcome that balances society's needs with those of the environment in a manner which meets agreed criteria for sustainability.

CHAPTER 5

The Role of Marketing Rural Food Products

Christopher Ritson and Sharron Kuznesof

INTRODUCTION

The future of the rural economy, rural society and rural landscape depends upon a viable farming community. The future of the farming community depends upon success in marketing.

(NFU, 1994)

The concept of marketing as a philosophy or business orientation has been identified as crucial to the success of organisations (Peters and Waterman, 1982). This chapter focuses on the marketing of rural food products as a means of examining the role of marketing in sustaining the rural economy. Rural food products are placed within the broader context of the agricultural industry to which they are linked by virtue of the industry's role as provider of raw materials for food production. It is acknowledged that marketing is of relevance to other industries which may have a contribution to make in sustaining the rural economy, such as tourism, for example (Tregear, et al, 1996). There are, however, three reasons for concentrating on rural food products in this chapter. First, agriculture is located in, and indigenous to, rural areas. There is nothing incidental about agriculture being 'rurally' based – it almost always *has* to be rurally based. Second, agriculture represents a significant area of economic activity within the rural economy. Third, the term 'marketing' is increasingly being applied to the agricultural industry as a means of improving the micro- and macro-level competitiveness of the farming/rural community, as indicated by the British National Farmers' Union (1994) quotation introducing this chapter.

Although effective marketing is central to the success of any business, urban or rural, this chapter is restricted to the role of marketing in the success of businesses containing attributes which are peculiar to the rural context, and it assesses the extent to which marketing-led success in rural activities is consistent with the sustaining of the rural economy. Sustainable development has been defined as 'managing the countryside in ways that meet current needs without compromising the ability of future generations to meet theirs' (DoE/MAFF, 1995). Two components of sustainable development are: meeting the economic and social needs of people who live and work in rural areas, ensuring that rural businesses are as efficient and competitive as they can be; and conserving the character of the countryside – its landscape, wildlife, agricultural, recreational and natural resource value (DoE/MAFF, 1995).

Within the context of the 'rural economy', these may coincide to produce a positive economic and environmentally sustainable outcome. Alternatively, initiatives may occur which place greater emphasis upon either environmental or economic sustainability. It is also possible to consider the most negative scenario of environmental and economic degradation. For example, over-grazing in upland areas may be detrimental to the sustaining of both the natural environment and the future viability of upland farming. Thus this chapter refers to the contribution of marketing to both sustaining the level of economic activity in rural areas and the success of initiatives directed towards (or at least consistent with) sustaining the natural rural environment.

The discussion begins with an overview of the modern marketing concept and its relationship to agricultural marketing, to provide background to the marketing of rural food products. This is followed by an analysis of the marketing advantages of location-specific production and the contribution of marketing to sustaining the rural economy, using three case studies for illustration.

MARKETING AND ITS CONTRIBUTION TO AGRICULTURE

The Modern Marketing Concept

Marketing is a relatively recent field of academic inquiry. It has developed from multidisciplinary foundations that sought to understand changes in market behaviour (Bartels, 1962), and later the process of exchange, as described by Bagozzi (1975).

A popular view of marketing is that it simply seeks to sell products. However, this undermines a more holistic concept of marketing which is possibly best described as a philosophy that places customer needs and wants central to an organisation's operations. For example:

> The marketing concept is a philosophy, not a system of marketing or an organisational structure, it is founded on the belief that profitable sales and satisfactory returns on investment can only be achieved by identifying, anticipating and satisfying customer needs and desires – in that order. It is an attitude of mind which places the customer at the very centre of a business activity and automatically orients a company towards its markets rather than towards its factories. It is a philosophy which rejects the proposition that production is an end in itself, and that the products manufactured to the satisfaction of the manufacturer merely remain to be sold.
>
> (Barwell, 1965)

An alternative definition of marketing is:

> Marketing is the process whereby, in order to fulfil its objectives, an organisation accurately identifies and meets its customers' wants and needs.
>
> (Ritson, 1986)

The method by which a firm can attempt successfully to meet the pre-identified needs and wants of its target market, occurs through the company's ability to influence a set of controllable variables or marketing tools coined by Borden (1964) as the 'marketing mix'. These marketing functions have been divided into four categories known as the four 'P's (McCarthy and Perreault, 1984): the product, its price, its promotion, and its distribution (or place). Thus the modern (business) marketing concept is based on a managerial philosophy that places identified target customer needs and wants as central to the organisation's operations, and uses a set of activities and techniques to achieve these objectives.

Marketing in the Agricultural Context

In contrast to, for example, tourism, services or industrial marketing, the marketing of agricultural products did not develop as a specialist application of modern marketing theory. In fact, agricultural marketing has a much longer pedigree than mainstream business marketing (Ritson, 1996). It developed during the early twentieth century, first in the major USA Midwest land-grant universities, and subsequently in Western Europe, as a branch of applied agricultural economics, concerned with understanding the behaviour and functions of agricultural commodity markets, and of government policies to control the marketing of agricultural products – as epitomised, for example by 'marketing orders' in the United States, and 'marketing boards' in the UK. It was associated with the increasing significance of the food marketing sector, and the belief that many of the problems confronting farmers originated in that sector. Thus marketing and agricultural marketing can be distinguished as separate subjects differentiated by their evolutionary paths (Figure 5.1).

Figure 5.1 The relationship between business and agricultural marketing

As a consequence, in the context of agriculture, the term 'marketing' is interpreted in three distinct, though related ways. First, marketing can be viewed as a set of economic activities that occur as produce moves from the farm to the final consumer. This is also sometimes known as the 'marketing margin'. This is relevant to the agricultural industry for, in some farming circles, there remains the widespread belief that effective marketing for agriculture is essentially about ensuring that the marketing margin is minimised, in order to get food to consumers as efficiently as possible. The (almost certainly false) corollary to this is that efficiency in this sense will entail a higher return to the farming sector by ensuring that a greater proportion of what the consumer pays reaches the farmer. However, efficiency within the agricultural sector does become important when one considers the issue of 'nation state competition'. This is something to which we return, but it is worth noting at this stage that the NFU 'Food from the Countryside' initiative can be seen in this way. For example the NFU (1994) suggests that success in agricultural and horticultural marketing depends on four key objectives:

1 strong marketing structures;
2 enhancement of operational competitiveness;
3 closer relationship with customers;
4 the development of a positive image for farm products.

A significant aspect of this interpretation of marketing for agriculture in terms of sustaining the rural economy concerns the critical issue of location. Successful farming is relevant to the rural economy because virtually all farming activity *has* to occur in rural areas, but as one moves through the food chain towards the consumer, there are a series of activities which may, or may not, occur within the rural economy. This issue is explored in the following section.

The second interpretation of marketing within the context of agriculture is the application of modern (business) marketing techniques and concepts to farm and agriculturally related businesses. This refers specifically to the adoption of the modern marketing concept as previously described. One aspect of the use of marketing techniques to achieve consumer-focused objectives is that it enables a company to achieve and retain a monopoly (or 'marketing') advantage. Thus a business can distinguish itself from, and achieve an edge against its competitors, by virtue of its 'marketing advantage'.

The third interpretation of marketing in the context of agriculture is the collective action by farmers to control the marketing of agricultural products. The application of modern marketing techniques is often said to be of little relevance to farmers. This is due to farmers being typically one of a large number of producers supplying a homogeneous or undifferentiated product, and in a position of price-taker, and therefore unable to influence market returns. Essentially most of the ways by which products can be transformed, promoted and where the power of pricing is achieved, occur beyond the farm-gate. There are, of course, exceptions – farmhouse cheese, self-pick operations, and so on. However, there are various ways in which farmers can become involved in 'marketing activity' – producers' groups, co-operatives, quality standards, generic advertising and so on. Such activities are characterised by the fact that there is almost always some government involvement, at its minimum in the form of enabling legislation but continuing right through to major finance of marketing-related initiatives such as structures, advertising and commodity programmes.

It follows that, if marketing is to sustain the rural economy, then presumably it must be by achieving a marketing (monopoly) advantage against the non-rural economy (the urban economy) which is, of course, a major challenge. If it is merely the sustaining of a specific rural area, then marketing may have much more to contribute. This distinction can be illustrated through the first of three product case studies around which the remainder of this chapter is built.

THE MARKETING ADVANTAGES OF LOCATION-SPECIFIC PRODUCTION

Case Study 1: Wensleydale Cheese

The first case study analyses the marketing of Wensleydale cheese produced in the Yorkshire Dales.* This creamery was closed in 1992 by Dairy Crest, at that time a wholly owned subsidiary of the Milk

* The information on Wensleydale Dairy Products Ltd, Hawes, Wensleydale, is taken primarily from Amsden (1994).

Marketing Board (MMB) of England and Wales. Dairy Crest intended to transfer the manufacture of Wensleydale cheese to a factory in Lancashire, as part of a cheese manufacturing consolidation exercise. The primary effect of the closure would have been the loss of 59 jobs, 20 per cent of the working population of Hawes. In addition the livelihoods of many small milk producers supplying the Wensleydale creamery were veiled by heightened uncertainty perpetuated by knowledge of the future divestiture of the MMB. Also, for the area's inhabitants, the creamery represented a part of their heritage. However, following six months of negotiation, Dairy Crest agreed to a management buy-out of the creamery. Since that period the new company has rapidly become very successful, securing more than 50 per cent of the UK market share for Wensleydale cheese.

The Wensleydale creamery represents a business interest that is unambiguously situated within the rural economy and which has had a significant economic impact on the area through the employment of local residents, and the sourcing of milk produced indigenously. The success of the creamery can be attributed at least in part to a successful marketing management philosophy, with two main features being:

1 the development of a product concept that has exploited the marketing advantage associated with the creamery being the only producers of Wensleydale cheese in Wensleydale, using raw materials sourced from local milk producers, and employing hand-crafted production methods by drawing on local cheese-making tradition and expertise; and

2 effective communication with its target market, specifically through the development of a visitor centre, thus capitalising on the one million or so visitors that the area attracts each year.

This business initiative is certainly contributing to sustaining the economy of Wensleydale; but is it sustaining *the* rural economy? In order to help to answer this question it is worth considering the various rural and non-rural competitive positions.

'The' Versus 'A' Rural Economy

Rural areas are in competition with each other in what they produce, and indeed in, for example, the tourists they attract, and quite different marketing issues arise if one is considering sustaining a specific rural area as opposed to the rural economy. This difference is highlighted by contrasting successful marketing, as it would have been understood in the Milk Marketing Board of England and Wales, and successful marketing from the perspective of a small number of dairy farmers in Wensleydale. The marketing mission of the MMB was at least in part to maximise the total return to *all* dairy farmers within England and Wales, with Dairy Crest developed predominantly as an outlet for the conversion of increasing volumes of milk production into butter and cheese. From a national perspective there clearly is a conflict between whether dairy farmers as a whole would benefit more from large-scale, efficient plants to manufacture what increasingly was becoming a CAP intervention product; or a smaller number of rurally based plants attempting to develop location-specific products. Clearly only some farmers would benefit from the latter.

Rural Versus Urban Competition
Tying the location of food processing activity to a rural area represents competition between rural and urban areas and is consistent with sustaining the rural economy. The idea is that the development of a speciality high-value food product attached to a specific rural area will induce consumers to pay on balance rather more money overall for (in this case) the cheese that they buy. Again, if a particular rural area can exploit a rural marketing advantage which enhances the overall value of a particular product category this can contribute to sustaining the rural economy overall.

One means through which such a marketing advantage for a regional food can be cemented within the rural economy has been addressed by the European Union Council regulation (EEC No. 2081/92) 'on the protection of geographical indications and designations of origin for agricultural products and foodstuffs' (Council Regulation (EEC) No. 2037/93 setting out the criteria). The following extracts from the Regulation will explain the background and philosophy involved.

> as part of the adjustment of the common agricultural policy the diversification of agricultural production should be encouraged so as to achieve a better balance between supply and demand on the markets; whereas the promotion of products having certain characteristics could be of considerable benefit to the rural economy, in particular to less-favoured or remote areas, by improving the incomes of farmers and by retaining the rural population in these areas;

... moreover, it has been observed in recent years that consumers are tending to attach greater importance to the quality of foodstuffs rather than to quantity; whereas this quest for specific products generates a growing demand for agricultural products or foodstuffs with an identifiable geographical origin;

... the desire to protect agricultural products or foodstuffs which have an identifiable geographical origin has led certain Member States to introduce 'registered designations of origin'; whereas these have proved successful with producers, who have secured higher incomes in return for a genuine effort to improve quality, and with consumers, who can purchase high quality products with guarantees as to the method of production and origin;

(Council Regulation (EEC) No. 2081/92)

Thus the introduction of a controlled designated name for a food from a specific geographical region has the potential to:

- enhance the value of raw material from a region through its use in the production of differentiated, premium products;
- ensure that processing activity occurs within the region (and thus within the rural economy); and
- grant a monopoly advantage to producers and processors within a specific area by restricting the use of area names to products genuinely supplied from the region.

Presently, a total of 318 agricultural and food products (including meats, cheeses, fruits and oil) have been registered as protected geographical indications (PGI) or protected designations of origin (PDO) under Article 17 of Regulation (EEC) No. 2081/92 from a first wave of 1400 applications. This list is expected to be extended in the future. This policy initiative favours rural economic sustainability. One outcome of this intervention for the marketing of rural food products is that, at its extreme, such an approach can give a marketing advantage to an area predominantly by control of quantity. For example, if the name 'Wensleydale' was restricted to cheese produced within Wensleydale from Wensleydale dairy farms, a successful marketing initiative which boosted the demand for Wensleydale cheese could eventually meet a supplier restriction and force up price. Thus in the future, price, rather than product and promotion would become a vital element in the marketing mix for Wensleydale cheese produced at the Hawes creamery.

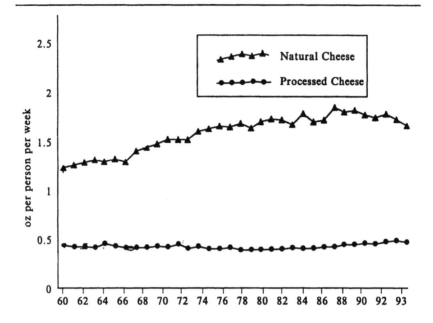

Figure 5.2 UK cheese purchases 1960–93
Source: calculated from National Food Survey data

Rural Versus Rural Competition

The above scenario indicates the potential for intra-rural competition. For example, Figure 5.2 shows that cheese consumption in the UK has been broadly static over a number of years, with a slight decline in consumption more recently. From this it follows that the adoption of marketing and the exploitation of a marketing advantage within Wensleydale by ensuring that dairy farmers in Wensleydale achieve a better return for the exclusive use of their milk for a high-value, premium-priced product is unambiguously at the cost of some other cheese-maker (and some other dairy farmer).

A parallel situation can be identified at a national level in terms of nation-state competition. It is increasingly understood that agricultural sectors of countries within the European Union can no longer achieve prosperity independently through government action directed against imported products. Thus the agriculture of Britain becomes a little like a food firm attempting to increase market share by product policy, promotion and efficient distribution. To a considerable extent a national marketing advantage might be acquired by an aggregate of regional marketing advantages (Scotch beef, Welsh lamb, and so on).

In this case study, the use of a marketing management philosophy has helped sustain the rural economy of Hawes through success in the manufacture of Wensleydale cheese by focusing in particular on a product concept and promotional strategy that exploited the marketing advantage of the creamery. This particular marketing mix strategy could, however, change in the future, if Wensleydale cheese is registered as a product of designated origin. This marketing advantage granted by the European legislation could ultimately result in a marketing strategy where the element of 'price' is given greater importance. Thus for some rural food products, government intervention through legislation (as seen above) features as an important factor in furthering a marketing advantage for rural products, with a resulting change in the relative emphasis of business strategies relating to the marketing mix, and enhancing rural economic sustainability.

Case Study 2: Scottish Farmed Salmon

The second case study analyses the issues of marketing and rural sustainability through the recently established salmon farming industry in Scotland. Although the first Scottish salmon farm was established in 1969, it was not until the 1980s that the industry witnessed rapid growth. By 1990, salmon farming had become a significant employment- and income-generator, comprising 170 companies occupying 350 sites and employing over 6000 people. For much of the 1980s the delivered price of salmon remained remarkably constant at around £2.50/lb (in real terms).

It has been argued by Ritson (1993) that the growth in the production of farmed salmon happened to coincide with a period which was particularly favourable from a demand perspective. Farmed salmon matched a number of factors which were influencing underlying trends in the patterns of food preference in Western Europe and hence satisfying a latent consumer demand. Marketing strategies incorporating promotional efforts, largely through generic advertising and distribution, led to increased consumer awareness of a luxury product and its wide availability through retail outlets, a contrast to the product's previous association with restaurant consumption. In addition, throughout this period, the quantity of farmed salmon

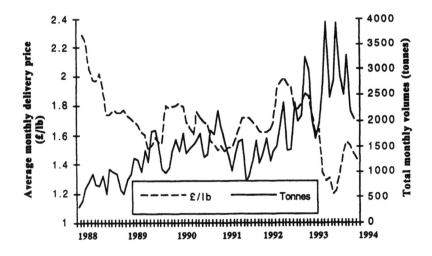

Figure 5.3 Scottish farmed salmon: production and prices, 1988–1994
Source: calculated from Salmon Growers' Association statistics

supplied to the market grew at roughly the same rate as that demanded by consumers, with resulting price stability.

Furthermore, the promotion of a national brand awareness for Scottish salmon enabled some of the larger companies to pursue market development strategies. Exports to a French market often perceived as impenetrable were particularly impressive, the Scottish farmed salmon even acquiring the French 'Label Rouge' quality mark.

However, the picture changed dramatically in 1988/89. The reason for this can be seen in Figure 5.3, with the annual rate of growth in the quantity of farmed salmon marketed suddenly exploding. During 1988 the delivery price plummeted and declined further in 1989. Since then the industry has been forced to cope with the marketing problems of a typical unstable commodity market. Production fluctuates wildly from month to month, predominantly for biological reasons. However, there is also evidence that price and production cycles are developing as large numbers of small producers react to short-term price rises and falls by expanding and contracting production accordingly. This has resulted in a number of fish-farm bankruptcies and considerable industry consolidation. Periodic attempts to protect the price of Scottish salmon in Western Europe have been made by the imposition of minimum import prices on competing Norwegian salmon and the growing recognition that in this particular case a marketing solution needs to contain some degree of producer organisation stability mechanism as provided for under the European Union's Common Fisheries Policy. To date the implementation of such a policy has been founded largely on the British Government's opposition to what is known as the 'extension of marketing discipline rule' which is intended to prevent the free-rider problem of individual producers not participating in collective action to support the market in times of chronic oversupply. At the same time, the larger companies in Scotland are progressively exploring the potential of obtaining marketing advantages by means of product differentiation such as branding and other company-related marketing initiatives.

The development of the farmed salmon industry is clearly relevant to sustaining the rural economy of Scotland, and government intervention in the salmon market is a testimony to this fact. The geography of Scotland gives it a unique advantage in the production of farmed salmon. Not only is this industry location-specific in the sense of any farm product being linked to rural areas, in this particular case the product *can only* be farmed in areas which are typically remote and otherwise disadvantaged within the rural economy.

However, to some extent, farmed salmon provides examples of a potential conflict between sustaining the rural economy in the sense of economic activity; and sustaining the natural environment. In terms of economic activity, the use of clean water as a primary raw material conflicts with other potential uses of clean water such as tourism, angling, drinking water abstraction, marine freshwater navigation and sewerage and waste disposal (Joyce, 1992). A selection of environmental problems caused by fish farming includes: the use of chemicals in cages where there is a free interchange with seawater; the visual impact in western lochs; and the possibility of disease infection to wild fish, and the introgression of wild salmon by escaped farm salmon which has been shown to have deleterious effects on the natural diversity of wild salmon species (Sattaur, 1989). Disease infection of wild fish is a particularly significant problem for Ireland, where it is alleged that farmed salmon has led to a severe demise of the sea trout (leisure) industry.

The adoption of marketing tools in satisfying an unmet consumer demand for salmon were formative in the early success of the Scottish farmed salmon industry and this has helped sustain rural economies in remote areas of Scotland. Government policies have been largely directed at maintaining this scenario despite potential adverse environmental effects.

Case Study 3: Northumbrian Bilberries

The last case study examines the potential for marketing to sustain both the rural economy and natural environment. The case study is purely hypothetical and centres on Northumberland bilberries. During the nineteenth century parts of the moors contained within the Northumberland National Park used to be covered by a mixture of heather and bilberry bushes, the fruits of which were collected by both rural and urban consumers. Today the bilberry bushes of Northumberland have largely disappeared due to overgrazing on the moorland, and bilberries are imported mainly from Eastern Europe. One of the objectives of the National Park is to reintroduce elements of landscape which existed prior to overgrazing and the question arises as to whether it might be possible, on either a self-pick or processed product basis, to exploit the bilberry itself. Given such a scenario it is superficially attractive to suggest that what is needed is 'some marketing'.

The idea that one could create a successful market for bilberries by the application of 'effective marketing' sits rather uncomfortably with the previous case study conclusions. These have highlighted the importance of:

- a managerial marketing philosophy which places the consumer central to the organisation's operation;
- an organisation satisfying pre-identified consumer needs through the application of the marketing tools within the organisation's control; and
- assessing the opportunities and threats posed by external operating factors, which are largely uncontrollable to the firm but which can affect its operations, such as legislation and government policy changes, and changing trends in demand.

However, recent developments in marketing theory give further insight into the application of marketing to Northumbrian bilberries and the potential simultaneously to sustain the natural and rural environment of Northumberland.

In so far as the marketing concept has been identified as 'an expression of the marketer's recognition of the importance of the consumer in the buying process' (Houston, 1986), the concept has been challenged as inapplicable to certain types of producers, in particular to artists and ideologists because of personal values and norms that categorise their production process (Hirschman, 1983). In one sense, National Parks (and perhaps many aspects of the rural economy) involve objectives which transcend the specific character-istics of individual products. The important message of marketing in these circumstances is not that everything must begin with the consumer, but that understanding the consumer is critical. For example, when a consumer buys a food product, she/he purchases a complicated bundle of attributes. Food purchases are not solely based on core attributes of hunger satiation, but the food decision-making process involves a well recognised a mixture of tangible and intangible factors such as taste, variety, prestige, convenience, animal welfare and care for the environment.

Linked to this change in emphasis of consumer understanding has been the challenge to the traditional view of marketing as an appropriate operating philosophy for organisations. The increasing divergence between private and social costs and benefits, such as rural depopulation resulting from urban industrial concentration, pollution, depletion of scarce resources, have raised the issue of businesses accepting 'social responsibility' in their management and operating procedures. Kotler (1980) succinctly highlights the dilemma:

> Some marketers have raised the question of whether the marketing concept is an appropriate organisational goal in an age of environmental deterioration, resource shortages, explosive population growth, world-wide inflation and neglected social services. The question is whether the firm that does an excellent job of sensing, servicing and satisfying individual consumer wants is necessarily acting in the best interests of consumers and society. The marketing concept side-steps the conflict between consumer wants, consumer interest, and long-run societal welfare.
>
> (Kotler, 1980)

In response to this, the marketing concept has been redefined and marketers now give credence to the 'societal marketing concept', defined as:

> a management orientation that holds that the key task of the organisation is to determine the needs and wants of target markets and to adapt the organisation to delivering the desired satisfactions more effectively and efficiently than its competitors in a way that preserves or enhances the consumers' and society's well-being.
>
> (Kotler, 1980)

The movement towards a societal marketing concept (more recent versions are 'green' or 'ethical' marketing) would suggest the possibility of some form of sustainability in Northumberland if the philosophy was used for the marketing of bilberries. In today's climate of heightened consumer awareness of the issues, it is possible for businesses with a profit motivation to make money by promoting themselves as socially responsible. Thus, from a managerial viewpoint, social responsibility or the adoption of a societal marketing orientation would make sound strategic sense in terms of securing a company's future viability. However, as Tregear (1996) suggests, the fact that food products are now being promoted with a unique selling point based on environmental sustainability or social concerns means that it is difficult to decipher the management motivations behind the product concepts, eg are they based on altruistic motivations (as typified by Hirschman's artists and ideological producers) or profit motivations.

In relation to Northumbrian bilberries, three points can be highlighted:

1 It is perfectly proper for the modern marketing concept to be adopted to meet the ideological/environmental objectives of National Parks.
2 'Success' means accurately identifying genuine consumer needs and matching them to these objectives.
3 Economic or environmental sustainability of rural Northumberland will be dependent upon the operating philosophy of the Northumbrian National Park.

CONCLUSIONS

In striving to identify whether or not marketing can have a role in sustaining the rural economy, a number of factors have been identified. The marketing of rural food products, particularly those with minimal processing, follow an agricultural marketing tradition where government intervention in the market is an important factor in the marketing strategies employed by a rural food business. As identified by the Wensleydale cheese case study, government intervention can alter the relative emphasis that a company may place on elements of the marketing mix. This situation is specific to a rural business rather than a rural economy. Alternatively, government intervention can help sustain the rural economy overall, as indicated in the case of Scottish farmed salmon. However, government intervention does not preclude a rural business from identifying the needs and wants of target consumers and producing a product to match their customers' needs and wants in a manner that is consistent with the company's objectives. Whether or not this approach will sustain the rural economy or rural environment will be largely dependent upon the organisation's managerial attitudes and operating philosophy, although government intervention can be influential in this situation. However, it is apparent that each of these factors should be assessed on a case-by-case basis to determine whether or not marketing has a role to play in sustaining the rural economy.

PART II

Rural Economy

CHAPTER 6

A Sustainable Rural Economy?

Paul Allanson

INTRODUCTION

Any discussion of the 'rural economy' immediately raises a series of questions. What is meant by the term 'rural'? Is there a distinct 'rural economy'? And, more recently, what might constitute a 'sustainable rural economy'? This chapter seeks to address these issues, though the main concern is to develop a coherent approach to the study of the rural economy and consider the implications for the design of sustainable development policies. The approach is ambitious because it attempts to inform various social science perspectives on the 'rural'; particularly those of agricultural economics and rural sociology. This is not to deny the distinctive methodological and substantive interests of the individual sub-disciplines, but the term 'rural economy' does echo the holistic traditions of classical 'political economy' where the economic, social and political were treated in the round.

Everyday usage of the term 'rural' typically reflects the distinctive spatial pattern of land use in rural areas. Thus Hoggart (1988) notes that the general public employs 'rural' as a common-sense category to refer to small settlements separated by stretches of open countryside, while Newby (1982, p 129) adopts a pragmatic definition of rural areas as 'geographical localities where size and density of population is relatively small'. Nevertheless, the definition of rural areas has itself become increasingly difficult in advanced industrial economies with the blurring of the distinction between urban and rural space, and this has led to various attempts to 'capture' the rural using quantitative methodologies. Examples include:

- simple population densities (Walford and Hockey, 1991);
- rurality indices combining population densities, rates of population change, age structure, occupancy rates and other relevant variables (Cloke and Edwards, 1986); and
- multivariate classification systems based on the main constituents of local economies, such as population, employment structure, house prices and location (Hodge and Monk, 1991).

While these studies are valuable in identifying key components of rurality, they are potentially misleading inasmuch as the 'rural' is represented as a static and coherent category. This gives rise to a number of problems when it comes to considering economic activity in rural areas. First, the nature of such activity is highly diverse so the 'rural' cannot simply be equated with particular sectors, certainly not just farming, forestry and raw materials. Indeed, 'Some rural areas have an employment structure which is more akin to that of successful urban areas' (DoE, 1992b). Overall, Table 6.1 shows that the importance of manufacturing as a direct employer in rural areas is little different from that in urban areas, while even in remote rural districts only about 6 per cent of employees work in agriculture. Second, the economic structure of rural areas is dynamic, as illustrated by the urban–rural shift in manufacturing industry which has led to an increase in manufacturing jobs in rural areas of 19 per cent compared to an overall decline of 37.5 per cent in Great Britain over the period 1960 to 1987 (DoE/MAFF, 1995), and by the growth of the service sector which is now the major source of employment in rural as in other areas. Finally, the processes of socio-economic change may extend far beyond the boundaries of the 'rural' and therefore undermine any static and spatially bounded categorisation. People commute from rural areas to work in urban centres, and many rural communities depend on visitors from towns for part of their livelihood. Moreover, Tables 6.2 and 6.3 show that the majority of the business of rural firms, both in terms of sales and purchases, is located beyond their immediate region: indeed, rural firms would appear to be less parochial in both their market and supply orientation than businesses in urban areas.

However, the rural economy can usefully be characterised as a complex system, open to the exchange of people, goods and services,

Table 6.1 Economic structure in urban and rural England, 1989

Percentage of employees	Metropolitan	Urban	Coalfield	Rural accessible	Rural remote	Total England
Other (public) services	30.0	29.2	25.5	28.3	26.9	29.1
Manufacturing	21.2	24.2	33.7	25.7	23.3	23.8
Distribution & hotels	19.9	21.7	17.9	22.0	23.8	21.2
Financial & business services	15.6	12.3	4.6	9.3	6.2	12.4
Transport & communications	6.9	6.1	4.2	4.9	6.0	6.2
Construction	4.5	4.3	5.4	4.9	5.3	4.6
Energy & water	1.7	1.8	7.2	1.9	2.2	1.9
Agriculture	0.1	0.4	1.0	3.0	6.2	1.3

Source: Tarling, et al (1993).
Note: The area classification is based on local authority districts.

Table 6.2 Market orientation of firms in rural and urban areas

Percentage of sales	Rural remote	Rural accessible	Urban
Locality (<10 miles)	15.7	11.8	23.3
Region (10–50 miles)	24.8	24.2	23.0
Rest of UK (>50 miles)	50.3	47.3	39.8
Exports	11.0	16.7	12.2

Source: Keeble et al (1992)
Figures are based on survey findings

Table 6.3 Supplier orientation of firms in rural and urban areas

Percentage of purchases	Rural remote	Rural accessible	Urban
Locality (<10 miles)	11.9	15.6	24.3
Region (10–50 miles)	25.1	28.5	25.8
Rest of UK (>50 miles)	52.2	38.9	39.4
Imports	10.8	17.0	10.5

Source: Keeble et al (1992)
Figures are based on survey findings

information and other flows. This explicitly recognises that the rural economy may encompass socio-economic processes which extend beyond rural areas to the regional, national or even global level. Interest is focused on the expression of these processes in rural localities by the distinctive material shape, social value and environmental qualities of these areas, though attention is not necessarily limited by their geographical boundaries. Accordingly, the rural economy is not to be seen as a discrete object of study per se, but rather as the context within which a specific range of issues may be amenable to analytical or policy resolution. For example, it makes sense to consider the impact of the planning system on patterns of land use, problems of accessibility in remote rural areas or the effect of agricultural intensification on the natural resource base from a rural economy standpoint, but not the maintenance of the balance of payments or the prevention of global warming which cannot be accomplished by intervention at this level.

AN EVOLUTIONARY PERSPECTIVE ON THE RURAL ECONOMY

Evolutionary theory has long been applied to social systems, but the paradigm has been given fresh impetus by the emerging science of complexity (Waldrop, 1992) and associated theories of self-organisation. In economics, the appropriation of evolutionary ideas dates back to the classical period: indeed, Darwin's work was partly inspired by reading Malthus' essay on human population (see Clark and Juma, 1988). However, neoclassical economics has favoured a Cartesian–Newtonian world view of a mechanical system operating according to strictly defined laws. The major exception to this perspective within modern economic thought was provided by Schumpeter (1934), who treated economic development not as a shifting balance of goods adjusted by prices but as an evolutionary process involving qualitative or structural changes brought about by endogenous forces. This tradition has been built upon by Nelson and Winter (1982) in formulating an evolutionary theory of economic change which has subsequently informed the work of, amongst others, Dosi et al (1988) on technical change, and North (1990) on institutional change and economic performance.

Sociology also has a long tradition of using biological metaphors: both Comte and Marx in the nineteenth century conceived of the social world as an 'organic whole' in the process of evolution towards an equilibrium state of a 'harmonious society' or 'communist utopia', respectively. This holistic vision has not been abandoned, though the teleological determinism of the resultant schools of structural functionalism and orthodox Marxism has been increasingly challenged. First, the emphasis on structural constraints has given way to a concern to integrate individual action and the requirements of the social system without reducing one to the other. For example, Bauman (1992) portrays 'a fluid, changeable social setting, kept in motion by the interaction of the plurality of autonomous and uncoordinated agents'. Second, the positivist attempt to discover universal laws and tendencies has given way to a recognition of the contingency of social patterns and regularities. Giddens (1987) argues that:

> Modern societies, together with the organizations that compose and straddle them, are like learning machines imbibing information in order to regularise their mastery of themselves.

These views are closely akin to recent evolutionary theory though modern sociology has largely avoided the explicit use of biological analogies.

An evolutionary perspective thus has the potential to inform both economic and sociological discourses on the rural economy as a system which is complex, open and dynamic. In particular, modern evolutionary theory stresses the capacity of such complex systems for 'self-organisation' (Silverberg, 1988): that is, the spontaneous emergence of structures at the aggregate or macroscopic level from the seemingly uncoordinated behaviour of individual agents at the microscopic level. In other words, individual agents within the rural economy are necessarily bound into networks (Lowe et al, 1995) which regulate the behaviour of each agent through (positive or negative) feedback mechanisms. For example, one might think of the role of markets in co-ordinating the buying and selling decisions of individuals through the price mechanism or the role of the planning system in regulating the pattern of development. Thus, within the rural economy, a number of interacting social, economic, cultural and political sub-systems can be identified and these may be conceived of as undergoing a process of mutual co-evolution.

Evolutionary change in complex systems may be seen as modifying the context which has previously structured behaviour and can arise in certain circumstances as a result of the interaction between internal variability and the external environment. By implication, the evolution of the rural economy will be a path-dependent process in which the developmental trajectory is contingent upon the initial state of the system and the chance nature and timing of human innovations, local anomalies, individual aberrations and other historical accidents. However, for such microscopic fluctuations to give rise to effects at the structural or macroscopic scale, interactions between (economic) units have to be both local and significantly non-linear; ie small changes in a given unit's action must be able to produce large effects on the actions of its neighbours under certain circumstances even though they do not have a uniform effect of that size (Scheinkman and Woodford, 1994). The density and coherence of local networks has been identified empirically as a key factor underlying the endogenous development of regions such as the agro-industrial districts of the 'Third Italy' (see Iacoponi et al, 1995; and Lowe et al, 1995, for discussion).

Evolutionary theory has been formally applied to the spatial analysis of regional development by Allen and Sanglier (1981; see also Krugman, 1994, on the 'new economic geography') who focus on the emergence of a central place system (Christaller, 1954). Their work explicitly recognises that local economies are complex, open systems such that 'the evolution of any neighbourhood, town or city can never be dissociated from that of the surrounding regions'. The spatial self-organisation of a region is held to be an outcome of the dynamic interaction between separate centres of production and distribution. Using computer simulation techniques, they explore the effects of the introduction, competition and co-operation of levels of economic functions as they structure employment and population within the region. The dynamic feedback mechanism between population and employment levels is found to give rise to a spatial structure that depends on the timing and location of the launching of each economic function. The same mix of functions can therefore give rise to many possible structures compatible with the underlying specification of the model.

However, it remains to be shown that an evolutionary approach actually proves useful in the study of specific rural economy issues. This can only be demonstrated through detailed empirical research, but one indication of the potential may be obtained from a review of the continuing debate on rural restructuring which reveals an interest in many of the central phenomena identified by the evolutionary approach. In particular, the differentiation of the countryside as a result of the local expression of broader political, social and economic processes has been a recurrent theme, both in the debate on uneven spatial development in the 1980s (see, for example, Rees, 1984) and in more recent discussion of local modes of social regulation (see Flynn and Marsden, 1995). Goodwin et al (1995, pp 1256–7) argue that rural change should not be expected to be in any way uniform or easily predictable, but instead should be viewed as a socially constructed and sometimes fairly localised process involving the reshaping and re-ordering of existing sets of social relations.

Allanson et al (1994) have also sought to illustrate the direct applicability of the evolutionary perspective to the rural economy by detailed consideration of three issues which touch directly on the concerns of both rural sociology and agricultural economics. First, the operation of the post-war planning system is shown to illustrate both the role of local feedback mechanisms in reinforcing particular developmental trajectories, and the consequent geographical diversity of rural change in spite of the application of a uniform policy framework. Second, the evolution of farm structures reveals the role of random processes in generating the characteristic skewness of the farm size distribution, and underlines the dynamic linkages between market forces, technological change and structural adjustment. Third, an examination of the social learning induced by current pesticide regulations emphasises the importance of such processes for the development of a sustainable agriculture.

There is not the space here to elaborate on these generic examples, but it is important to recognise that the processes which underlie these issues are co-evolutionary, both shaping and being shaped by the overall trajectory of the rural economy. The 1947 Agriculture and Town and Country Planning Acts have common roots in the Scott Report of 1942 (Ministry of Works and Planning, 1942), with the agricultural support system designed to promote modernisation through farm rationalisation, mechanisation and intensification, while the planning system protected agricultural land from urban encroachment. However, this post-war policy 'regime', in which rural space was equated with agricultural space, has been placed under increasing pressure by subsequent developments. One particular focus of concern has been the environment, with the spread of modern agricultural production techniques leading to problems of pollution and degradation of natural habitats, at the same time as demands on the countryside as a consumption space have increased due to rising prosperity and the changing social composition of rural areas. This has induced both changes in agricultural policy to encourage more environmentally friendly farming practices (though in part these also serve to reduce over-production) and calls for the extension of the planning system to regulate farming practice and agricultural developments.

THE DESIGN OF SUSTAINABLE RURAL DEVELOPMENT POLICIES

The evolutionary perspective on the rural economy, in emphasising the complexity and inter-relatedness of human and natural sub-systems, provides an appropriate vantage from which to consider the 'integrative' concept of sustainability. Accordingly, the view of the rural economy as a complex, open, dynamic system is used to define the set of issues which has to be taken into account in the design of sustainable rural development policies. This does not lead to a single blueprint for the development of rural areas since there are many possible states which might legitimately conform to some vision of a sustainable rural economy. Thus, the discussion is restricted to the guiding principles rather than the substance of sustainable development policies in order to avoid a fruitless debate about the ultimate goal of sustainability. However, it does focus attention on possible pathways of deliberate change and improvement which maintain the ability of the rural economy to withstand or adapt to endogenous or exogenous change indefinitely while answering the needs of the present population (see Dovers and Handmer, 1992).

The fundamental insight of the evolutionary perspective is that the future development of the rural economy is inherently uncertain due to the capacity for self-organisation and the complexity of the process interactions. The capacity for self-organisation is evident in the proliferation of middle-class pressure groups which have exploited the public participation mechanisms of the planning system to create an 'exclusive' rurality, and in the elaboration of a legislative framework to regulate the novel externalities generated by the introduction and diffusion of agricultural chemical technologies. In the face of the pervasive uncertainty created by these unforeseen structural innovations, the neoclassical concept of sustainability underlying the commitment of the government to manage 'the countryside in ways that meet current needs without compromising the ability of future generations to meet theirs' (DoE/MAFF, 1995, p 9) is inoperative since it is not possible to define in advance either the choice set or the social and environmental constraints. Moreover, overall measures of system performance may be vitiated over time by the restructuring of value systems which are themselves subject to social learning processes (see Allen and Lesser, 1991).

Yet, even in the absence of some unequivocal measure of progress, maintaining the adaptive capacity of the rural economy will lead to a loss in static efficiency (see Allen, 1988). First, it must be understood that adaptivity or resilience is not the same as stability (Holling, 1973; Common and Perrings, 1992): the objective of 'protect[ing] the countryside for its own sake' (DoE/MAFF, 1987) is likely to be counter-productive in the longer term since the rural economy is open to social and economic fluxes induced by external changes. Rather, resilience requires the retention of some minimum level of diversity, which will be sub-optimal in the short-run, but is necessary to maintain the capacity to explore alternative development paths in the face of unforeseen change.

Clearly, the definition of the requisite level of diversity is problematic, though it is arguable that the post-war priority given to the agricultural use of rural land has been detrimental, because the constraints on alternative development uses have left some rural areas particularly vulnerable to the retrenchment of agricultural support policies, others dependent on single employers such as defence establishments or rural collieries, and still others reliant on the maintenance of commuting patterns which have developed in an era of relatively low energy prices. In recognition, UK government policy since the mid-1980s has increasingly sought to promote diversification both on and off farms, and in the rural economy at large (see Elson et al, 1995). For example, the original Planning Policy Guidance note 7 (DoE, 1988) states the need 'to foster the diversification of the rural economy so as to open up wider and more varied employment opportunities' and this emphasis has been maintained in the revised version published in 1992 (DoE, 1992c). Ironically, even though the modern pattern of economic activity in rural areas is far less diverse than in the past, these attempts to generate a more resilient rural economy face resistance from social groups attempting to impose their particular image of the 'authentic' countryside.

The capacity for self-organisation further implies that the rural economy cannot be assumed to be an inert system that can be 'optimally controlled' by the policy maker (Allen, 1982). Thus emphasis must be placed on the role of adaptive management strategies which will require institutions capable of reacting flexibly and responsively to changing ecological, economic and social conditions (Batie, 1991). The need for monitoring has long been recognised by the government in the agricultural sector with the production of the Annual Review White Paper on the state of the industry, and this practice has been extended to the environmental sphere following the publication of the White Paper *This Common Inheritance* (DoE, 1990), though the Rural White Paper *Rural England* (DoE/MAFF, 1995) significantly fails to include a similar commitment. Formal policy evaluation and review mechanisms are less common, although examples, such as the mandatory evaluation of Environmentally Sensitive Area schemes and the decennial reviews of all pesticides, do exist.

However, if monitoring is to serve as a reliable guide for policy appraisal and review, there is a further need to understand the processes which underlie both the general pattern of change and specific reactions to policy. This is not straightforward since knowledge of the existing structure of the rural economy is not sufficient to explore the set of possible configurations that may evolve in the future. Policy impacts will depend on the location and timing of intervention as the rural economy is spatially heterogeneous and may display irreversible changes due to hysteresis and threshold phenomena (Silverberg, 1988). For example, the impact of agricultural commodity support programmes will change over time because farm enterprise choices which are conditional upon existing farm structures, will in turn influence the future course of structural change. Or consider the viability of rural services such as public transport, village shops and local schools which generally will depend upon the size and social composition of a community but, if once withdrawn, are unlikely to be readily reinstated, with long-term consequences for the future of a locality. In general, the possibility of irreversibility does not seem to have been adequately assimilated into social and economic policy-making, though it is well recognised in the environmental field through the development of concepts such as the precautionary principle and safe minimum standards.

Furthermore, the complex inter-relatedness of ecological, economic and social conditions calls for a holistic approach to policy formulation. Rural concerns have historically been largely equated with agricultural issues, with MAFF taking a major role in rural land use policy. Yet, the sectoral responsibilities of MAFF leave it poorly equipped to tackle the emergence of a broader set of social and environmental problems. Thus, agricultural price-support policies, which promote farm rationalisation and intensification, are maintained at the same time as concern is expressed about the social fabric of rural areas (Commission of the European Communities, 1991a) and compensation is offered to farmers to encourage them to farm in a less intensive manner. The incoherence of such incremental policy changes points to the inadequacy of organisational conservatism in the face of continuing change.

The only realistic alternative is to orchestrate the totality of ecological, economic and social processes within the rural economy through a territorial system of governance. However, the evolution of any particular administrative area can never be dissociated from broader developments, while policies implemented by any one area will have more widespread consequences. This interdependence raises problems of co-ordination between different spatial levels of governance which in the UK have traditionally been addressed in a hierarchical manner rather than through a partnership approach based on principles of subsidiarity and co-operation, which would potentially be more flexible and spatially responsive (Ward, 1994b). Thus the current perception of the ten Government Regional Offices, established in 1994, is as outposts of central government implementing policy at a regional level rather than as representatives of the regions for which they are responsible (House of Commons Environment Committee, 1996). A more satisfactory basis on which a working relationship between the different levels of governance might be accomplished is through the reconciliation of strategic plans that co-ordinate the intentions of locally significant commercial and public organisations within a framework of community aspirations and environmental constraints. This approach to policy formulation is already employed to some extent in the implementation of European Union Objective 5b and LEADER II programmes. More generally, the preparation of Rural Strategies (Countryside Commission, English Nature and Rural Development Commission, 1993) provides a model that has been implemented in roughly half of all English County Councils though not as yet formally incorporated into the planning system.

Finally, the implementation of sustainable development policies requires the design of appropriate policy instruments. This design problem raises a vast and irresolvable complex of issues. However, it is worth pointing out that it does not reduce to a simple choice between market mechanisms and state intervention: North (1990) argues that custom and regulation reduce uncertainty and hence facilitate development by lowering search and transaction costs, while Marquand (1988) observes that the proper functioning of any market is dependent on the existence of the state to define and enforce property rights. Rather, the fundamental policy problem lies in the continuing development of institutional structures capable of internalising the benefits and costs generated by technological and cultural change (see Nelson and Soete, 1988).

Thus the canonical externality problem of neoclassical theory cannot be treated as a straightforward issue of 'market failure', even though the creation of private property rights in environmental media could in principle lead to a less exploitative use of natural resources. Another approach has been the formation and activities of Conservation, Amenity and Recreational Trusts (Hodge, 1988). Alternatively, the government may wish either to offer incentives for the preservation of public good attributes, through mechanisms such as the Environmentally Sensitive Area schemes, or to preclude certain forms of development through regulation. Historically, parliamentary enclosures, and more recent modifications in fiscal provisions and security of tenure, have profoundly influenced the pattern of agricultural and rural change.

CONCLUSION

In conclusion, the management of a complex, open, dynamic rural economy requires a society which is both information-rich and information-sensitive (Dovers and Handmer, 1992). The evolutionary perspective does not provide a grand synthesis of the disparate social-science disciplines, but rather a common focus on the processes of social and economic change which underlie the development of the rural economy. As such, the approach represents a move away from building precise descriptive models of the momentary states of a particular system, and challenges neoclassical concepts of optimality and dynamic control. Instead it focuses on the need for a holistic understanding of the complex of interrelated processes which constitute the rural economy in order to inform and manage a range of possible policy directions.

CHAPTER 7

The Planning of Rural Britain

Jonathan Murdoch

INTRODUCTION

This chapter considers the emergence and consolidation of the British nation state and the subsequent re-positioning of rural areas in the context of the nation. It will argue that the formation of the British nation state has entailed specifying the role that rural areas should play in national life. In general the dominant requirement has been increasing food production and the commercialisation of the agricultural sector which reached its apotheosis in the immediate post-war period with the development of a comprehensive agricultural policy. More recently, however, the rationale underpinning agricultural policy has been reassessed and this may signal a shift to a new specification for rural areas, one which draws upon other national considerations. Accordingly, the chapter goes on to trace the emergence of an alternative national discourse on rurality, one which identifies the essence of nationhood with the 'countryside' and which seeks to preserve the countryside in order to preserve the 'well-spring' of national identity. This concern has been incorporated into the planning system and it is now being bolstered by middle-class groups who have moved into rural areas in recent years and who seek to preserve a 'traditional' rural environment. Moreover, this emerging form of rurality is much more concerned with local diversity than the previously dominant agricultural regime and may lead to a new mix of the local and national in rural affairs. The chapter concludes with some thoughts on future patterns of rural development.

A HISTORICAL PREAMBLE ON AGRICULTURE AND PLANNING

In her excellent book *Britons*, Linda Colley (1994) dates the birth of the British state as the Act of Union with Scotland in 1707. At this time England, Scotland and Wales were brought together within one state for the first time. However, while this Act marked the formal emergence of a British state, it overlay strong local, regional and other national attachments. It was some time before people began to identify themselves as 'British'. Partly this was because a British nation was hard to discern. After the Act of Union, Scotland, for instance, still retained its own distinctive religious organisation and social structure, as well as its own legal and educational systems. And, in the first half of the eighteenth century, poor transport, inadequate maps and the sheer distance separating Scotland from London meant that for many (particularly Southern) English people Scotland seemed a distant and strange place, not one with which they felt much affinity.

Moreover, while it is sometimes assumed that the Act of Union was a piece of cultural and political imperialism, foisted on the Scots by their stronger Southern neighbour, this view disregards the hostility felt by many English people. To some of the latter, union with Scotland seemed a blatant affront to older identities, and they bitterly disapproved of 'English' and 'England' giving way to 'British' and 'Great Britain'. English nationalists were much less repelled by the union with Wales, mainly because the connection was so much older. Yet in many respects Wales was a more aloof and distinctive country even than Scotland. This was particularly so because the Welsh had their own language (even as late as the end of the nineteenth century three out of four of the inhabitants of Wales spoke Welsh).

Colley (1994) remarks that, at the time of its formal inception, Great Britain 'was like the Christian doctrine of the Trinity, both three and one, and altogether something of a mystery'. The inhabitants of Wales, Scotland and England were separated from each other by history, culture and, in some cases, by language. And they were not only separate from each other. Within each of these countries, communities in different places were also distinguished by:

different folklores, different sports, different costumes, different

building styles, different agricultural practices, different weights
and measures, and different cuisines.

(Colley, 1994)

The inhabitants of Wales, Scotland, and England did not even possess
an overwhelming sense of themselves as English, Scots or Welsh. For
instance:

in terms of language, religion, levels of literacy, social organisation
and ethnicity, Scottish lowlanders had far more in common with
the inhabitants of Northern England than they did with their
Highland countrymen.

(Colley, 1994, p 14)

And the degree to which the Welsh were able to see themselves as one
people was constrained by a North–South divide, marked by the
country's central range of mountains, making trade, communications
and human contact between counties in the North and those in the
South extremely difficult.

Although England was more centralised – with one language and
better communications – there was still only limited uniformity in
terms of culture. Northumberland, for instance, in the way that its
people lived, was much closer to being a Scottish than an English
county. Scottish books and newspapers were far more common than
those produced in England, Scottish accents were more familiar than
those of the Southern English (it is worth noting that as late as 1861 a
parliamentary inquiry on coal-mining needed an interpreter for
witnesses from Northumberland – see Lowenthal, 1991), and the
lowland Scots and Northern English shared many of the same tastes
and customs. Colley (1994) cites one small illustration of this: in
Northumberland, as in the Scottish lowlands, the poor as a matter of
routine consumed oatmeal. Yet this was a cereal, as Samuel Johnson
remarked in his dictionary, that the more affluent Southern English
regarded as being only fit for animals.

Many of the same general comments could be made about
Shropshire and Herefordshire with relation to Wales: here, as in the
case of Northumberland, centuries of cross-border trade, migration and
marriage had forged a distinctive but 'hybrid' culture. However, even
those parts of England which were not close to the Welsh or Scottish
borders were characterised by massive diversity:

How could they not be, when scenery and soil types varied enormously even over short distances, when the bulk of roads and people were too poor for long-distance travel to be common, and when no one – however rich – could journey faster on land than a horse, that is at ten miles an hour at the most? 'I had never been above eight miles from home in my life' the labouring poet John Clare would write of his youth in Northamptonshire, 'and I could not fancy England much larger than the part I know'.

> (Colley, 1994, p 17)

Thus, Colley remarks, the Union of Great Britain should be considered as:

> much less a trinity of three self-contained and self-conscious nations than a *patchwork* in which uncertain areas of Welshness, Scottishness and Englishness were cut across by strong regional attachments and scored over again by loyalties to village, town, family and landscape. In other words, like virtually every other part of Europe in this period, Great Britain was infinitely diverse in terms of the customs and cultures of its inhabitants.
>
> (Colley, 1994, emphasis added)

From this time on, however, the story is one of increasing cohesion, heralded by advances in road and postal communication, by the proliferation of print and by the operation of free trade throughout the island. The Act of Union had done away with all internal custom duties and trade barriers. The increased trade links between the countries necessitated better transport links (new turnpike roads). The movement of goods between different parts of Britain was accompanied by an incessant movement of people. England and Scotland, though not Wales, experienced a much faster rate of urban growth in the eighteenth century than did any other part of Europe. Moreover, country dwellers were drawn out of their seclusion to trade; farmers and farm labourers were forced regularly to visit nearby towns so as to sell produce and buy goods. Thus Colley argues:

> The idea ... that Great Britain at this time was a land of small inward-looking communities, frozen in custom and cut-off from trade and communications, is at best only a half-truth. The majority of men and women simply could not afford entirely self-centred lives. The business of earning a living drove them,

whether they wanted it or not, to towns, to markets, to pedlars
and at some stage to travel.

(Colley, 1994, p 40)

The extent to which Britain began to experience some genuine sense of
cohesion during the eighteenth century marked it out from its
continental neighbours:

> In terms of its agricultural productivity, the range and volume of
> its commerce, the geographical mobility of its people, the vibrancy
> of its towns, and ubiquity of print, Britain's economic experience
> in this period *was* markedly different from that enjoyed by much
> of Continental Europe.
>
> (Colley, 1994, p 43, emphasis in the original)

Thus it was not just the increased interconnections between them
which gave people a sense of being British but a sense also that they
were different from those living beyond their shores, and, in particular,
different from their prime enemy the French.

As Britain and Britishness became more tangible aspects of people's
lives, and as other more local identities were undermined by the
increasing networks of links that tied places together, so rural areas
became increasingly incorporated into national patterns of development. We can trace two aspects of this: first, industrialisation,
agricultural specialisation and strategic concerns about food production; second, the desire to preserve rural land as part and parcel of
maintaining national identity in the face of rapid industrialisation,
urbanisation and two world wars. Each will be briefly dealt with in
turn.

INDUSTRIALISATION AND THE
COMMERCIALISATION OF AGRICULTURE

The increased connectedness of the different parts of Britain has
continued since the Act of Union until the present day. With the
industrial revolution, and the establishment of the factory system,
industry became concentrated in certain towns and these grew rapidly
to form new agglomerations. At the beginning of the nineteenth
century a fifth of the population lived in towns, increasing to four fifths

by the end of the century (Lowe and Buller, 1990). As Britain industrialised, the concentration of economic activities and urbanisation ensured that rural areas became progressively emptied of diverse economic activities. They came to rely more and more upon agriculture. Furthermore, agriculture was becoming increasingly commercialised, with labour leaving the industry from the 1850s onwards (between 1861 and 1911 the proportion of the working population in agriculture fell by 10 per cent (Bellerby, 1958)).

While it would be an overstatement to claim that these trends – industrialisation, urbanisation and commercialisation – were eradicating diversity – both in agricultural practices and the relationships between agriculture and other sectors (what we now term diversification or pluriactivity) – there is little doubt that the strong local and regional distinctions noted by Colley (1994) were being undermined. Rural areas, in particular, came to play a highly specialised role, being devoted almost exclusively to primary production.

The commercialisation of the agricultural sector was slowed, however, by the expansion of new territories in the Americas which, when allied to Britain's traditional free trade policy, stimulated the ever-increasing importation of food to nourish an overwhelmingly urbanised population. The consequent reduction in prices led to the agricultural depression in the latter half of the nineteenth century. Not only did the depression slow the development of the agricultural sector, it also left the country in a strategically vulnerable position with the outbreak of the First World War. Thus at this time a system of state support was introduced to boost domestic production. Intervention consisted mainly of a system of county committees to direct agricultural production, along with modest price guarantees. The state's involvement was not, however, carried through into the post-war period. With the collapse in the world market in 1920, the cost of state support increased rapidly, leading to the abandonment of agricultural policy in 1921 (the so-called 'Great Betrayal' – see Self and Storing, 1962).

A fully fledged agricultural policy was not introduced until the beginning of the Second World War, and, again, it was a response to the need for increased production from domestic resources. The success of the policy meant that by the end of the war a broad consensus had emerged that state involvement in the industry should be maintained in the post-war period. For instance, in 1944 the National Farmers Union, the Royal Agricultural Society, the Country

Landowners Association, the National Union of Agricultural Workers, and the Chartered Surveyors Institute issued a joint statement claiming that 'It is essential on *national* grounds that British agriculture should be maintained in a healthy condition' (quoted in Self and Storing, 1962, p 21, emphasis added). Such concerns fed directly into the 1947 Agriculture Act. The objectives of this measure were presented as:

> promoting and maintaining by the provision of guaranteed prices and assured markets ... a stable and efficient agricultural industry capable of producing such a part of the *nation's* food and other *national* produce as it is desirable to produce in the UK and of producing it at minimum prices consistently with proper remuneration and living conditions for farmers and workers in agriculture and an adequate return on capital invested in the industry (emphasis added).

It was agreed that nothing short of guaranteed prices and markets in agriculture would ensure success in reaching these objectives; farmers would now be required to produce as much as possible, as efficiently as possible. Here we see it quite clearly stated that rural areas have a national role: they must be incorporated into a set of national objectives for increased and efficient food production.

Agricultural efficiency would be promoted by three main components of the new policy:

1 direct public funding for agricultural research and development and the promotion of labour-saving technologies;
2 the use of support policies which would encourage farmers to take up these new technologies (these would promote a stable business environment, confidence for the longer term, and increased profits);
3 the state proposed to encourage the amalgamation of farms with the aim of establishing agriculture on a 'commercial' footing. (Importantly, a 'commercial farm' was defined at this time as one capable of providing full-time occupation for a farmer and one worker).

Many of the objectives and concerns of post-war agriculture policy were reinforced by Britain's entry to the Common Agricultural Policy in the mid-1970s and commercialisation and rationalisation of agriculture continued after the UK's entry to the EC. Thus over the period 1950–1990 the numbers employed in British agriculture fell from almost one million to under 300 000 (Body, 1991). Mean farm size has exhibited sustained growth since the Second World War, having been either stable or declining throughout the period 1875 to 1939, when no comprehensive policy existed (Allanson, 1992).

In general terms agricultural policy was oriented towards increasing the uniformity of UK agriculture through its promotion of a rationalised farm structure, standardised business practices and widespread use of particular technologies and inputs. In the process much of the previous diversity of the industry was lost but this was regarded as a price worth paying to get the sector on a commercial footing. The development of the industry along such lines also ensured the 'gradual dissociation of modern agriculture from rural society' (Buller and Lowe, 1990, p 28).

A turning point in the direction of policy may now have been reached, however, for two main reasons: firstly, food shortages and food security have given way to food surpluses, trade wars and concern over the budgetary costs of agricultural support; and, secondly, the environmental 'costs' of the policy have become plain for all to see, including the loss of important wildlife habitats, landscape change, water pollution, soil erosion and so forth. These pressures have resulted in a discernible shift in agricultural policy, with a breakdown in the post-war consensus over its operation.

PRESERVATION, NATIONAL IDENTITY AND THE ROLE OF PLANNING

The incorporation of rural areas into the national economy as a specialised zone for agriculture is not the only national role that they have played. Rural areas are also characterised as 'countryside' and, as such, have long been seen as a national treasure to be protected against the ravages of modern patterns of development. During the nineteenth century Britain became an industrial and urban society. The rapidity with which the processes of industrialisation and urbanisation unfolded, coupled with their unregulated nature, resulted in urban areas becoming wracked with what many commentators regarded as acute social ills: 'Even as [the country's economy] grew, belief in untrammelled progress was being questioned' (Marsh, 1982, p 2).

Pollution, ill-health, overcrowding, unemployment, destitution, poverty and so forth afflicted the largest cities and became favourite themes for artists and painters, such as Dickens, Dore and Gissing, who represented the modern city as 'the obvious antithesis not merely of culture, but of humanity itself' (Chambers, 1990, p 30).

The despair generated by the urban situation had two main effects: first, there was a widespread inclination to turn away from the city back to the 'timeless sanctuary' (Chambers, 1990, p 32) of the country. For many, this was realised within the suburbs but there was also at this time a noticeable inclination to re-present the countryside in rustic and recreational panoramas, for instance the paintings of Gainsborough and Constable, in which the working figures disappeared from view, and the misery of rural life was obscured by a tranquil pastoralism. This countryside seemed to reflect, in a way the cities could not, a British way of life:

> it offered a world neatly separated from the dirty, utilitarian logic of industry and commerce; a world in which it became possible to imagine the lost community and real nature of Britishness.
>
> (Chambers, 1990, p 33)

The other response was social reform. The growing middle classes became more and more concerned for the urban poor. Thus public health, education and eventually social security measures were introduced. But a feeling persisted that the urban environment itself should be modified. Such a concern is evident in planning philosophy at the turn of the century, most notably Ebenezer Howard's Garden Cities concept. Broadly speaking, Howard equated the urban with accessibility and the countryside with environmental quality. He wished to maximise the benefits of each in a new settlement form – the 'social city' – which would enable residents to gain the benefits of modern societies – jobs, amenities, services – while retaining a vital connection to nature. He thus advocated urban containment and the development of garden cities.

These two responses to the problems of urban life were combined during the inter-war period by Patrick Abercrombie who was regarded by some commentators to be 'the most influential professional planner in the 1930s and 1940s' (Hall, et al, 1973, p 45) (it is worth noting that Abercrombie was also a founder member of the Council for the Protection of Rural England – CPRE). Abercrombie adopted the principle of urban containment but was primarily concerned to protect the countryside on much more explicitly aesthetic grounds. He was particularly anxious to prevent any blurring of the distinction between the urban and the rural. As he famously stated in his book *Town and Country Planning*, published in 1933:

> The essence of the aesthetic of town and country planning consists in the frank recognition of these two elements, *town* and *country*, as representing opposite but complementary poles of influence ... With these two opposites constantly in view, a great deal of confused thinking and acting is washed away: the town should indeed be frankly artificial, urban; the country natural, rural.
>
> (Abercrombie 1933, pp 18–19)

Urban containment was to be employed primarily to prevent the remorseless expansion of the cities and to protect rural areas. The countryside was held to be worthy of preservation for reasons of national significance; it was seen as a national treasure, worthy of preservation in its own right. This view derived from a version of British, or, perhaps more accurately, English, nationalism in which the countryside enshrined all the finest qualities of national identity. As David Lowenthal says: 'Nowhere else is landscape so freighted as legacy. Nowhere else does the very term suggest ... quintessential national virtues' (1991, p 213). Here, for instance, is Stanley Baldwin's vision of England:

> The sounds of England, the tinkle of the hammer on the anvil in the country smithy, the corncrake on a dewy morning, the sound of the scythe against the whetstone, and the sight of a plough team coming over the brow of the hill, the sight that has been England since England was a land, and may be seen in England long after the Empire has perished and every works in England has ceased to function, for centuries the one eternal sight of England.
>
> (Baldwin, 1926)

The countryside was therefore to be preserved because it defined and reflected Englishness. As the planner Thomas Sharp put it in 1940: 'the English countryside may be claimed to be one of the supreme achievements of civilisation' (quoted in Lowenthal, 1991). And, again, during wartime this 'supreme achievement' became especially valued. HJ Massingham wrote in 1945:

> What ... prevents us from falling into the degradation of modern Germany? ... The greater depth and rootedness of our rural traditions, our profounder and more experienced sense of individual and institutional liberties derived from strength of character, and our richer cultural inheritance.
>
> (quoted in Lowenthal, 1991)

This protective stance towards the countryside, reflecting its emblematic qualities, and the wartime and post-war requirement to boost food production in the face of acute shortages and rationing seemed to require a policy of physical controls to preserve rural land. Under the 1947 Planning Act the administrative counties and county boroughs were thus given the power to oversee land development. In order to fulfil this role the authorities were required to undertake two main tasks: first, prepare a Development Plan for land use in the local authority area for a period of twenty years, reviewed every five years; and, secondly, control land development in the light of the approved plan ('development control work'). All proposals for development were to be submitted to the planning authority and were to be judged in accordance with the plan. The right to decide which land could be developed, and for what use, was to be lodged with local planning authorities and these authorities had the power to grant or withhold planning permission. A government ministry was given overall responsibility for planning matters and it also operated an appeal mechanism which gave developers the opportunity to object to planning authority refusals.

Agriculture itself, however, was excluded from planning control (thus development plans were drawn up only for urban areas); it was to be given the freedom to develop into an efficient, modern industry. Rural planning was, therefore, primarily about containing the spread of the urban, in order to maintain a national *treasure* (the countryside for the preservationists) and a national *resource* (agricultural land for food production).

A WEAKENED AGRICULTURE AND STRONGER PLANNING: TOWARDS A NEW RURALITY?

The 1947 Agriculture and Town and Country Planning Acts were wrapped around one another: planning's main function in rural areas was to contain settlements and protect agricultural land; agricultural policy was aimed at producing as much food, in as efficient a manner as possible, from that land. Thus the modernisation, and perhaps homogenisation, of rural areas was increasingly to be brought about through the 'twin pillars' of rural policy. With the rational planning of settlements and the rationalisation of agriculture (a viable farm structure and efficient agricultural practices) rural areas would become more alike; they would eventually lose those idiosyncratic distinctions that could only hinder their 'rational' organisation.

In tandem with these national policy goals, rural areas became increasingly bound into a 'national' space through communication and transport networks. First, railway and latterly road links ensured that distances between places were rendered less significant by ease of travel. Secondly, the utility networks were extended ever further into rural areas so that electrification became widespread. Following electrification came the ubiquity of the electronic media, first the wireless, then telephones, television, the fax and so on. Thirdly, national services such as health and education were made available in rural areas (generally concentrated in key settlements/growth centres). Arguably these developments further eroded local distinctiveness.

Taken together it might seem that all these measures and innovations should have rendered rural areas pretty uniform. The operation of a national agricultural policy aimed at standardising agricultural practices and structures, and a national planning system, attempting to rationalise the settlement structure, would seem guaranteed to render rural Britain much more homogenous, certainly than in the times described by Linda Colley (1994). It should be remembered, however, that there are limits to how far such processes can go, mainly given by topography, landscape, soils, climate, proximity to urban areas, etc. Local distinctiveness has not disappeared altogether.

These developments also had some unforeseen social consequences. Most notably, transport and communication links have allowed for a reversal of the long-standing trend of migration from the countryside into the towns and cities. Since the 1960s the population of rural areas has been rising. For instance between 1951 and 1961 the population of rural areas fell by 0.5 per cent; between 1961 and 1971 it increased by 5.7 per cent, between 1971 and 1981 it increased by 9.4 per cent; and between 1981 and 1991 by 7.9 per cent (Champion, 1994). Now what is significant about this shift is that, along with the decline in the agricultural labour force, it has ensured that rural areas are now more middle-class; by definition, those with the freedom to move to desirable new locations are those with high or middle incomes. The true significance of the changed social complexion of rural areas only becomes evident, however, when we place it in the context of the change in the orientation of agricultural policy.

The crisis in the agricultural policy sphere – surpluses, budgetary pressures, environmental degradation – led to a recognition that rural areas should not be so dependent upon the single industry of agriculture. Thus, in the 1980s the diversification of the farm economy became a major policy objective. The Government was concerned to rejuvenate the rural economy and suggested that farming should be seen as a land use only on a par with other economic uses. However, this change in emphasis was seen by conservation groups as potentially lowering the barriers to development in the countryside and a storm of protest followed. The Government thus promised to protect the countryside for 'its own sake' (as stated in Planning Policy Guidance Note 7, (DoE, 1988)), a sentiment which gelled quite easily with the preservationist strands inherent in the planning system.

The huge amount of political pressure on the Government from many of its 'natural' middle-class supporters in the countryside swung the tide against deregulation. Thus the tentative moves to 'free up' the planning system in the mid-1980s had, by the end of the decade, been replaced by a commitment to protecting rural land from sporadic development. The 1991 Planning and Compensation Act strengthened the role of planning by bringing all rural areas under the local development-plan-making process for the first time. The plan was now to be paramount, with all development control decisions being made in accordance with the plan. Moreover, if we add to this a recognition that participation in the planning system 'is left largely to the more articulate, assertive and educated sections of society, more often than not the middle classes' (Cloke and Little, 1990, p 231) then as planning increases its hold over rural land use policy so, by definition, does the middle class.

What is truly distinctive about this development is that it marks the end of the 'national' farm and the rational modernisation of rural areas. The way rural areas now develop is going to depend upon the local balance of social and political forces rather than nationally imposed, spatially undifferentiated policies. In those areas where there is still a preponderance of the 'traditional' rural population – landowners, farmers, developers, rural working class – it may well be that they can continue to 'modernise' the rural economy along the lines of the post-war model. However, in those areas where there is a preponderance of politically active middle-class residents there is likely to be a moratorium on most types of development except those that fit in with the local 'aesthetic'. Preservationism will rule. Thus traditional buildings will be restored to a pristine state, distinctive landscapes will be protected and local features of interest will be upheld as 'sacred' goods. Even 'traditional' communities may be 're-invented', and local customs may be re-enacted. In short, diversity may once again begin to flourish.

In this new situation the resources that different rural areas possess – environmental, natural and architectural – will become crucial in determining how they develop (or whether in fact they develop at all). But these resources need mobilising by political groups. The most 'treasured', 'beautiful' and 'unspoilt' areas attract the most able and committed members of the middle class, who fight to preserve what they have 'bought' their way into. The most degraded places are likely to be unattractive to such groups and will not be so readily fought over. If development *has* to take place in rural areas it is likely to gravitate to the latter areas. Thus different areas will now be on sharply differing development trajectories (where once we believed they were all heading in the same general direction; see Murdoch and Marsden, 1994).

There are, however, limits to how far this process may go and these are provided by the legacy of the 'national' framework. Instead of national demands (eg for food) determining the shape of all rural areas, they are likely to do so quite selectively. Moreover these national demands will have to be considered as in a complex relationship to those existing at the local level. For instance, rural areas are still governed by a national planning system, albeit one administered locally. The effect of national policies such as protecting the countryside 'for its own sake' (DoE, 1987, p 3) will mesh with the variable local conditions found in diverse rural localities and produce a range of outcomes.

SOME CONCLUDING COMMENTS: FROM DIFFERENTIATION TO SEGREGATION

Raymond Williams has argued that in understanding the 'rural economy':

> it is always necessary to distinguish the 'country[side]' as a place of first livelihood ... and the 'country[side]' as place of rest, withdrawal, alternative enjoyment and consumption, for those whose first livelihood is elsewhere. (1990, p 8)

In the light of the analysis presented above we can conclude that the relative balance between the use of the countryside as a place of employment and its use as place of leisure or residence has changed markedly in recent years. With the steep decline in agricultural employment, agriculture's hold over rural society has been virtually lost. The consequences of this shift are only now becoming clear.

First, the value of rural areas is no longer simply, or primarily, assessed through the lens of increased food production. Planning, for instance, now concerns itself with protecting the countryside 'for its own sake', with 'scenic beauty', 'conservation interests', 'amenity value', 'landscape diversity' and 'visual appearance' (all the latter are taken from a recent County Structure Plan). Planning will, therefore, make some provision for development within rural settlements, as long as this is small-scale and in sympathy with its surroundings. In land outside settlements (now covered by district-wide plans) new building will be strictly controlled and other forms of development will only be permitted if they too are in keeping with their surroundings (thus curtailing many avenues of diversification for farmers).

Planning will most likely operate in this fashion where there is a strong middle-class constituency. Middle-class networks will seek to ensure that development plans are restrictive and they will fight specific proposals which go against the types of countryside they wish to preserve. And these middle-class groups will possess many resources which can be mobilised in this fight (resources which can make the networks strong and, therefore, powerful).

Second, these 'powerful' networks of middle-class actors will not be found in all rural areas. As previously noted, they will gravitate to the most desirable places in the most accessible areas. So some rural areas (such as many districts in the South of England) will be marked by increasing restrictions on development (including agricultural development). Other localities, however, may become overdeveloped. Yet other areas will continue to be marked by agricultural specialisation. These will be places where agricultural development has already denuded the countryside of any distinctive features (eg so-called 'prairie landscapes') or will be places that are inaccessible and dependent upon traditional primary industries (eg parts of mid-Wales). The likely future shape of these different areas will depend on a whole range of factors which will be as much to do with the regional economic and social context as with any national policies.

Recently we (Marsden et al, 1993) have distinguished four types of countryside which serve merely to show the types of diversity that are likely:

1 The *preserved countryside*: this is perhaps evident throughout the English lowlands, as well as in attractive and accessible upland areas, and is characterised by anti-development and preservationist attitudes and decision-making. Such concerns are expressed mainly by new (middle-class) social groups in the countryside who will impose their views through the planning system on would-be developers. In addition, demand from these new social groups will provide the basis for new development activities associated with leisure, industry and residential property. Thus the reconstitution of rurality is often highly contested by articulate consumption interests who use the local political system to protect their 'positional goods'. (Hirsch, 1976)

2 The *contested countryside*: this refers to types of countryside which lie outside the main commuter catchments and may be of no special environmental quality. Here farmers, as landowners, and development interests, may be politically dominant and thus able to push through development proposals. These are increasingly opposed by incomers who adopt the positions which are so effective in the *preserved countryside*. Thus the development process is marked by increasing conflict between old and new groups.

3 The *paternalistic countryside* refers to areas where large private estates and big farms still dominate and the development process is decisively shaped by established landowners. Many of the large estates and farms may be faced with falling incomes and are thus looking for new sources of income. They will seek out diversification opportunities and are likely to be able to implement these relatively unproblematically. They are still likely to take a long-term management view of their property and adopt a traditional paternalistic role.

These areas are likely to be less subject to external development pressure than either of the above two types.

4 The *clientelist countryside*: this is likely to be found in remote rural areas where agriculture and its associated political institutions still hold sway but where farming can only be sustained by state subsidy (such as Less-Favoured-Area headage payments and welfare transfers). Processes of rural development are dominated by farming, landowning, local capital and state agencies, usually working in close (corporatist) relationships. Farmers will be dependent on systems of direct agricultural support and any external investment is likely to be dependent upon state aid. Local politics will be dominated by employment concerns and the welfare of the 'community'.

In conclusion then, we can say that, in general, the defining characteristic of rurality is no longer derived from a dominant conception of a national agricultural space. Instead there are now much more complex processes in operation where the *relationship* between national requirements and local social structures is much more significant. This is not, of course, a return to the diversified, relatively isolated rural areas of earlier centuries. Modern technologies make such a return unthinkable. It is, however, clear that diversity and distinctiveness have now been made virtues in their own right. Thus in the future we can expect to see some novel forms of rurality emerging as, against the uniformity and standardisation that are believed to permeate so much of modern urban life, more and more people turn back to the countryside. The forum in which we would expect to find these sentiments expressed will be the planning system. The attempt by the Thatcher Government to 'free up' the rural planning system in the mid-1980s came to nought and resulted in commitment to strengthen certain aspects of the planning system, most notably in the 1991 Planning and Compensation Act which brought all rural areas under the local development plan-making process for the first time. This development will ensure that articulate sets of interests within rural localities will be heard within the planning process and may give voice to a whole new set of rural concerns.

Perhaps what these 'new voices' will seek are the more palatable of those features identified by Linda Colley (1994) as characteristic of eighteenth century England. These features are now wrapped up in romantic conceptions of the countryside, summed up in the following quote by Frazer Harrison:

The ordinary places and objects that make up our everyday landscape, our personal countryside, stand as living monuments to our continuing survival and feeling response to the world. Without such monuments... our sense of identity begins to crumble and warp. We need little, low, unspectacular corners which can carry special resonances for us alone... this complex intermingling of our emotions and their reflection in nature makes possible a birth of a powerful sense of rootedness and meaning in a world which otherwise yields little but confusion and futility.

(Harrison, 1986, quoted in Matless, 1994)

It is perhaps strange that the hard economic calculus that has dominated rural development for much of the last three hundred years should be giving way to such emotional celebrations of distinctiveness and diversity. But these latter concerns are now effectively driving a much more localised set of differentiated rural policies. The planning system will be the key mediator of rural development trends. It is disturbing to note that the operation of this system has still not taken account of the social and economic processes of change that drive the rural economy and the danger emerges that planning will come under the influence of dominant groups seeking to impose their own exclusive concerns. Diversity might be celebrated as a good in itself but can often result in efforts by one group to distinguish itself from others. The differentiated countryside may then become the segregated countryside.

CHAPTER 8

Local Rural Development and the LEADER I Programme

Christopher Ray

INTRODUCTION

The concept of 'the community' (and therefore of 'community development') has come to dominate many aspects of policy and society: as in community health initiatives, community policing, community schools, art in the community, planning-for-real exercises. Indeed, the redesign of policy so as to reflect, and to be implemented at, the level of the community has become virtually the new orthodoxy. This is no more so than in rural areas where, for many, the term community assumes almost definitional power. Tied in with this is the three-fold character of the concept: descriptive (a category of the 'real' world), normative (a set of values) and prescriptive (an ideal to pursue).

The roots of the community development approach are manifold and complex but include the theory and practice of Third World development which, since the 1970s, has been evolving 'bottom-up' approaches as an alternative to the somewhat discredited 'top-down', large-scale theory, policies and schemes (see, for example, Schuurman, 1993). Not unconnected to this is another major source of the new orthodoxy: the reaction to certain perceived trends of modernity, particularly the trajectories towards a centralised, homogenised and anonymous society (via the growth of the nation state and forces of globalisation) with the consequent reduction of cultural diversity, a perceived rise in social problems, increased vulnerability to 'the restless flow of capital' and the geographical polarisation of political and economic power (Harvey, 1990). Reactions to these trends of modernism have been expressed at least since the Romantic writers of the last century but took on a greater significance from the 1960s onwards with the rise of popular environmentalism and cultural (and political) regionalism. Added to this was a growing awareness of, and concern for, the plight of certain rural areas that were in a process of continuous socio-economic decline as people indigenous to the area migrated out (to be replaced, in some areas, by in-migration with its attendant impact of cultural dilution and gentrification).

These factors fed the growth of the intellectual climate that challenged the ascendancy of 'top-down', universal policy models of development that used the state, or even the region, as the unit of intervention. Instead, theory and practice began to explore ideas of local rural development and in the process rediscovered local context, diversity and local participation.

In 1991, the European Commission introduced a policy initiative in the form of the LEADER I programme (*Liaisons Entre Actions de Développement de l'Economie Rurale*). In essence, this new, experimental programme aimed to animate endogenous, rural development at the local (ie sub-state or sub-region) level. The programme lasted for three years, to be superseded at the end of 1994 by the five-year, LEADER II programme. It is, however, the experience of LEADER I that is of interest here and, in particular, the way in which that experience reflects on the processes at work in the socio-economically disadvantaged rural areas of the United Kingdom and on the evolving relationship between those areas and the institutions of policy formation.

This chapter introduces some of the key concepts contained within the term 'local rural development' and then goes on to consider the way in which the approach became adopted within EU structural policy. The chapter proceeds with a case study of how the LEADER I programme was interpreted and implemented by a local development initiative in South Pembrokeshire, Wales. Finally, the perspective is broadened out again in order to reflect more generally upon the LEADER experience and the potential, future trajectories for development activity and policy in rural areas.

GENERAL FEATURES OF LOCAL RURAL DEVELOPMENT

The term 'local rural development' lacks precise definition, as do the three component terms. However, embedded within it is a perspective on the geographic scale at which development activity should be 'organised'. In practice, this scale means something smaller than the state or, indeed, the region. Thus the 'local' can refer to: the village or township community; the local administrative area; or to a number of other geographic and institutional scales.

Local rural development also implies a particular conceptualisation of the organisation of the local economy. This has two elements: the small-scale (including the very small) enterprise and the endogenous enterprise. The emphasis on the small-scale enterprise comes directly from Schumacher (1973) and makes an implicit appeal to ecological thought by arguing that a local economy ('community') will be more robust to shocks if economic activity is dispersed throughout a large number of sectors ('species') and enterprises ('organisms').

Greater robustness is also said to be promoted by an emphasis on endogenous enterprises in that these will be more geographically fixed than enterprises or branches coming into an area from the outside. The approach is, in part, to move towards a model of self-reliance through the encouragement of local enterprise opportunities which are based on the employment of the human and physical resources of the locality (Ray, 1991). As a result, according to the model, local trends of socio-economic decline and demographic outflow will be reversed. However, it should be noted that among practitioners of local development there will be found different emphases, ranging from the pragmatist, who will allow a place for exogenous enterprises within the local model, to the purist to whom any relaxation of the endogenous principle would fundamentally undermine the model.

It should also be noted that the use here of the term self-reliance is not meant to infer the practice of a Gandhian-style 'village economy'. Rather a major component of the model (if one can talk of a West European 'model' of local rural development) would be inter-regional and international trade in the form of, for example, tourism and agricultural products marketed under a local identity.

Finally, local development seems to offer the prospect of a new understanding of the ends and means of 'development'. Included in this would be the dissolution of the orthodox dichotomy between the so-called 'hard' (economic, 'concrete') and 'soft' (social, community) forms of development. Local development also defines itself by making 'environmentally friendly'/sustainable development activity fundamental to the approach.

In a very general sense, local rural development defines itself as much by process as by outcome and the process is participation. Through the local development approach, the territory is enabled to participate more fully in the socio-economic realms of national, European and Western 'society'. Simultaneously, this process of enablement translates as participation by the individuals, groups and enterprises in the design and enactment of local development.

Thus, in the document that presented the European Commission's rationale for the reform of Structural Policy, the new approach was described as:

> making the most of all the advantages that the particular rural area has: space and landscape beauty, high quality agricultural and forestry products specific to the area, artistic heritage, innovatory ideas, availability of labour, industries and services already existing, all to be exploited with regional capital and human resources.
>
> (Commission of the European Communities 1988b, p 48)

In general terms, then, local rural development shifts the focus of activity from a sectoral to a territorial approach and seeks context-specific responses to socio-economic-cultural problems: responses that are identified and implemented, as far as possible, by the people of the locality.

LOCAL RURAL DEVELOPMENT AND EUROPEAN UNION POLICY

The Reform of the Structural Funds announced in *The Future of Rural Society* signalled a change from Regional Policy, that had been in operation since 1975, to a Rural Policy. Through Objective 1 and Objective 5b, Structural Funds were to be employed to target, more directly, areas of socio-economic disadvantage. Underpinning this new approach was the belief that horizontal policy measures needed to be supplemented by a more spatially specific approach that would enhance the prospects of socio-economic convergence into the Single European Market: the rationale was to be the pursuit of European rather than purely national objectives (O'Donnell, 1992).

Through Objectives I and 5b, the European Union was redirecting money from the Structural Funds towards particular rural regions. The initiative to apply for either status lay in the hands of the regions which were required to demonstrate that their socio-economic situation was below the European average.

Objective I status was reserved for those areas that could be considered to be 'structurally backward': ie with a Gross Domestic Product (GDP) per head not greater than 75 per cent of the average for the European Union. Successful applicants would be required to produce a comprehensive, five-year development programme that represented 'an overall policy of structural adjustment' (Commission of the European Communities 1988b, p 60). The programme was to identify, in broad terms, the use to which each of the three Structural Funds was to be put (the European Social Fund – with a training focus, the Guidance section of the European Agricultural Guidance and Guarantee Fund – assistance to the agricultural sector to adapt to CAP reform, and the European Rural Development Fund – development of the rural economy).

Objective 5b status was to be conferred on 'more limited rural areas' and to incorporate 'a more flexible approach when identifying and tackling rural problems' (Commission of the European Communities 1988b, p 61). The criteria for selection of an area as Objective 5b were: a below (European Union) average level of economic development; an employment profile in which agriculture played a very prominent role; and an agricultural sector suffering from low levels of income. Applications could also draw upon secondary criteria, particularly: problems caused by peripherality; depopulation; and a particular vulnerability to further CAP reforms (Commission of the European Communities, 1988c).

For the 1988–1993 period, Objective I status was given to Northern Ireland, whilst four areas: Dyfed–Gwynedd–Powys (Wales); Devon–Cornwall (England); Dumfries–Galloway and The Highlands and Islands (Scotland) acquired Objective 5b status.

Through the designation of Objective I and 5b areas, a policy channel had been opened between the European Commission and the sub-national level, albeit mediated by the nation state (Jones and Keating, 1995): the development programme for an Objective 1/5b area would be the outcome of negotiation between the area, the nation state and the Commission. Thus, although the Commission retained ultimate power over the approval of plans and area definition and the state could exercise a veto, the local level had acquired significant, new access to development-programme design. This access increased the potential to mould development programmes so as to reflect contextual factors.

The new policy style also signalled a move away from sectoral and single Fund programmes and towards the negotiation of frameworks which would incorporate the three Structural Funds into an integrated development plan for the particular territory.

THE LEADER I PROGRAMME

The same environment that led to the reform of the Structural Funds also conferred on the Commission the power to instigate programmes of its own (Community Initiatives), one of which was LEADER I.

LEADER represented a development of the policy approach introduced via Objective 1/5b. It was to be applicable only within these designated areas but to be implemented at a yet smaller spatial scale – for areas whose population numbered less than 100,000. A local organisation – existing or newly created for the purpose and having been approved as a 'competent body' by the state government – would be able to submit a three-year development-plan proposal for the local area. The plan was required to be compatible with the relevant Objective 1/5b programme and also to respect certain guidelines laid down by the Commission as to broad categories of development measures and other general principles.

The 'competent body' (called a Local Action Group) could come from the public sector (a local authority, an association of local authorities, etc.) or the private sector (a 'not-for-profit' private company such as a Local Enterprise Company or Training and Enterprise Company). But what was more crucial was that the local action group had legitimacy in local terms by demonstrating that its membership consisted of 'leading figures in the local economy and society' (Commission of the European Communities, 1992a). This would facilitate a feeling of ownership and commitment and would harness local expertise in the design and implementation of the LEADER programme. The local development plan was to be a product of local consultation and to be implemented through a principle of participation.

Certain guidelines were laid down by the Commission regarding the type of development activity allowable under the LEADER programme and these were formalised under five headings (Commission of the European Communities, 1991a):

1 Technical Support was for 'action to discover and assess local potential'. Essentially, this allowed LEADER funds to be used to establish the local structures that would enable the local development process as, for example, in the creation of a network of community *animateurs*.

2 Vocational Training was to be interpreted broadly and to include any means that would develop the skills of local people and so enable them to participate more fully in the local economy and socio-cultural life.

3 Rural Tourism was one of the sectors to be given specific assistance. The debate that culminated in *The Future of Rural Society* (Commission of the European Communities, 1988b) had identified low-key, 'green/heritage' tourism as an economic activity in which the LEADER areas would have a ready-made comparative advantage. Indeed, in the negotiation stage with the European Commission, a prospective Local Action Group was required to demonstrate the local potential for such tourism development. The logic of green/heritage tourism required development activity to be sensitive to the local culture and the natural environment as these were the essential resources. They were resources not only in an economic sense of the word but also in the sense of promoting an identity within the local population and to the outside world.

4 Local Agricultural and Fishery Products was to cover schemes to add value to food products by exploiting local identity and perceptions of environmental quality. In marketing parlance, this meant the development of niche markets.

5 Small Firms, Craft Enterprises and Local Services placed emphasis on small and very small enterprises and on the structures to be created that would help the development of the sector.

But perhaps more important than the titles of these categories was that: (a) the fact that they were broad categories and thus open to interpretation according to local context; and (b) that the main principle driving LEADER was to be the search for innovative solutions to local problems. Thus, the combination of a small, 'grass-roots' Local Action Group, the flexibility of a global grant system (using all three Structural Funds) and the principle of innovative development projects marked LEADER I as, potentially, a radical departure in policy style. The very local level was being allowed an input into policy design and implementation: the local context could influence the general characteristics of the development plan at the design stage and during the implementation phase (in which specific projects could arise through a process of interpretation of the local plan).

Finally, LEADER money could only be used to part-finance projects: matching funding for each project had to be obtained from the public or private sectors or from a project proposer. In this way, LEADER was to be a partnership between the European Commission and the local area.

A CASE STUDY OF LEADER I

According to the logic of local rural development, the 217 LEADER I initiatives throughout the European Union were more likely to be characterised by their diversity than by commonality and this has been demonstrated through a number of evaluation studies in the United Kingdom (Arkleton Trust and Aberdeen University 1994, Venus 1994, Ray 1996). This section presents a summary of a study (Midmore, Ray and Tregear, 1994) of one particular LEADER initiative in rural South-West Wales: South Pembrokeshire Action with Rural Communities (SPARC).

South Pembrokeshire has traditionally been regarded as relatively prosperous in Welsh terms, benefiting from high-grade agricultural land, a mild climate and a tourism industry based on its coastal resorts. Subsequent economic decline, particularly in the agricultural sector, has, however, highlighted the polarised nature of economic activity at certain towns and resorts with the 'residual' interior suffering from many of the standard, rural problems. Culturally, the area has a split identity, the northern part with vestiges of a Welsh-language culture whereas the southern part has, for most of this century, been almost exclusively Anglophone.

LEADER initiatives in general can be seen as operating on three inter-related spatial scales:

1 The area of the initiative which in this case lies within the administrative district of South Pembrokeshire. This was the level of strategic activity by the Local Action Group as it built a local development infrastructure. A South Pembrokeshire LEADER identity and set of structures had to be established in order to enable the process of local development.

2 This territorial/local action group identity enabled the group to cultivate links between the LEADER area and the wider institutional environment and also between the local action group and other local development initiatives.

3 Within the LEADER area, were the individuals, communities, groups and businesses that were to be the direct target of animation, a process that was to be assisted by their being linked into the territorial-level identity and networks.

The relationship between a Local Action Group as an institution/ identity and the wider institutional level (upward links) was different in each LEADER initiative. For SPARC, these links were necessary in order to secure project co-funding and also to attempt to integrate the various sources and spatial levels of policy making with the activities of the LEADER initiative. Some bodies represented regional-level policy (eg the Welsh Office and the Wales Tourist Board), others had sub-regional remits (eg the Welsh Development Agency, Dyfed County Council – since disbanded, South Pembrokeshire District Council and the Pembrokeshire Coast National Park). As far as SPARC was concerned, the objective was to extract from these bodies all available assistance for its territorial approach.

Somewhat unusually, the LEADER programme had been anticipated in SPARC's case by a local development initiative which had been developing a particular philosophy and method. Consequently, SPARC was in many ways ahead of the field in terms of having a coherent rationale for its actions by the time that LEADER was announced. As a result, SPARC had acquired a self-confidence in its own territorial and organisational identity and this in turn enabled

SPARC to engage in a continuous dialogue with the other institutional partners of the initiative in order to develop these relations.

The nature of some of these relations was crucial in that the organisations represented the sources from which matching funding for individual LEADER projects had to be obtained. Other organisations were important, at least potentially, as links between SPARC and the makers of policy that might impinge on the LEADER area. Formally, these upward links occurred through the representation of organisations on a Consultative Committee within the SPARC structure. Informally, the strength of the links were a function of the relationships at a personal level between the co-ordinator of the Local Action Group and key individuals within the organisations concerned.

The strength of these institutional links was recognised as being very important to the rate of progress for the SPARC initiative. However, SPARC saw this aspect as solely a means to an end and that end was the improvement in the socio-economic well-being of the people of the area. And it is the concept of 'the community' and the people within it, that informed the SPARC ethos, community being both an end and a means:

> The South Pembrokeshire LEADER project is a people's partnership which has an explicit focus on the development of communities, by providing them with the means to improve their social relationships, economic circumstances and the environment in which they live and by fostering the confidence within them *as communities* to be able to bring about these actions themselves.
>
> (Midmore, Ray and Tregear, 1994)

The process of animating community development within SPARC had, to a certain extent, been formalised into a blueprint. It began with an invitation to a community (a village or cluster of villages) to engage in the process which would be initiated by the creation of a committee of local people (a Community Association). The association would then undertake a household survey of needs and local issues using a questionnaire form which was standard to SPARC but which could be modified by the association according to local context. The results of the survey would then be analysed and put into the local action plan for the area (although any items outside the competence of a local development initiative had to be excluded).

A number of issues follow from this approach to community

development. First, there is the nature of participation. This, in certain cases, could be rather limited given that the questionnaire survey was, strictly, an exercise in consultation and that involvement in the community association tended to decline after the initial meetings. Furthermore, a great deal of the practical work identified in an action plan would be organised by SPARC technical officers rather than by the people of the community. It is a moot point whether community development as participatory development needs to be defined by continuous popular participation or whether one should focus on the possibilities for participation created by the process of developing the action plan and community association.

A second issue relates to legitimacy and accountability. The community association may, or may not, have been 'elected' from within the community population; it depended on the percentage of the community which attended the initial meetings.

Then there was the legitimacy of the contents of the action plan. This was only a problem if there was not universal accord as to the needs of the community. On the one hand, it could be argued that everyone had been actively canvassed on their views and that everyone would have been able to contribute to the debate prior to finalising the action plan. But the membership of a community association, whilst theoretically accountable, was not subject to any formal means of election. Sometimes it was far from clear whether the approach could be described as participatory or whether it was simply a more effective way of 'getting things done': was it general participation, participation by a few activists or the creation of a framework that would allow participation? It should be noted that the community associations were, quite deliberately, set up parallel to, but autonomous from, the community councils which, in a democratic sense, could claim to be legitimate organisations. Occasionally, this was the cause of some resentment in that the community council might feel that it had been sidelined by SPARC which was much more powerful in that it had far greater access to development funds and contacts with development agencies.

Such issues were exacerbated by the status of SPARC itself. The structure included a presence for councillors from the District Council. Individuals from the community associations were also appointed to both the consultative and management structures within SPARC but the method of appointment was not regulated by the usual rules of a democratic electoral system and re-selection.

Much of the content of local action plans was concerned with improvements to village appearance and facilities. Typical projects that appeared in the action plans were: village hall renovation; providing play areas for children; improving car-parking facilities for residents; landscaping and tree-planting; and local tourism development through the restoration and interpretation of historical and archaeological features.

Another aspect of SPARC community development concerned the encouragement of, and support for, local history associations and this had two complementary roles. First, they were a means to generate material that could be fed into the development of heritage tourism organised at the village level as well as being synthesised into area-level marketing identities. Second, the activity of uncovering and interpreting local history through landscape features, village archaeology, personal biographies, etc., helped to promote among the inhabitants a personal sense of identity (belonging and commitment) with the community as well as raising local consciousness as to what would constitute 'sensitive' development.

Community development as a process was defined mainly in terms of a process of identifying communal problems and then implementing the solutions. It equates with an improvement in the quality of life. The discussion on local history and tourism shows that there can also be an economic effect. The same process of animating community development also produced examples of community enterprises (based on a community association) which can be seen as another facet of participation and, potentially, a step towards a more self-reliant form of community development.

Another major component of local development in SPARC was the tourism sector. South Pembrokeshire has had a long history of coastal resort tourism and, somewhat more recently, green tourism associated with the coastal National Park. But inland from the coastal fringe, there has been relatively little activity and this was to be the emphasis of LEADER. SPARC did not, however, see tourism only in terms of an economic sector to be developed. As has already been noted, there was an intimate relationship between tourism and community development. Tourism was also related to: environmental enhancement work in the local action plans through the opening-up of circular, local footpaths and linking these into a network of theme walks, and the SPARC agricultural strategy through farm conservation and the marketing of agricultural products under a local image. Thus, tourism was seen as both an end and a means.

In common with a number of local development areas, the policy adopted in the SPARC plan was to develop tourism activity that exploited the renowned quality of the natural environment and the local heritage. A three-pronged approach was pursued. At the 'corporate' level, SPARC developed an area-level tourism identity, established a central reservation agency and animated area-level trade associations of tourism-operators. Second, SPARC embarked on a programme to professionalise the sector by providing training courses for tourism operators. Third, SPARC, through a combination of community associations, local history associations and its own officers, animated the collection and interpretation of village-level information. This approach to tourism offered the potential for a more sustainable form of economic activity by basing it on local resources and indigenous, small enterprises.

Another major component of SPARC activity was small business support. In particular, this concerned the provision of advice, support (providing practical assistance with business plans and grant applications) and training courses to very small enterprises. To some extent this activity focused on enterprises already in existence as the general feeling locally was that this sector had been poorly served by existing sources of business support which were not particularly able to respond to the needs of the very small enterprise characteristic of the SPARC area. But SPARC did become involved in supporting the establishment of some new enterprises – eg community enterprises that came out of the community development process – although this was essentially by SPARC working in a responsive mode. But it should perhaps be emphasised that it is somewhat misleading to think of business support as being separate to the other activities of SPARC. For example, much SPARC activity under this heading would also have related to enterprises within the tourism sector.

Finally, the SPARC plan included an Agriculture, the Countryside and the Rural Environment heading although, again, this could overlap with tourism, business support and, through work on local footpath networks, with community associations. The production of an agricultural strategy by a working group of local interests organised by SPARC prepared the ground for future activity. The strategy included: the establishment of local networks of advice and aid; a skills survey to be undertaken within the farming population and the development of training courses; the development of labour- and machinery-sharing rings; and the exploration and development of farm diversification ideas, particularly in local identity products, farm tourism and farm woodland products.

However, it was the conceptual and practical integration of the themes of community associations, tourism, business advice, environmental enhancement and agriculture into an ethos and *modus operandi* that described the SPARC approach to local rural development and LEADER.

THE EXPERIENCE OF LEADER I AND RURAL CHANGE

The above case study has avoided, deliberately, any attempt to quantify the impact of the LEADER initiative. Conventional policy analysis would expect to count the number of jobs created or new businesses started and so evaluate the effectiveness of the initiative. Output might then be juxtaposed with the value of funds put into the initiative, the set of objectives originally set out in the development plan or the record of other initiatives. However, Midmore et al (1994) and Ray (1996) argue that a formal approach to policy analysis would, in the case of LEADER as well as other local/participative initiatives, be both premature and inappropriate. In the first place, the LEADER approach was concerned with changing perceptions (identity), raising the level of confidence within the area so as to begin to animate local development and establishing local-level structures. Considering that the rural areas in which LEADER was introduced were starting from a very low base, it would have been unrealistic to expect to be able to measure the impacts after, in some cases, only two or three years of the programme. The LEADER programme was also meant to search for innovative approaches to rural development, and innovation, almost by definition, can include ideas that are experimental, longer-term and whose impact may be, at first, difficult to foretell.

LEADER I undoubtedly produced some immediate and tangible output but to focus on this would be to sell the approach short. Crucial to participative forms of local development is the need to see them as processes. Their dynamic nature means that they can, and should, be in a constant state of social learning (Wight, 1985) as they experiment with new ideas and redefine objectives and practices.

A number of interesting issues arise from the study of the LEADER programme and similar approaches to rural development. Of particular interest is the potential for creating new social, economic, cultural (and even political) spaces. There was a need to establish, or create, an identity for the area and for the Local Action Group. This identity had a number of functions. It was aimed at an internal audience in order to cultivate a sense of ownership by local people, businesses and institutions. It was also aimed at an external audience, in the first place in order to construct an argument that the proposed initiative had a certain coherence, economically and culturally. This identity also had an external function in terms of creating niche markets for local businesses, most notably in the sectors of tourism and local craft and agricultural products.

What is interesting about these identities is that they are very often constructions, using rhetoric in order to claim an authenticity (historically, ethnically, etc.). Sometimes the rhetoric, especially when underpinned by an ethnic discourse, makes an appeal to historical revisionism; in other words, an historical territory is being re-discovered. The SPARC initiative revived the historical identity of the *Landsker* for part of the area (a Nordic episode that resulted in the area developing a monolingual, English tradition) and, for another part, an identity that recognised the parallel presence of the Welsh language. This can be compared with the Hebridean LEADER initiative, which arose out of a local discourse to re-legitimise the dual identity of the Gael and the crofter (Ray, 1996).

A number of local rural development initiatives have included an ethnic or cultural component in the rationale for the 'new' area. This can provide a resource for economic exploitation, particularly in the form of ethnotourism. But in some areas where there is a pre-existing cultural (political) regionalist movement, a relationship can develop between the local development initiative and the cultural region. The attempts in north-western Highlands and Islands to reintroduce the Gaelic language into public domains, particularly that of business, offers a good example of this. In the cultural regions of the UK and abroad, the idea of language planning as a means of stemming demographic and capital outflow is gaining in popularity. And, whilst the local LEADER programme did not actively pursue an ethnic discourse, the potential nonetheless exists for such initiatives to contribute to a regionalist agenda. Thus, local development feeds into the creation of another type of new space as the regions negotiate their relationship to the nation state.

The marketing of places by re-legitimising and exploiting historical identities is a growing phenomenon in local development and tourism (Kearns and Philo, 1993). But, whilst one cannot cast this in terms of a restructuring process because the existing institutional infrastructure usually remains untouched (although, see Ray, 1996), there is at least the potential for the creation of new policy, and therefore political, relationships.

The precedent set by Objective 1/5b and by LEADER has also created channels of communication and policy negotiation between the regional/local area and the European Commission. This does not, as yet, seriously challenge the position of the nation state as the latter retains a mediating role in this relationship. But the situation is dynamic. In the first place, the degree of local–Commission policy dialogue has increased for the period 1994 to 1999 through the expansion in the number (and sometimes size) of Objective 1 and 5b areas and LEADER II initiatives. The new 5b areas are: the English Northern Uplands, Lincolnshire and the Fens, the English Midland Uplands and the Southern Scottish Highlands whilst the Highlands and Islands of Scotland has been re-designated as Objective 1 and each of these areas includes LEADER II initiatives.

From the European Union's point of view, the objective of political and economic convergence may well be assisted by cultivating support from the sub-state level by appearing to be more sympathetic to the needs of the region and offering them access to the policy process (and funds). From the perspective of the peripheral regions, this situation appears to offer the means by which to solve their problems, that the state appears unable or unwilling to solve. The evolving relationship between the regions/local area and the European Commission is possibly being enhanced as the development professionals in the regions become increasingly Europhile in their outlook and the regional institutions professionalise their approach to marketing the region to the Commission and elsewhere.

At the very local level, development initiatives have the potential to 'empower' communities. A momentum may be started in which the community progressively assumes greater control of its future. The setting-up of village community enterprises (co-operatives, etc), community development trusts, credit unions and communal land-owning trusts are examples of how a community can acquire significant power and control over the local socio-economic environment.

Still at the local level, community development can sometimes introduce a new dynamism that challenges the community status quo. Entrenched, reactionary interests may be circumvented by a new community group supported by a LEADER initiative.

Finally, one can reflect on the ideology of rural development. On the one hand, much action within local development initiatives concerns the cultivation of networks and co-operative arrangements such as area-marketing associations and machinery-sharing groups. In this sense, one is talking about territorial economies of co-operation (Boswell, 1990). In the same way, much LEADER activity has sought to animate village communities, although the emphasis on this varied greatly between initiatives. On the other hand, few initiatives confine themselves to a single 'blueprint' and try, instead, to animate development in a more anarchic, 'bottom-up' way. The philosophy of local rural development includes, to varying degrees, the perspectives of communitarianism and of individualism. Some commentators on society suggest that by focusing on social interests rather than on community as the primary unit of development and policy, then the development needs of both the private individual and the social/co-operative person can be met (Frazer and Lacey, 1993). Thus, local rural development becomes redefined as participative development and then transformed again into personal growth.

CHAPTER 9

Losers and Gainers from Rural Policies

Martin Whitby[1]

INTRODUCTION

A particular focus of the sustainability debate has been that the criterion of sustainability should be that present consumption levels should not constrain those of future generations. At the centre of the argument is a concern for the distribution of the benefits of economic development between different time periods, which reflects a pre-existing interest in the distribution of income within time periods.

The wider literature on economic evaluation of policies postulates two main economic outcomes which must be recognised: the total volume of welfare which policies produce and the way in which benefits and costs are shared between the groups or members of society. Most of the published analysis of policies tends to focus on the so-called efficiency gains from policy – assessing policies in terms of total financial or resource costs (see Harvey, this volume, for example). However, policies invariably impose costs on society as well as delivering benefits: usually those who pay for policies are different from those who gain. Where this occurs, society is making choices which explicitly change the balance of welfare between its members. This pervasive aspect of policy also requires consideration yet it is commonly overlooked in economic analysis although politicians are sensitive to such effects. Yet political sustainability requires that distributional outcomes of policy must also be acceptable: some analysis of the present distribution of benefits and costs of policies would logically precede any change of policy.

This chapter therefore explores the intricate question of the distribution of the proceeds of policies, both positive and negative, amongst the population in the recent past. It begins with a review of the way in which the distribution of income before and after tax has changed in the last fifteen years and then deals with four case studies of individual policies – agricultural policy, land development policy, conservation policy and recreation policy – focusing on their redistributive impact, before drawing some general conclusions.

DISTRIBUTING THE PROCEEDS OF DEVELOPMENT

In a democratic state there is an expectation that policies chosen by governments shall be acceptable in some broad (political) sense and this must include the issue of the distribution of the proceeds of development as well as the aggregate rate of development over time. This is a basic characteristic of development itself. There is quite general agreement amongst economists and many others that development is not only about increasing aggregate welfare – measured perhaps by Gross National Product – but that societies are also concerned about the way in which it is shared out amongst their members. That applies to both the within-generation changes in distribution and to those arising between generations. This is also important to politicians who frequently find themselves embroiled in distributional issues about which electorates care very strongly and are often divided.

Because rural policies are so numerous and pervasive and other chapters in this book have discussed them in detail, it is necessary to be selective in the issues discussed. Only a few particular policies can be dealt with in the space available, asking who gains and who loses as a result of them.

Most economic studies focus directly on questions of efficiency – the way in which resources are allocated, the size of the output produced from those allocations, the rates of change of productivity and so on. As a result, questions such as who gains and who loses from particular policies, the way in which different groups in society are able to capture various resources and benefits, the extent to which incomes are equitably distributed, are too often overlooked. To illustrate the pervasive importance of the issue, policies have been selected which are of particular interest from the point of view of their distributional impact. Before presenting the case studies, a few simple methodological points must be made about how distribution may be measured.

METHODOLOGY

To examine income distribution among a population we need a basis for measuring differences in distributions. For example, we need to know the way they change over time and how they vary between different situations. For example Figure 9.1 shows the cumulative distribution of income before tax in the UK in 1979 and 1987 using the device of the Lorenz curve. On the vertical axis the cumulative share of income of the population is plotted and the population groups, in this case those earning each of five successive income groups (or quintiles) is displayed on the horizontal axis. This is a standard method of presenting such distributions and the amount of inequality they imply is easily measured from such a graph by calculating the extent to which the curve sags away from a 45° ray drawn through the origin.

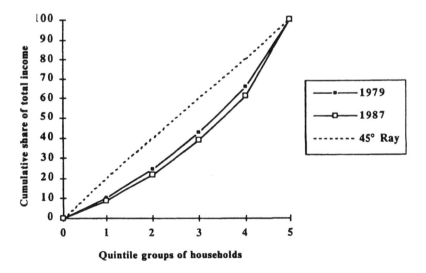

Figure 9.1 Change in distribution of income before tax (UK)
Source: Social Trends, 1982 and 1989

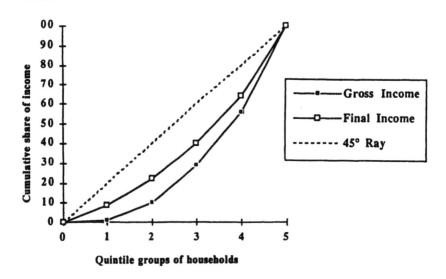

Figure 9.2 Cumulative distribution of gross and final income (UK), 1979
Source: Social Trends, 1982

The curve for 1987 is also shown on the graph and, because it sags further away from the 45° line than the 1979 curve it implies that incomes before tax were less equally distributed in 1987 than in 1979.

Figure 9.2 presents a more detailed picture for 1979, displaying two different measures of income. First, gross income records everything a household receives in the way of income. But, as we know, the tax and benefit system modifies the result of this by taking income from the relatively well off and redistributing it to the less well off. That produces a measure called final income which is the amount received by the household from work and benefits of all kinds and after paying income taxes. Notice that the curve of final income is above that of gross income, which means that, in 1979, there was a substantial amount of redistribution from richer to poorer quintiles. The size of the gap measures the extent to which the poorest groups in society had their incomes augmented to give them a higher share of total income. The smaller the gap between the two curves, the less the redistribution.

Figure 9.3 shows that by 1993 the situation had changed and the extent of redistribution passing through the benefit system was reduced whilst the tax system was taking less away from the rich. The result is that the gross and the final income curves lie practically on top of each other but the story does not end there.

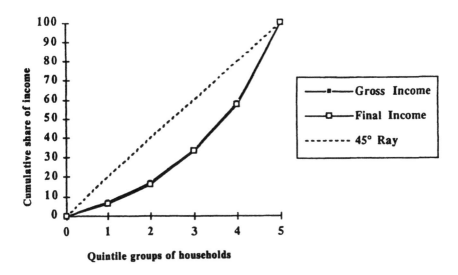

Figure 9.3 Cumulative distribution of gross and final income (UK) 1993
Source: Social Trends, 1995

There are of course many difficulties with this analysis. We are not able to measure incomes particularly accurately and the extent to which the taxation systems correct inequalities is only approximately measured by this approach. Moreover, dividing all households into only five groups gives a very crude view of distribution. However, the analysis of pre-tax incomes over this period does receive broad support from an Organisation for Economic Co-operation and Development (OECD) study (Atkinson et al, 1995) which shows a steady increase in the inequality of incomes in the UK from the 1970s to the early 1980s.

There is another reason for the reduction in the effective level of redistribution, as the balance of taxation has shifted from income to expenditure taxes. In addition to income tax and benefits there are also major expenditure taxes used to raise revenue in society which take a proportion of consumer expenditure. The changes are displayed in Figure 9.4. These sources of government revenue have changed substantially between 1978/9 and 1993, particularly showing a major increase in the revenue of governments through expenditure taxes. Notice that in Figure 9.4 the revenue bar chart shows the importance of taxes on income has declined over the period whilst those on expenditure have increased steeply. These expenditure taxes tend to be

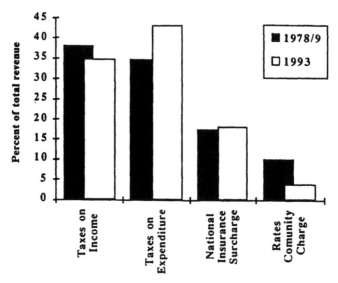

Figure 9.4 Distribution of government revenue 1978/9 and 1993
Source: Social Trends, 1995

regressive in nature, they affect the poor more than the rich, so these changes have probably had an adverse impact on the situation of the poor in our society over the period.

The trend shown in Figures 9.1–9.4 indicates that recent macro-economic policies have notably increased the inequality of income distribution under the impact of taxation. We now turn to some other major policies that affect rural areas and consider their distributional implications in a somewhat broader framework, in particular to examine:

- agricultural policy;
- land development policy;
- conservation policy; and
- recreation policy.

REDISTRIBUTION THROUGH AGRICULTURAL POLICY

One obvious rural policy relates to agriculture in this country, which has for several decades had an objective of supporting farm incomes.

This objective has always been vaguely specified rather than saying exactly how high the level of incomes should be for farmers. The 1947 Agriculture Act states that the aim of agricultural policy was then to promote and maintain:

> a stable and efficient agricultural industry capable of producing such part of the nation's food and other agricultural produce as in the national interest it is desirable to produce in the United Kingdom, and of producing it at minimum prices *consistently with proper remuneration and living conditions for farmers and workers in agriculture* and an adequate return on capital invested in the industry.
>
> (Agriculture Act, 1947, emphasis added)

For decades the agricultural policy that has been pursued in this country has been based on supporting the prices that farmers receive in the markets either through deficiency payments or, since we joined the EC, through import controls and surplus disposal mechanisms. That is now in the process of change (as Harvey spelt out in some detail in Chapter 1 above) but how fast it will change still remains to be seen, although there is no doubt that the policy is paid for by consumers and taxpayers and affects the incomes of farmers. Despite these changes in policy mechanisms used, the aims of the policy remain essentially unchanged.

A useful critique of the CAP (Harvey and Hall, 1989) found that the efficiency of this policy in transferring income to farmers, measured as the addition to farm incomes it induced, as a percentage of policy costs, was 32 per cent for the EC as a whole whereas in Britain it was only 19 per cent. This is serious indictment of the policy at the aggregate level and focuses on an important aspect of it. By showing that only 19 per cent of policy expenditure reaches its destination they imply that 81 per cent does not!

But the extent to which farms of different size benefit from agricultural policy has been studied remarkably little although the problem is well known amongst agricultural economists. It was drawn to public attention in the 1950s by a senior civil servant in the Ministry of Food (Lloyd, 1955a; 1955b) who became concerned about the impact of policies designed to maintain incomes by boosting the price of farm products on the grounds that not only was this inefficient, but it was also liable to enrich further the richer farmers leaving the less well off comparatively impoverished. After that it was 17 years before the next serious piece of work on agricultural policy, focusing on the distributive aspects of it in this country, was undertaken by Josling and Hamway (1972) using Lorenz curves. They concluded that agricultural policy was essentially regressive across different sizes of farm and was in fact making the rich richer and leaving the situation of poorer farmers approximately unchanged. They also warned that the policy would become even more regressive to those paying for it when we joined the EC because the burden of funding it would be shifted from the taxpayer to the consumer.

Twenty years further on, this work has recently been revised in a study (Renwick, 1992) applying the same basic methodology as Josling and Hamway to produce estimates of the inequality generated by agricultural policy in Britain. The study shows that the policy continues to improve the lot of the rich at the expense of the poor in this country, concluding that:

> The results highlight the downside of support policies. First, they are a 'hidden' cost. Second, they are borne disproportionately by low income households. Third, the majority of support goes to those with higher than average income. Clearly it would be difficult to defend this system as a 'fair' one, as it acts to accentuate income inequality in the UK.
>
> (Renwick, p 266)

Two 'health warnings' should be attached to this conclusion. First, that we do not know to what extent taxation and other redistributive mechanisms have corrected the inequalities induced by this policy. They should go some way to offset its worst effects but it is barely conceivable (see Figure 9.4 above) that they would completely correct the inequalities these policies introduce. Second, this is an essentially static model and what is really needed here is an evolutionary approach to measuring the long-term response to farm support systems as they develop (see Allanson, Chapter 6 above). From the evidence on the way in which the tax and benefit system has changed one would not expect them to have gone far to offset the regressive impact of agricultural policies.

REDISTRIBUTION THROUGH LAND DEVELOPMENT POLICY

Meanwhile, one of the major changes that has been made in this country during the last century has been a substantial extension of the urban area. This extension proceeded particularly rapidly during the 1920s and 1930s when suburban Britain was being developed but since then it has continued at a steady pace as our demand for housing, factories, roads and airports has taken land from primary production.

Despite this very considerable amount of investment and major developmental activities we still have only a small proportion of the UK surface area (up to 13 per cent, (DoE, 1996)) under urban use.[2] During this century the amount of urban land has increased steeply under this series of forces: and we now find that there are some three million hectares of our surface area under non-agricultural use (Best, 1981; DoE, 1995).

These data indicate that we have converted roughly one million hectares from agricultural to urban use since 1947. This increase in urban space has been achieved through the planning system which was brought into operation by the Town and Country Planning Act of 1947. That Act was important because it made a major change in the structure of property rights in this country at a stroke. Thus it reassigned the existing pattern of rights, which gave all landowners comparative freedom to develop their land, and decreed that from the date of its entry on to the statute book, development (as defined in the Act) would only occur with permission of the planning authorities. In order to change use, land owners had to receive prior permission. To the extent that the planning system rationed the supply of land for development, the result would be that the value of development land would increase.

Those who were able to obtain planning permission to convert land from, say, agriculture, to urban uses, were consequently able to obtain substantial capital gains and for many years this was a popular way of financing farm investment. Farmers who could sell a few building plots were able to obtain many times the agricultural value of that land and this provided them with a convenient source of investment capital. The 1993 value of building land in England and Wales was more than £300 000 per hectare (having fallen from a peak of £578 000 in 1987 (DoE, 1995)). That figure will be influenced by prices in and around

London but it would be reasonable to take, say, £100,000 as an indicator of the increase in the value of agricultural land being converted today. At that price the increase in the current value of the land converted would be very large indeed – £100 billion accruing to a comparatively small group of individuals, even spread over nearly half a century.[3] It may well be that the pace of realisation of these gains has varied widely over this period with periods of development booms characterised by steep rises in value, some of which have proved ephemeral.

There are two aspects of the cost of development here. One is the extra value of land under one use compared with another. This would be revealed in a perfectly working market if such existed. But there is also the cost of the planning system itself. This would include all of the extra costs associated with the transactions of planning. Cheshire and Sheppard (1989) have published some economic estimates of the cost of the planning system, concluding that the cost of operating the system, (salaries and operating costs of planning departments) amounts to £13 per household per annum throughout the country. Further, on the basis of comparing the housing markets of Darlington and Reading they suggest that the impact of the planning system in generating an artificial scarcity of land and housing has added between 3 and 8 per cent to the price of all houses. Precisely who acquires the benefit of extra house prices would require a very intricate study in itself, but an obvious starting point would be the development gains realised on new housing. A short list of beneficiaries would include landowners, developers and some householders.

This is an interesting example of redistribution of wealth taking place through the land development system. It could be argued that the gainers from this process are those who have managed to obtain planning permission. The losers are those who fail to obtain planning permission and those who have to pay higher prices than otherwise for building sites.

Speculating about the accretion in asset values acquired by those owning development land over the last half century it could be estimated at around £100bn at contemporary prices. This is very much a current value estimate and the fact that it is spread over a long period is important. Some of this gain has, of course, been picked up through the tax system, where it has applied, but it is unlikely to have succeeded fully in redressing the distributional windfall gains from the conversion of land for development.

REDISTRIBUTION THROUGH CONSERVATION POLICY

The third example is taken from conservation policy where we have tried to conserve land for a variety of different purposes – usually centring on recreation or conservation, by methods which commonly involve drawing lines on maps. This process of identifying areas which are deemed to be important for particular activities or for the avoidance of particular activities is called designation and it is remarkable how much of it we now do in this country (Table 9.1). It was recently claimed that there are 30 different types of designation in use in this country and a map (Ordnance Survey, 1994) has recently been published showing some of the spatially important forms of designation currently in use.

Table 9.1 Area of major conservation designations in the UK

Designation	Area covered	
	(million hectares)	(Percentage of UK total)
National Parks	1.373	5.7
Areas of Outstanding Natural Beauty	3.390	14.1
National Nature Reserves	0.193	0.8
Sites of Special Scientific Interest	1.943	8.1
Environmentally Sensitive Areas	3.160	13.1

Source: DoE, 1996

These designations are completely public: maps are generally available and to a large extent it is known where their boundaries fall. It is important that this should be the case if such designations are be effectively monitored. The distributional implications of these measures are compared first by examining two designations currently in use which are aimed at similar results – namely conservation – but which proceed by importantly different means – and second by examining the use of tax allowances to secure landscape conservation. The two designations compared are Sites of Special Scientific Interest (SSSIs) and Environmentally Sensitive Areas (ESAs). SSSIs are designated under the 1949, 1968 and 1981 Acts which set them up. We now have 6103 of them in the UK (DoE, 1996) and they are an important element in the armoury of conservation measures undertaken by English Nature and its equivalents in other parts of the UK. Under the legislation which establishes them, once the boundary has been drawn, farmers and landowners in SSSIs must notify the conservation authorities if they want to carry out any of the proscribed operations, known as Potentially Damaging Operations or PDOs. Within these areas, the state has powers of compulsion with regard to the carrying out of PDOs and these powers, if carried through and fully used, can ultimately result in the making of a conservation order or in public purchase of the land.

Where farmers within an SSSI wish to carry out a PDO they now have to notify the conservation authorities, in effect asking for permission to proceed. If the conservation authorities does not want them to carry out the PDO then it may offer them a management agreement which will compensate them for not being able to undertake the development they wish.

The important point is that the state, in the act of designating an SSSI, changes the rights of farmers and landowners within the area and assigns to the state the right to prevent them undertaking particular activities. There is a compensation mechanism which works through management agreements, in contrast with the development planning system, but it is taken up by comparatively few farmers on only a small part of the SSSI area. The result has been that we now have many agreements relating to SSSIs in various parts of the country although only 11.5 per cent of the SSSI area in Britain is under management agreements (DoE, 1996). It can be seen from this that although farmers may understandably object to having their property rights curtailed, they are not sufficiently concerned about this to attempt to do more than carrying on farming within the limitations imposed. Whilst a few farmers within SSSIs have tried to develop and have obtained management agreements the remainder are apparently prepared to suffer any loss of asset value resulting from designation without compensation.

This situation contrasts with what has happened in ESAs. These areas were defined under the European Structures Regulation of 1985 (797/85, Article 19), as implemented through the UK Agriculture Act of 1986. The latter provided for the designation of ESAs within which farmers who undertook to farm within stated management guidelines would be paid pre-determined sums in compensation (Whitby, 1994).

This policy was popular with farmers and has been taken up by many thousands of them in the comparatively short period for which these areas have been running. We now have over three million hectares under ESA designation and there are some 10,000 management agreements currently running on them, relating to rather more than half the total area.

The interesting aspect of the ESA mechanism is that, although in common with SSSIs, it offers management agreements to farmers, it is crucially different from SSSIs. In the case of ESAs, farmers are simply offered an opportunity to claim money in return for not undertaking particular activities or working within set constraints. In the case of SSSIs, farmers have to claim that they wish to develop and go through detailed negotiations about the compensation they are to be paid through a management agreement which is specific to their farm.

These two policies differ in a number of important ways. First, the designation of SSSI actually changes the rights of farmers which is an important act on the impact on government policy. By contrast ESAs do not change what farmers are allowed to do and simply provides them with an opportunity of which they may avail themselves if they wish.

Second, ESA agreements are not negotiated in the same way as SSSI agreements. The basis of compensation is essentially similar between the two in that it is based on the notion of income forgone from complying with the particular policies. But in the case of ESAs, the income forgone is estimated on a standard basis in relation to a particular set of management guidelines which are determined for the ESA as a whole. In the case of SSSIs, individual negotiations produce quite considerable variation in the amounts of payment made, from a modest level for the majority of agreements up to extremely high levels for a small number (Whitby and Saunders, 1996).

The third characteristic in which SSSIs are different is that they are comparatively expensive to administer. The nature of individual negotiations and the rather more complex procedure for designation of an SSSI which follows from the fact that it changes property rights, requires much more administrative and bureaucratic effort then does the designation of an ESA where the boundary is subject to comparatively slight argument. As a result the cost of administering an SSSI, including negotiation costs, is much greater than that of an ESA. Although the amounts paid out in compensation within SSSIs are smaller per hectare than they are in the ESA, they are nevertheless expensive to administer and this is an important attribute to bear in mind in deciding whether to proceed with that policy.

This characteristic has distributional aspects as well. In particular, where there are high administrative costs incurred, an important share of the cost of the policy is 'siphoned off' into what is called the transacting sector of the economy. This would include the civil servants responsible for running the policy as well as any legal, surveying or other professionals who may be involved in helping to negotiate the agreement.

According to recent estimates (Whitby and Ray, 1996) the difference between SSSIs and ESAs is that the share of the total cost of SSSIs which goes on administration is approaching 50 per cent whereas the share devoted to administration of ESAs is closer to 30 per cent according to the most recent data (Hansard, 6 February 1996). Consequently the extent to which these policies create employment in the public sector differs importantly and the distributional effect of the policy as far as bureaucratic and professional workers are concerned also differs.

One other policy instrument aimed at securing conservation of landscape and wildlife has comparatively minor use but has significant distributional implications. This policy has rather similar aims and objectives to ESAs and SSSIs through the designation of what are called Heritage Landscapes which allows their owners, by designating them Heritage Landscapes, to avoid paying inheritance tax on them when the estate is passed from one generation to another.

This policy was introduced in the 1970s but changed in the 1980s when inheritance tax was modified. It has important and obvious distributional implications because it is providing people with a means of avoiding paying taxes which were originally introduced to improve the equality of the distribution of wealth.

In return for this tax concession the relevant landowners are required to provide access to the relevant land. Unfortunately, because matters relating to taxation are regarded as highly confidential – in particular by the government, who will not release details of any individual's personal taxation position – the fact that landscapes had acquired this status was often not generally known. As a result, although the public at large may have had rights of access to these landscapes, they have not been aware of this and have not been able to avail themselves of that right. Debate about Heritage Landscapes in Parliament has led to modifications of the system so that new Heritage Landscapes are now being given some publicity and the public will know where they have rights of access to such landscapes. In some cases landowners have waived their right to secrecy and have personally announced that their land is available for access. The current area under such arrangements is 51,000 hectares and the estimated cost to taxpayers is over £3 million without allowance for transactions costs.

The redistributional aspects of this policy are obvious in that they allow people to avoid paying taxes and as such are regressive. Where government is using the tax system to raise necessary revenue, the use of tax breaks such as this inevitably increases the rates of taxation elsewhere in the system. In efficiency terms the situation is even worse if people are unable to gain access to these areas because of ignorance of them. However, it is very important that progress has been made in guaranteeing the provision of access in return for society's waiving of an important tax obligation.

REDISTRIBUTION THROUGH RECREATIONAL POLICY

Finally, we turn to the distributional aspects of recreational policy which are a complex area for research and one which is not well served by the data currently collected regarding recreation. This argument draws on the work of Curry (1994) who has assembled the available survey evidence regarding the class basis of participation in countryside recreation and gains some support from the work of environmental economists.

The most recent recreation survey published (UKVDS Consortium, 1996) showed that in 1994 there were some 2610 million leisure visits of all kinds made from home in that year. One thousand two hundred and fifty three million visits were made for recreational purposes to the countryside and a further 173 million to countryside and coast. This massive total of day visits to coast and countryside has very major importance as a leisure activity. Curry (1994) examined the previous series of recreational surveys over the last 20 years and his conclusions and those of other agencies point unambiguously to high participation of the middle classes in countryside recreation (Table 9.2). By dividing

Table 9.2 Summer recreational participation by class, 1994

Social class	Visits to coast and countryside (million)	Number of adults (15+) in class (million)	Annual visits per person
A	84	1.4	60
B	353	8.7	41
C1	346	12.5	28
C2	325	10.3	32
DE	319	12.8	25
Total	1427	45.7	31

Sources: UKDVS Consortium, 1996
       Advertising Association, 1996

the numbers from each class participating by the total number in the group, we obtain a picture of the relative strength of visiting from each class. The series in the right hand column shows a clear decline across the classes with the number of visits from the large DE group being less than half that of the A group. The more or less steady progression across the classes confirms Curry's argument that class is a major determinant of recreational participation.

This result is not surprising because car ownership is an income-related phenomenon and one would expect the upper and middle classes to have more cars available for the purpose of countryside recreation. Curry also claims that many working class people are not particularly interested in countryside recreation and that, given the choice, they would choose to visit centres which provide more set-piece entertainments (eg Alton Towers) than to attempt recreation of a more typical outdoor kind in the National Parks and other open areas. The data presented here are not fine-grained enough to allow us to test that hypothesis.

Gratton and Taylor (1985) recognise that there may be a case for subsidising rural recreation to ensure that the less well-off are able to consume outdoor recreation opportunities and derive benefit from the positive externalities it provides up to the level where marginal cost of provision equates with the value of social demand. They also point out the substantial expenditure involved, much of it unnecessary, through a policy of subsidising supply for all. However, they also recognise the difficulty of making the appropriate measurements to identify that ideal position and hence of implementing an appropriate change in policy.

Given that the basis of recreational participation in the countryside is heavily dominated by the middle classes, one must ask who pays for this recreation. Much of it is paid for out of taxation revenue which comes from a number of different sectors in the society depending on how progressive the tax system is. This therefore brings us back to the question of how the population in this country is taxed. Under a progressive system of taxation the middle classes will both pay for and enjoy the benefits of a state-funded recreation system but as the tax system becomes less progressive (more regressive) the recreation of the rich is increasingly paid for by the poor.

Recreation differs from the other policies described above in that it is generally made available to all. Participation is not deliberately determined by policy but is an outcome of it. Policy determines provision, largely through the designation system combined with various subsidies, and use is a matter of choice. These circumstances offer two approaches to targeting provision. First, if it is thought desirable to broaden the basis of use of these facilities, means will have to be found for encouraging those who do not have access to private transport to reach the countryside for recreation. Past experiments with provision are generally deemed to have been discouraging, but that need not prevent further examination of the possibilities. There are many recreation sites which are, or could be, accessible by public transport and this option should not be ignored when decisions about provision are being made. The use of public or collective transport could still be encouraged through countryside clubs associated with relevant facilities.

Second, for those who can afford to, it has to be asked whether there should be a more emphatic policy for encouraging people to pay for recreational access, where possible, as a basis for funding this provision. Because the better-off members of society are the main users of these facilities it would be more equitable to distribute these benefits on a pay-as-you-go basis. That would allow those who do not enjoy countryside recreation to do other things without having to pay for the benefits of others.

The result of the current level of public provision is that taxpayers are paying for the recreation of society as a whole whether they want to participate or not. Individually taxpayers would be better off if they only paid for what they consumed. Moreover the price mechanism could be more widely used to remove countryside congestion at peak use periods. Peak-load pricing could provide a ready means of managing congestion at individual sites. There is, of course, a problem of the transactions cost of collecting the money here but many countryside sites are already partly funded by entry fees. The National Trust takes in more than ten million paying visitors a year and there are other sites for which paid access is the norm. What proportion of the 1.4 billion visits to the countryside could be paid for is not known but it probably is the case that a significant proportion are already subject to some form of payment, whether through club membership, by turnstiles or by parking charges. The current debate about road pricing might also lead to the introduction of charging mechanisms which could be extended to cover payment for countryside public goods. For example, the 'smart card' charging systems which receive radio signals when they pass electronic turnstiles, once introduced, could be adapted for charging for any part of the road system as a means of raising revenue. So the cost of charging varies over time and this is a case where technological change is very likely to reduce costs in the future.

CONCLUSIONS

The above examples of the distributive effects of policy indicate that, even where we are explicitly trying to redistribute income, it is difficult to achieve the desired result. Our willingness to redistribute benefits through the public sector has diminished sharply in the last 15 years, as the burden of taxation has been shifted from the rich to the poor, and the result is to heighten the importance of any redistribution which can be achieved through other polices.

In the case of agricultural policy it has to be admitted that the objectives do not precisely say what they mean by 'ensuring adequate incomes'. But it is difficult to believe that we are happy to divert the vast amount of public funds that go to agricultural policy without gaining better results than are achieved, in terms of both equity and efficiency. The current state of flux of agricultural policy may provide an opportunity to improve this situation but there are as yet no signs of serious thought being given to distributional aspects of the policy. The series of international conferences planned in the next few years will offer an opportunity to focus attention on these aspects more clearly.

Nor should we overlook the fact that most of our fellow EU Member States see agricultural policy as an important way of redistributing income to small farmers. Because most of them have more small farmers than we do, this will be a significant policy objective they will not easily give up. In this country, where our most serious poverty is urban, the approach to the redistribution issue has been rather different.

The major conversion of agricultural land to urban use in the last half century has allowed realisation of considerable capital gains, many of them resulting from decisions about the location of development, and some from the planning system itself. We have little systematic information about the size of these large transfers or who receives them. Have farmers and landowners managed to benefit from them or have the gains been acquired by the developers? To what extent has the transacting sector acquired them by growing in size? A society concerned with justice should be able to find answers to such questions and use them to tighten up its policies with regard to the taxation of wealth.

Conservation policy produces contrasting policy instruments which work in very different ways from the distributional point of view. Some do and some do not change the assignment of property rights, but all have an impact on the distribution of wealth either by changing property rights or by more direct means. ESAs leave property rights unchanged but add to the income-earning opportunities of some farmers within their boundaries. SSSI designation has clear effects on property values by changing the assignment of property rights to farmers and landowners which will be transferred to property values and some of them are compensated for such losses. Meanwhile Heritage Landscape designation goes in the other direction rewarding some landowners for designation but failing to ensure that the relevant public goods are in fact delivered! The redistribution through the transacting sector which these policies entail should at least be revealed through a more open disclosure system. As a matter of efficiency such magnitudes should also enter into the calculus for selecting new policies.

Recreational policy has encouraged the use of rural areas for recreation and has thereby provided benefits on a large scale for car owners who are mainly of middle-class origin. But the middle classes could afford to pay for many of the goods they enjoy along with countryside recreation, and equity would be better served by encouraging them to convert their revealed willingness to pay into actual cash payments. Such a move, sensitively implemented, could bring the twin benefits of easing congestion at peak times through selective use of peak-load pricing and improving the flow of funds into the provision of desired public goods. Publicly funded provision combined with distribution according to market forces is most unlikely to serve the purposes of equity.

No doubt it will be a long time before we have mastered the art of producing policies which are sustainable because they combine efficiency and equity in politically acceptable proportions. If this chapter has highlighted some of the necessary steps on that road then it will have served its purpose.

Notes

1 I am grateful for thoughtful comments on this chapter from Ian Hodge. Errors remain my own.
2 It is only *up to* 13 per cent because that category also includes 'land not otherwise specified', in other words, various non-urban types of land which have been included in that category making it difficult to measure trends accurately.
3 These gains would have been taxed in various ways over this period and to that extent £100bn will overstate the size of this transfer. Offsetting this, it may also be an underestimate of the actual accretion in value due to development.

CHAPTER 10

Blueprint for a Rural Economy

Philip Lowe

Rural communities are inextricably part of the wider society. Policies for and affecting rural areas inevitably reflect that relationship and depend ultimately upon the wider society's interest in and sensitivity towards them. Rural policy must therefore share society's broad objectives. Perhaps the three most salient objectives are those of efficiency, equity, and sustainability.

Efficiency refers to society's interest in the effective use of its human and material resources in the fulfilment of its goals and the maintenance of its competitiveness. Equity refers to the interest a society has in tackling injustice and in ensuring that all who belong to the society can participate in its benefits and opportunities. Finally, sustainability refers to the need to look ahead: it projects the objectives of efficiency and equity into the future, seeking to anticipate possible risks to the society and the security of its resources and to ensure that present use does not compromise the ability to meet future needs.

These three societal objectives translate into the following broad principles of rural policy and justifications for state intervention:

- to help ensure the efficiency of the rural economy;
- to overcome the specific disadvantages of rural living;
- to safeguard rural resources vital to the public interest.

These principles have an enduring quality. Yet the way they have been pursued in specific policies differs considerably between the post-war period and the present, reflecting not only changed social and political circumstances, but also a shift in the underlying model of development.

This chapter first examines how these principles were expressed in post-war policy, revealing its essentially exogenous (top-down) assumptions about rural development. Those assumptions are no longer tenable and recent policy for rural areas reveals quite different thinking. The second section of the chapter, therefore, examines the 1995 Rural White Papers and clarifies their endogenous (bottom-up) perspective on rural development. The final section then formulates revised objectives for the efficient, equitable and sustainable management of the rural economy in the light of our changed understanding of the forces that animate and shape it.

RURAL POLICY IN THE POST-WAR PERIOD

In the post-war period, the efficiency of the rural economy was seen in terms of primary production, particularly the agricultural sector. The disadvantages of rural living were seen in terms of the low incomes arising from employment-dependency on primary production, and of remoteness from urban-based services and jobs. The vital rural resources were seen as those that ensured domestic food supplies.

Economic efficiency was therefore pursued through promoting increased production and productivity in the primary sector. Agriculture was cast as an industrial sector within the post-war model of an integrated national economy composed of articulated sectors. Agricultural research and development were strongly supported and, through the state advisory services, grants and price support, farmers were encouraged to adopt new technologies and increase their efficiency.

The disadvantages of rural living were addressed in the context of a corporatist, interventionist welfare state. Agricultural policy had deliberate redistributive intentions: its various price supports and subsidies were meant not only to boost production and efficiency but also to enhance incomes in farming relative to those in the rest of the economy. At the same time, the universal access rules (and internal cross-subsidisation) of the welfare state and nationalised utilities ensured access to basic services throughout the rural areas.

The over-riding public interest in food security, in the aftermath of a war in which food supplies had become critical, was addressed through a range of production subsidies and supports for agriculture to increase self-sufficiency and planning controls to safeguard rural land from urban development and for agricultural production.

Note the key significance of agricultural support policies: to promote the efficiency of an important national sector; to overcome rural disadvantage; and to protect a strategic natural resource. As discussed in the Introduction to this volume, the essence of rural policy in this period was that, in the pursuit of domestic self-sufficiency and economic efficiency in food production, farming should be supported by the state and this in turn would both ensure the wellbeing, and sustain the resources, of rural areas.

Implicit in this policy were certain fundamental assumptions:

- that the prosperity of the countryside equated with the prosperity of farming;
- that the production of food was the overriding purpose of agriculture; and
- that Britain's food security equated with increased domestic self-sufficiency.

Thus various meanings were elided in the following equation:

THE COUNTRYSIDE = FARMING = FOOD PRODUCTION.

This was an oversimplification even in the 1950s and 1960s, but it gave a clear sense of purpose to various groups and organisations. For example, the role of official agricultural policy was to increase output while containing costs. The remit of agricultural scientists was to boost yields. The remit of planners was to preserve, as far as possible, every acre of farm land. The remit of agricultural economists was to evaluate the efficiency of these developments in terms of their use of human and capital resources.

The framing of rural policy in these terms is incidentally also the reason why there is no institutionalised rural sociology in Britain. Unlike most other European countries, there was no peasantry (crofters apart) to be weaned off the land (Lowe and Bodiguel, 1990). Elsewhere in Europe, post-war agricultural modernisation saw not only massive technical and structural change in farming, but also involved the absorption of the rural population into civil society. The widespread social upheaval and its political reverberations could not be ignored. Agricultural modernisation could not possibly be conceived – as it was in Britain – as a technical exercise in the management of markets and the promotion of new technologies. To help understand and ease the wider social changes, rural sociology developed as a sister discipline to agricultural economics.

In Britain, by comparison, sociological enquiry into the rural world is not so longstanding and is of lower status. Agricultural modernisation in Britain did imply considerable social change but that never became a major object of public policy or academic enquiry. Put simply, the rural dispossessed did not riot; instead, many simply departed. The term used to describe the changes – farm adjustment – robbed them of any wider sociological significance. This anodyne term was meant to characterise what the historian Gordon Mingay (1990) has judged the only agricultural revolution ever worthy of the title.

Insofar as a rural development problem was recognised in Britain, it was conceived in terms of peripherality (or marginality), which was discerned in its most extreme form in the experience of particularly problematic rural areas – such as Mid-Wales, the Highlands and Islands and the Northern Uplands – whose high and persistent levels of rural depopulation were taken as a stark social response to and indicator of peripherality. These regions extrapolated the general experience of those living in rural areas of physical exclusion from urban-based services and jobs. Low productivity in primary industries was seen to compound such difficulties, condemning rural people to a low standard of living.

Peripherality also served as a metonym for other types of distance. Rural areas were distant technically, socio-economically and culturally. In all of these respects they were seen to be backwards or lagging behind. That entailed a fundamentally exogenous perspective on rural development (ie one which conceived the main forces of modern development as emanating from outside rural areas) (Whitby and Powe, 1995). While steps could be taken to encourage the transfer of progressive models, technologies and practices from dynamic sectors and centres, it was only through overcoming peripherality that rural backwaters could be reconnected to the mainstream currents of economic and social modernisation. The main means of achieving this were through the industrialisation of agriculture and its full integration as a modern sector in the national economy and through the encouragement of labour and capital mobility. In the problematic rural regions these measures were later supplemented and orchestrated by interventionist planning boards armed with additional powers to force the pace of rural development and to reintegrate these regions into the economic mainstream.

Rural areas, their populations and their economic activities have undergone profound changes in the past fifty years. The consequence has been to undermine the simple post-war equation of the country-side, farming, and food production and to discredit exogenous models of rural development (Marsden et al, 1993). First, increased farm production has brought food surpluses, whose management and disposal have led to mounting budgetary costs, distortions in world trade and international disputes. At the same time, the broad post-war political settlement between farmers and urban consumers has been undermined by changes in food demand. With food in surfeit, there has been a shift to a more discerning and a more capricious consumer. Food is no longer seen as merely basic nutrition, but as an aspect of diverse lifestyles or of health-conscious living. A production-oriented agricultural policy locked into a European framework has experienced considerable difficulty coming to grips with this increasing fragmentation and sophistication of food markets. No longer with any clear sense of purpose or long-term objectives, contemporary agricultural policy has dissolved into a succession of crises – of food surpluses, budgetary excesses, environmental problems, health scares, and animal welfare protests. Policy making is not so much the art of muddling through as perpetual crisis management.

Second, the tremendous increase in farm labour productivity, based on the use of manufactured inputs, has detached agriculture from the rural economy. Even in the most rural of areas, agriculture and related industries rarely account for more than 1 in 7 of the employed population. At the same time, the technologies of transport and communications – the motor car, the telephone, telecommunications – have each successively facilitated the decentring and dispersal of activity and people from urban areas. Rural out-migration, though still continuing, has been cancelled out by in-migration which has contributed to a demographic buoyancy in all rural regions.

Third, social change in the countryside has transformed rural society. The influx of an articulate middle-class population has displaced farmers and landowners from positions of social leadership. New demands have arisen particularly for urban levels of service provision and for a protected countryside. At the same time, the intensification of agricultural production has diminished the variety of rural landscapes and wildlife habitats and led to an increase in farm pollution, as farmers have treated the countryside as their factory floor. These pressures on the rural environment have become a focus of concern for new middle-class inhabitants.

Together these developments have transformed the economy and society of rural areas. The rural economy is no longer dependent on primary production but is largely a service economy. Rural society is in many areas predominantly middle class. Increased mobility and improved rural infrastructure have given most rural families access to a range of services and facilities. Nowadays, rather than rural disadvantage, the impression is often one of a superior quality of life. In consequence, not only have traditional notions of rural peripherality and marginality been undermined but also most of the justifications for established policies based on exogenous models of rural development are no longer relevant. There is a clear need for a new strategy for rural areas – one which recognises the changing and heterogeneous nature of the economy and society of rural areas.

THE RURAL WHITE PAPERS: NEW VISION OF ENDOGENOUS DEVELOPMENT

October 1995 saw the Government publish *Rural England: A Nation Committed to a Living Countryside* (parallel documents were issued for rural Scotland and rural Wales). It had been 17 years since the last White Paper on agriculture and over that period the basic under-pinnings of agricultural policy had been removed. A fundamental review of policy therefore seemed timely, if not overdue, and its rural, rather than farming, orientation represented a welcome recognition of the changing and heterogeneous nature of the economy and society of rural areas. The shift from a sectoral to a spatial focus was reflected in the preparation of the three separate national White Papers. In keeping with this shift, the English White Paper was jointly produced by the Department of the Environment and MAFF (the other two, by the Scottish and Welsh Offices respectively), thereby providing an opportunity not only to review existing policies but also to examine the problems that fall between departmental responsibilities and to consider basic resource and institutional questions. Its preparation included an extensive consultation exercise involving some 380 organisations, sectoral and regional seminars and various commissioned studies. All of this served to raise expectations, only some of which could be fulfilled. When it was published, though, the White Paper was generally dismissed by the press who could see little of substance that was new in it. It does, indeed, lack any identifiable strategy, and has few new proposals, targets or tangible resource commitments. And it makes a virtue out of rejecting new controls or regulations.

What the White Paper does not lack is vision, even if at times the vision is soft-focused. The countryside is seen as a precious 'national asset' and the rural way of life as the repository of the essential spirit of Englishness (or Scottishness or Welshness, as the case may be). Policies must be founded on the principle of sustainable development which means 'managing the countryside in ways that meet current needs without compromising the ability of future generations to meet theirs'. At the heart of this is a vision of rural communities as: 'active communities which take the initiative to solve their problems themselves'; that are 'close-knit and balanced'; and that nurture 'traditions of independence, partnership and voluntary action'.

True to this vision and its implication that 'local people are generally best placed to identify their own needs and the solutions to them', the White Paper places considerable emphasis on being responsive to rural communities, on encouraging them to express their own needs and on expanding the scope for these needs to be met locally through community effort. Thus it proposes a much more active role for parish councils in managing local affairs, through greater delegation of functions from district and county councils and through taking on additional responsibilities, for example, for crime prevention and community transport. Voluntary organisations are seen to have a key role in rural community development, countryside management and the provision of certain rural services. Local authorities are urged to be more sensitive to their rural areas, for example, in preparing Rural Strategies and promoting community development, and legislation is proposed to provide a framework of formal consultation between parish and county and district councils. A range of agencies – from the Training and Enterprise Councils to the Housing Corporation, to the Ambulance Service, to transport operators – are pressed to be more responsive to specifically rural requirements, and a Rural Citizen's Charter Initiative is promised to help ensure that public service providers address the needs of their rural customers.

The Government for its part promises to 'listen to what people in the countryside have to say' and 'to work in partnership with local people rather than impose top-down solutions'. Far from being the last word, therefore, the White Paper is intended to act as a catalyst for further debate. To improve the Government's own responsiveness to rural issues, the remit of the Cabinet Committee dealing with the environment will be expanded to include oversight of rural dimensions of policies across government, including responsibility for reviewing progress with the implementation of the White Paper. The Government Offices for the Regions are also directed to meet regularly with representatives of rural communities and to work closely with the countryside agencies and the separate regional organisations of MAFF. Already the Welsh Office and particularly the Scottish Office have their own detailed arrangements for consulting rural interests.

The White Paper's vision is in keeping with endogenous models of rural development. Such models have superseded exogenous models on the assumption that the specific resources of an area – natural, human and cultural – hold the key to its sustainable development. In promoting rural economies, therefore, the objective of policy has become to help rural communities help themselves, to diminish rather than increase rural dependency. Public intervention is seen as playing an enabling role, where it has a role at all. The emphasis is on: rural diversification, facilitating community development, support for indigenous businesses, the encouragement of local initiative and enterprise, the reskilling of workers shed from traditional industries, and the provision of suitable training and support for those previously excluded from the labour market.

However, it is difficult to find a clear justification for endogenous development models grounded in an analysis of the changing context for rural development, and certainly there is none in the rural White Paper. Pragmatism informed by rural populism seems to be the prevailing rationale. However, endogenous approaches to rural development also appeal to new Right, deregulatory governments keen to scrap traditional regional policy and to extol the virtues of self-help and the freeing-up of entrepreneurship (Lowe et al, 1995).

What is required is some conceptualisation of the relationship between the local economy and society and wider forces of change. After all, the consequences of globalisation and European integration are likely to lead to more complex inter-regional links and erase any sense of regional autarky. Rural areas are thus increasingly subject to external forces which are integrating them ever closer into the broader economy and society. This is true in all sectors of economic activity, but also in consumption patterns and lifestyles as well as in production. Structural economic changes have important implications for rural areas, including the establishment of new industries and production processes based around flexible specialisation, differentiated markets and customised products, the growth of information services and the establishment of new organisational principles and communication systems which improve the scope for decentralisation and spatial dispersal. At the same time, new flows of people, consumption patterns, and cultural images promoted by international media and marketing giants are superimposed on cultural vernaculars and traditional social identities. In pursuing particular forms of rural development it is important to be clear about the changing roles of rural areas within this global restructuring.

Certain characteristics of rural areas are contributing to their new roles. These include:

- a relatively low-wage and non-unionised workforce;
- reduction in migration flows from rural to urban areas, as a result of both the urban production crisis and better accessibility, helping to stabilise rural labour supply;
- a small-scale business structure and a culture of entrepreneurship which provides conditions for rapid economic adjustment;
- state support for agriculture, which has been capitalised in land values, giving rural landowners sources of collateral to invest in new businesses, and which provides support systems designed to encourage farmers and rural landowners to diversify;
- greater accessibility for rural areas as a result of improvements in telecommunications and transportation systems;
- the favouring of rural locations by some of the new-wave technologies, particularly biotechnology and information technology;
- the high priority given to non-material and positional goods by influential and affluent sections of society, who place increasing value on the opportunities rural areas provide for living space, recreation, the enjoyment of amenity and wildlife, and a wholesome and pleasant environment.

Of course, the above characteristics are not uniformly present. For many rural areas, though, specific combinations of them have catalysed a deep-seated shift away from an emphasis on traditional, primary production and towards consumption activities, including housing, leisure, conservation and the service sector. Agriculture is still called upon to ensure supplies of basic foodstuffs but increasingly it is judged by the quality of the goods and environments it produces and this is leading to a greater differentiation of products and places. Likewise, the countryside remains a relatively cheap location for some activities (eg tourism and food processing) as well as a necessary space for others (eg mineral extraction) and potentially for new forms of primary production (eg energy crops and biomass). No longer so subject to the imperatives of a single industry, the development trajectories of rural areas are diverging, leading to a more differentiated countryside. This is heightened by the increasing competition within and between regions to attract or resist external forces of change. Certain areas are seen to offer comparative social, locational and environmental advantages to the technologies and processes of flexible production and have benefited from the decentralisation of economic activity. These areas, in part through their attractiveness to the professional classes, have a good skill base and local business services distant from urban markets. Other areas – particularly ones with poor communications infrastructure or distant from urban markets, with difficult or unattractive environmental conditions, or with a weak skill base – continue to suffer from rural decline.

What must be clear from the above analysis is that rural areas are subject to both localising and globalising tendencies. This is why the exogenous/endogenous distinction presents a false dichotomy. Most forms of development in capitalist societies involve the welding of local with extra-local labour and resources. The crucial question is how local circuits of production, consumption and meaning articulate with extra-local circuits. For many, if not most, producers, this articulation occurs at the point of exchange and thus the terms on which it occurs are of critical importance in determining the exchange value of their products. From this point of view the key issue is the interplay between local and external forces in the control of development processes. Effective rural development strategies must seek to build up the economic and political institutions, particularly at the regional level, which help to ensure favourable terms of trade with the external world.

THE EFFICIENT, EQUITABLE AND SUSTAINABLE MANAGEMENT OF THE RURAL ECONOMY

In the light of these developments, how should we now understand the justifications for state intervention in rural areas? Below we examine in turn the categories of efficiency, equity and sustainability.

Promoting the Efficiency of the Rural Economy

The recent reforms of the CAP have involved a partial opening-up of European agriculture to world markets, and increasingly EU agricultural policy will be subject to international rule under the auspices of the World Trade Organization. The Union is also preparing to open up its agricultural market to the countries of Central and Eastern Europe which have been undergoing their own painful transitions to world market conditions.

Declining farm incomes are encouraging farm families to look for additional income sources, and so-called pluriactivity (multiple job-holding) is seen as an important means of maintaining the farming population. The opportunities to diversify farm incomes depend crucially upon the strength and diversity of the local and regional economy. In other words, the prosperity of farm families increasingly depends on the rural economy, which in turn depends less and less on the performance of an agricultural sector that is increasingly integrated into global markets. The focus of intervention to promote rural development and employment should therefore be the rural and regional economy and not the agricultural sector.

Analysis of the place of rural areas and regions in global restructuring helps to specify what exactly diversification might mean for particular regions. Although there seems to be consensus about diversification as the strategy for rural areas, the concept can be defined in quite different ways, making agreement over what it means at a local level very difficult to achieve. For some, the basis of the definition is the word 'diversity'; hence the aim is broadly to ensure that the rural economy has a range of activities, that farm families have multiple income sources, that school leavers have a choice of jobs. Such an approach follows from the view that the past over-dependence of rural areas on a single sector narrowed the options and concentrated the risks too much. For others, the definition has more to do with transformation and the development of new and distinctive economic functions as rural areas redefine their comparative advantage in a changing world.

The crucial questions to be resolved are: what is our long-term goal for the rural areas? Are we aiming for a permanent state of hedging our bets, or is it a temporary transition from one form of specialisation to another? Is diversification something that can be left entirely to local decision making and incentives, or should we be planning at a larger scale? The approach to rural development in some other European countries is based on a less piecemeal approach than ours, and leads to local specialisation rather than diversity. The German approach, for example, concentrates on diversity between areas of 'indigenous potential', encouraging local specialisation where a village or town has a natural advantage. For them, diversification should be based on a systematic exploration of the possibilities for 'decentralised concentrations' of services and functions, aiming to distribute these between local areas. Such an approach makes the concept of diversification much more useful as a tool for rural development, and reduces the risk of local economies in rural areas becoming fragmented by small-scale diversification. However, it also suggests a more planned approach at the regional level than would be the norm in Britain. Without such an approach, however, it is difficult to allocate public resources sensibly for such things as training programmes, infrastructural development, business advice and support, or regional economic promotion and marketing.

Overcoming the Specific Disadvantages of Rural Living

What nowadays are the specific disadvantages of rural living? Not remoteness per se, nor dependency on the primary sector. Instead, they are problems of social exclusion, especially experienced by those tied to a locality and suffering restricted choice through low income or lack of transport. In other words, the prosperity and mobility of the rural majority causes acute problems for the minority. Paradoxically, the efforts of those promoting endogenous rural development to fix rural labour may actually exacerbate matters.

The domination of rural areas by a very mobile, prosperous and conservation-minded middle class has a number of consequences:

- Conservation-motivated restrictions on housing development coupled with strong market demand lead to difficulties for local people of modest incomes in gaining access to accommodation.
- Localised services diminish as commercial and public services respond to the buying power and demands of mobile middle-class consumers;
- Reduction of public transport patronage leads to higher fares and/or service cuts (which in turn lead to reduced use).
- There are growing problems of access to basic services for the rural car-less (which may include for most of the time all those in car-owning households except for the one person who must use the car to get to work).

A recent survey of lifestyles in rural England, as well as finding extensive evidence of these problems, also reported many local residents feeling:

being 'left out' or marginalised in what they thought of as their own place, as others moved in and brought with them relative affluence, influence, different political and social ambitions, and even a different view of what rurality was all about.

(Cloke et al, 1994)

Contemporary rural society is highly mobile. Levels of car ownership are much higher than in urban areas. But a significant minority of people in rural areas do not have ready access to a car, including car-less households, those without a licence, the young, the old and the infirm. Given the withdrawal of rural railway services in the 1950s and 1960s, followed by the inexorable decline of rural bus services in the 1970s and 1980s, such groups enjoy levels of mobility less than those of villagers of 50 or 100 years ago. That is shocking, but should be even more so when it is recalled that most villages that once had a local school, a local post office, a local general store, a local garage, a local nurse, a local policeman now have none of these. The rural transport-poor suffer real deprivation.

Moreover, shifts in policy over service delivery may be exacerbating the problem. The truncation of the welfare state and the privatisation of various utilities and services involve the replacement of a public service ethos with a customer/profit ethos and the erosion of the principles of universal access, uniform provision and cross-subsidisation. Increasingly, those with market power will get better quality service; those without will have to make do with poorer and less accessible services. However, the solution is not necessarily widespread subsidisation of rural services which would be inefficient and could also be inequitable. A survey of people moving in to rural Devon (Bolton and Chalkley, 1989) found that many were being attracted there because of the better quality of life – why should the rest of society have to subsidise such choices? Moreover, non-selective rural subsidies may exacerbate the problem, encouraging even more people to move into rural areas and demand subsidised services.

Nevertheless, cost-squeezed public services and privatised utilities under commercial pressure do need some rules to indicate how extensive or localised their coverage should be. At the nub of the matter is our changing notion of citizenship. In other words, what services should be available as a right to all citizens wherever they live? Education, health and police services, mains electricity and water supply seem obvious ones, but what about a public telephone? Or a daily postal service? Or a mobile library? Or child-care facilities? Or weekly refuse collection? The answer should surely be those services that people need to be able to participate fully in society. That issue goes to the heart of contemporary political debate. From the welfare state to the Citizen's Charter is a shift in the expectations of what the state should provide for people and what people should provide for themselves. However, social, economic and technological change also alter our notions of the basic entitlement people need to be effective citizens. Once that might have been a village church; then a village school. These days a certain level of mobility is essential. And in the future, access to information technology will be equally vital.

Sustaining Vital Rural Resources

Turning to the third strand of rural policy: what is the overriding public interest in rural areas? Our society looks to the countryside as a reservoir of environmental and cultural resources and values. Some of these may be critical to our survival, and others may not but are still regarded as invaluable because they are part of our cultural or natural heritage or are considered key components of the good life. As a society we would be immeasurably impoverished by their loss – rural landscapes, habitats, the natural fauna and flora, and the cultural heritage of villages, market towns and historic houses.

In the post-war period the critical rural resources were considered to be those that underpinned national food security, ie agricultural land and the productive capacity of its soils. The sustainability debate has broadened our notion of critical rural resources in two respects. First, concern has spread to other resources. In recent years, for example, parts of Britain have been threatened by water shortages, not by food shortages (one of the causes of those shortages has been the growing abstraction demands from agriculture). A move toward a more resource-conserving society emphasises the role of rural areas as sites for the supply and replenishment of renewable resources (plants, animals, the soil, air and fresh water) and continuing resources (wind, solar energy, water power). Second, the emphasis has shifted to the maintenance of environmental capacity rather than resource flows, to safeguarding natural capital rather than the specific rates of consumption which may be unsustainable. In certain cases, for example, the pursuit of food self-sufficiency is depleting the productive resource. The classic instance is the Fens, as well as other drained organic soils, where current high productivity, brought about through drainage, is wasting the soil resource and will inevitably lead to impoverished mineral soils.

The overriding public interest in rural areas is in safeguarding, managing and enhancing their function as an environmental reservoir. This is classically a public good and cannot be left to market forces. The *safeguarding* of this environmental reservoir is the chief purpose and justification of rural planning. The *maintenance* of the reservoir and society's access to it depend upon those who own and manage rural land: this must be the prime justification for any continuation of state intervention in or support for agriculture. So we have arrived at renewed justifications for rural planning and for agricultural support. But this should be no cause for complacency or succour for vested interests. There is a risk of this: of sustainability becoming yet another excuse for rural planners in saying no to development, and of the environment becoming yet another excuse for continuing to subsidise farmers. On the contrary, what is suggested is a fundamental review of the objectives and means of rural planning and agricultural policy.

For rural planning this will involve a move away from the preoccupation with defending the entire agricultural land base. The classification of rural land for planning purposes should no longer rest solely on its food-growing potential, but should embrace other sustainability criteria. What is needed is a system that gives more assured protection to the environmental reservoir functions and assets of rural areas. This requires both a more strategic approach to rural planning at the regional level and an altered outlook to development control. On the one hand, policies whose main rationale is urban containment such as green belt and village envelopes, must be questioned, and there should be a presumption in favour of developments which facilitate the sustained utilisation of natural resources, for example for renewable energy. On the other hand, planning control in some cases needs to be more restrictive, for example to regulate the ploughing up of grassland beside water courses or in sensitive catchments and to include a presumption against destructive agricultural development in Sites of Special Scientific Interest or National Parks.

Agricultural policy, in turn, becomes rural environmental management policy. A number of farming groups have accepted this logic, and conversely it is clear that public finance will be needed to support the management of the rural environment. However, if significant sums of public money are to be spent in this way it is important that certain criteria should be applied:

- The public benefits must be clear and proportionate.
- Institutional mechanisms need to be put in place to ensure that tangible and long-lasting environmental benefits result.
- Payments need to be targeted to ensure cost-effectiveness.
- The level and targeting of funds need to be responsive to public demand. (After all, it is the public who will be paying and are the supposed beneficiaries. What structures could be established to allow local community groups, villages, towns, cities or counties to purchase the environmental amenities that they wish?)

The efficient, equitable and sustainable management of the rural economy clearly requires significant policy changes. These need to be matched by institutional developments focused at the regional level. At that level, many of the conflicting economic, social and environmental pressures can be resolved, and rural communities and regions can be better equipped to face the demands of the wider world. This calls for strong and accountable economic and political institutions, sensitive to rural needs and concerns.

References

Abercrombie, P (1933) *Town and Country Planning* Butterworth, London

Acilladelis, B, Schwarzkopf, A and Cines, M (1987) 'A study of innovation in the pesticide industry: analysis of the innovation record of an industrial sector' *Research Policy*, 16, pp 175–212

Adams, W M (1996) *Future Nature* Earthscan, London

Advertising Association (1996) *The Marketing Pocket Book* NT Publications Ltd, Henley-on-Thames

Agricultural Economics Research Institute (1995) *Proceedings from the European Union 'Concerted Action' Workshop on Pesticides*, August 1995, Netherlands: Wageningen Agricultural University, Department of Agricultural Economics

Allanson, P (1992) 'Farm size structure in England and Wales 1939–1989' *Journal of Agricultural Economics*, 43, pp 137–148

Allanson, P and Moxey, A (1996) 'Agricultural land use change in England and Wales, 1892–1992' *Journal of Environmental Planning and Management*, 39 (2), pp 243–254

Allanson, P, Murdoch, J, Garrod, G and Lowe, P (1995) 'Sustainability and the Rural Economy: an Evolutionary Perspective', *Environment and Planning A 1797–1814*

Allen, P M (1982) 'Evolution, modelling and design in a complex world' *Environment and Planning B*, 9, pp 95–111

Allen, P M (1988) 'Evolution, innovation and economics', in Dosi, G, Freeman, C, Nelson, R, Silverberg, G and Soete, L (eds), *Technical Change and Economic Theory* Pinter, London

Allen, P M and Lesser, M (1991) 'Evolutionary human systems: learning, ignorance and subjectivity', in Saviotti, P P and Metcalfe, J S (eds), *Evolutionary Theories of Economic and Technological Change* Harwood Academic Publishers, Reading

Allen, P M and Sanglier, M (1981) 'Evolution, self-organisation and decision-making' *Environment and Planning A*, 13, pp 167–183

Amsden, A (1994) *Grabbing the Market – The Initiative Takers: Wensleydale Cheese*, Proceedings from The Great North Meet, November 16th

Arkleton Trust and Aberdeen University (1994) *WILS LEADER Evaluation: Final Report*

Arrow, K J and Fisher, A C (1974) 'Environmental preservation, uncertainty and irreversibility' *Quarterly Journal of Economics*, 88, pp 312–319

Arrow, K J, Solow, R, Portney, P R, Leamer, E E, Radner, R and Schumann, H (1993) 'Report of the National Oceanic and Atmospheric Administration Panel on Contingent Valuation' *Federal Register*, 58, pp 4610–4614

Atkinson, A B, Rainwater, L, and Smeeding, T L (1995) *Income Distribution in OECD Countries: Evidence from the Luxembourg Income Study, Social Policy Studies Number 18* OECD, Paris

Bagozzi, R P (1975) 'Marketing as exchange' *Journal of Marketing*, 39, pp 32–39

Baldwin, S (1926) *On England* London

Bartels, R (1962) *The Development of Marketing Thought* Richard D Irwin, Homewood, Illinois

Barwell, C (1965) 'The marketing concept', in Wilson, A (ed), *The Marketing of Industrial Products* Hutchinson, London

Batie, S (1991) *Sustainable development: concepts and strategies* paper presented to the 21st International Conference of Agricultural Economists, August 22–29, Tokyo, Japan

Bauman, Z (1992) *Intimations of postmodernity* Routledge, London

Bellerby, J R (1958) 'Distribution of manpower in agriculture and industry, 1851–1951' *The Farm Economist*, 9, pp 1–11

Best, R H (1981) *Land Use and Living Space* Methuen, London

Blowers, A (1980) *The Limits to Power: the Politics of Local Planning* Pergamon, Oxford

Body, R (1991) *Our Food, Our Land: Why Contemporary Farming Practices Must Change* Rider, London

Bolton, N and Chalkley, B (1989) 'Counter-urbanisation – disposing of the myths' *Town and Country Planning*, September 1989 pp 249–250

Borden, N H (1964) 'The concept of the marketing mix' *Journal of Advertising Research*, 4, pp 2–7

Boswell, J (1990) *Community and the Economy – The Theory of Public Cooperation* Routledge, London

Bowers, J (1985) 'British agricultural policy since the Second World War' *Agricultural History Review*, 33, pp 66–77

Bowers, J (1991) 'The consequences of declining support for agriculture', in Bowers, J (ed), *Agriculture and Rural Land Use: into the 1990s* ESRC, Swindon

Bradbury, P, Howard, D C, Bunce, R G H and Deane, G C (1989) 'Production of maps and estimates of area', in Bunce, R G H (ed), *Heather in England and Wales* ITE, Merlewood

Buller, H and Lowe, P (1990) 'Rural Developments in Post War Britain and France', in Lowe, P and Bodiguel, M (eds), *Rural Studies in Britain and France* Belhaven, London

Carson, R (1962) *Silent Spring* Hamish Hamilton, London

Chambers, I (1990) *Border Dialogues* Routledge, London

Champion, A G (1994) 'Population change and migration in Britain since 1981: evidence for continuing deconcentration' *Environment and Planning A*, 26, pp 1501–1520

Cheshire, P and Sheppard, S (1989) 'British planning policy and access to housing: some empirical estimates' *Urban Studies* 26, pp 468–485

Christaller, W (1954) *Central places in South Germany* Dover, New York

Clark, N and Juma, C (1988) 'Evolutionary theories in economic thought', in Dosi, G, Freeman, C, Nelson, R, Silverberg, G and Soete, L (ed), *Technical Change and Economic Theory* Pinter, London

Clawson, M and Knetsch, J L (1966) *Economics of Outdoor Recreation* Johns Hopkins University Press, Baltimore

Cloke, P (1983) *An introduction to rural settlement planning* Methuen, London

Cloke, P and Edwards, G (1986) 'Rurality in England and Wales: a replication of the 1971 index' *Regional Studies*, 20, pp 289–306

Cloke, P and Little, J (1990) *The Rural State? The Limits to Planning in Rural Society* Oxford University Press, Oxford

Cloke, P, Milbourne, P and Thomas, C (1994) *Lifestyles in Rural England* Rural Development Commission, Rural Research Report No. 18 University of Bristol, Department of Geography

Clover, C (1993) 'Eight out of 10 are ready to pay for preserving the countryside' *Daily Telegraph* 20 September, p 4

Coase, R (1960) 'The problem of social cost' *Journal of Law and Economics*, 1, pp 10–44

Colley, L (1994) *Britons* Pimlico, London

Colman, D (1994) 'Comparative evaluation of environmental policies', in Whitby, M C (ed), *Incentives for Countryside Management* CAB, Wallingford

Commission of the European Communities (1985) *Perspectives for the Common Agricultural Policy* Green Europe Newsflash No. 43

Commission of the European Communities (1988a) *The Future of Rural Society* COM(88) 501 final Brussels

Commission of the European Communities (1988b) *The Future of Rural Society: Bulletin Supplement 4/88*

Commission of the European Communities (1988c) *Regulation L374*, Brussels

Commission of the European Communities (1991a) *The Development and Future of the CAP – Reflections paper of the Commission* COM (91) 100 final, 1 February, Brussels

Commission of the European Communities (1991b) *Official Journal*, C73, 19 March, Brussels

Commission of the European Communities (1992a) Council Regulation No. 2081/92, 14 July, Brussels

Commission of the European Communities (1992b) LEADER (*Brochure*)

Commission of the European Communities (1993) Council Regulation No. 2037/93, 27 July, Brussels

Common, M and Perrings, C (1992) 'Towards an ecological economics of sustainability' *Ecological Economics*, 6, pp 7–34

Countryside Commission, English Nature and Rural Development Commission (1993) *Rural Strategies* CC, EN & RDC, Cheltenham

Court, W H B (1967) *A Concise Economic History of Britain* Cambridge University Press, Cambridge

Curry, N (1994) *Countryside Recreation, Access and Land Use Planning*, Spon, London, xix, 255

Dahlman, C (1980) *The Open Fields and Beyond*, Cambridge University Press, Cambridge, i–viii, 1–234

Department of the Environment (1983) *Agriculture and Pollution: The Government's Response to the Seventh Report of the Royal Commission on Environmental Pollution*, Pollution Paper 21, HMSO, London

Department of the Environment (1987) *The Countryside and the Rural Economy* Planning Policy Guidance Note 7, Department of the Environment, London

Department of the Environment (1988) *Rural Enterprise and Development Planning Policy* Guidance Note 7 HMSO, London

Department of the Environment (1990) *This Common Inheritance* Cmnd 1200 HMSO, London

Department of the Environment (1991) *Policy Appraisal and the Environment* HMSO, London

Department of the Environment (1992a) *The Countryside and the Rural Economy* Planning Policy Guidance Note 7 HMSO, London

Department of the Environment (1992b) *Action for the Countryside* HMSO, London

Department of the Environment (1992c) *The Countryside and the Rural Economy* PPG7 (revised) HMSO, London

Department of the Environment (1993) *Agriculture and Pollution: The Government's Response to the Seventh Report of the Royal Commission on Environmental Pollution* Pollution Paper, No. 21 HMSO, London

Department of the Environment (1994) *Environmental Appraisal in Government Departments* HMSO, London

Department of the Environment (1996) *Digest of Environmental Statistics* HMSO, London

Department of the Environment and Ministry of Agriculture, Fisheries and Food (1987) *Farming and Rural Enterprise* HMSO, London

Department of the Environment and Ministry of Agriculture, Fisheries and Food (1995) *Rural England: a Nation Committed to a Living Countryside* HMSO, London

Dixon, J A and Hufschmidt, M M (1986) *Economic Valuation Techniques for the Environment: A Case Study Workbook* Johns Hopkins University Press, Baltimore

Dosi, G, Freeman, C, Nelson, R, Silverberg, G and Soete, L (1988) *Technical Change and Economic Theory*, Pinter, London

Dovers, S R and Handmer, J W (1992) 'Uncertainty, sustainability and change' *Global Environmental Change*, 1, pp 262–276

Elliott, J (1980) 'Weed control: past, present and future – a historical perspective', in Hurd, R, Biscoe, P and Dennis, C (eds), *Opportunities for Increasing Crop Yields* Pitman, London

Elson, M, MacDonald, R and Steenburg C with Broom, G (1995) *Planning for Rural Diversification* Department of the Environment Research Programme HMSO, London

Environmental Data Services (ENDS) (1990) 'Rivers authority outlines ideas on pesticide controls' *ENDS Report*, (184), pp 7–8

Environmental Data Services (ENDS) (1992a) 'Ban on straw burning may increase pesticide threats to waters' *ENDS Report*, (205), pp 10

Environmental Data Services (ENDS) (1992b) 'Pesticide removal to cost water industry £800 million' *ENDS Report*, (206), pp 9–10

Environmental Data Services (ENDS) (1992c) 'Ban on non-agricultural uses of atrazine and simazine' *ENDS Report*, (208), pp 33

Environmental Data Services (ENDS) (1994) 'EC opens debate on sustainable pesticides policy' *ENDS Report*, (233), pp 38

European Commission (1988) *The Future of Rural Society* European Commission, Brussels

Evans, R (1990) 'Water erosion in British farmers' fields: some causes, impacts, predictions' *Progress in Physical Geography*, 14, pp 199–219

Flynn, A and Marsden, T K (1995) 'Guest editorial' *Environment and Planning A*, 27, pp 1180–1192

Frazer, E and Lacey, N (1993) *The Politics of Community – A Feminist Critique of the Liberal–Communitarian Debate* Harvester Wheatsheaf, Hemel Hempstead

Frazer, I M (1995) 'An analysis of management agreement bargaining under asymmetric information' *Journal of Agricultural Economics*, 46, pp 20–32

Friends of the Earth (1988) *An Investigation of Pesticide Pollution in Drinking Water in England and Wales* Friends of the Earth, London

Friends of the Earth (1993) 'Millions supplied with illegally polluted drinking water' *Friends of the Earth Press Release* 28 July

Froud, J (1994) 'Upland moorland with complex property rights', in Whitby, M C (ed), *Incentives for Countryside Management: the Case of Environmentally Sensitive Areas* CAB International, Wallingford

Garrod, G D and Willis, K G (1992) 'Valuing landscape: a contingent valuation approach' *Journal of Environmental Management*, 37, pp 1–22

Garrod, G D and Willis, K G (1994) 'Valuing biodiversity and nature conservation at a local level' *Biodiversity and Conservation*, 3, pp 555–565

Garrod, G D and Willis, K G (1995) 'Valuing the benefits of the South Downs Environmentally Sensitive Area' *Journal of Agricultural Economics*, 46, pp 160–173

Gasson, R M (1988) *The Economics of Part-Time Farming* Longman, Harlow

Giddens, A (1987) 'What do sociologists do?', in Giddens, A (ed),

Social Theory and Modern Sociology Polity, Cambridge

Goodman, D and Redclift, M (1991) *Refashioning Nature: Food, Ecology and Culture* Routledge, London

Goodwin, M, Cloke, P and Milbourne, P (1995) 'Regulation theory and rural research: theorising contemporary rural change' *Environment and Planning A*, 27, pp 1245–1260

Graham-Tomasi, T (1995) 'Quasi-option Value', in Bromley, D (ed), *The Handbook of Environmental Economics* Blackwell, Oxford

Grant, R M (1975) 'Economic problems, economic theory and the role of Government', in Grant, R M and Shaw, G K (eds), *Current Issues in Economic Policy* Philip Allan, Deddington

Grant, S A (1971) 'Interactions of grazing and burning on heather moors. 2. Effects on primary production and level of utilisation' *Journal of the British Grassland Society*, 23, pp 285–293

Grant, S A and Armstrong, H M (1993) 'Grazing ecology and the conservation of heather moorland' *Biodiversity and Conservation*, 2, pp 79–94

Gratton, C and Taylor, P (1985) *Sport and Recreation: an Economic Analysis* Spon, London

Grigg, D (1989) *English Agriculture: an Historical Perspective* Basil Blackwell, Oxford

Hall, P, Gracey, H, Drewett, R and Thomas, R (1973) *The Containment of Urban England Vol 2*, Allen & Unwin, London

Hanemann, W M (1994) *Valuing the Environment through Contingent Valuation* Working Paper 728 Department of Agricultural and Resource Economics, University of California, Berkeley

Hanley, N (1995) 'The role of environmental valuation in cost-benefit analysis', in Willis, K G and Corkindale, J T (eds), *Environmental Valuation New Perspectives* CAB International, Wallingford

Hanley, N, Kirkpatrick, H, Oglethorpe, D and Simpson, I (1996) *The Provision of Public Goods from Agriculture: Modelling the 'Provider Gets Principle' for Moorland Conservation in Scotland* Paper presented at the Agricultural Economics Society Conference, Newcastle upon Tyne

Hargrove, C (1992) 'Weak anthropocentric intrinsic value' *The Monist*, 75, pp 183–207

Harrison, F (1986) *The Living Landscape* Pluto, London

Harvey, D (1990) *The Condition of Postmodernity – An Inquiry into the Origin of Cultural Change* Blackwell, Oxford

Harvey, D R (1990) *The Economics of the Farmland Market* Proceedings of AES One Day Conference: The Agricultural Land Market, Department of Agricultural Economics and Food Marketing, University of Newcastle upon Tyne

Harvey, D R (1991) 'Agriculture and the environment: the way ahead?', in Hanley, N (ed), *Farming and the Countryside: an Economic Analysis of External Costs and Benefits* CAB International, Wallingford

Harvey, D R (1995) 'European Union cereals policy: an evolutionary interpretation' *Australian Journal of Agricultural Economics, 35* (3), pp 193–217

Harvey, D R and Hall, J (1989) *PSEs, Producer Benefits and Transfer Efficiency of the CAP and Alternatives* Department of Agricultural Economics & Food Marketing, Newcastle upon Tyne

Hawkins, E (1991) *Changing Technologies: Negotiating Autonomy on Cheshire Farms* Unpublished PhD thesis, South Bank Polytechnic, London

Hill, B and Young, N (1989) *Evaluating Support to Rural Areas* Land Use for Agriculture, Forestry and Rural Development: 20th Symposium of the EAAE, Department of Agricultural Economics and Food Marketing, University of Newcastle upon Tyne

Hirsch, F (1976) *The Limits of Growth* Harvard University Press, Cambridge, Mass

Hirsch, F (1977) *Social Limits to Growth* Routledge & Kegan Paul, London

Hirschman, E C (1983) 'Aesthetics, ideologies and the limits of the marketing concept' *Journal of Marketing, 47* (3), pp 45–55

HM Treasury (1991) *Economic Appraisal in Central Government: a Technical Guide for Government Departments* HMSO, London

Hodge, I (1988) 'Property institutions and environmental improvement' *Journal of Agricultural Economics, 39*, (3), pp 369–375

Hodge, I (1995) 'Public policies for land conservation', in Bromley (ed), *The Handbook of Environmental Economics* Blackwell, Oxford

Hodge, I and Monk, S (1991) *In search of a rural economy: patterns and differentiation in non-metropolitan England* Monograph 20 Department of Land Economy, Cambridge University, Cambridge

Hoggart, K (1988) 'Not a definition of the rural' *Area, 20*, pp 35–40

Holling, C S (1973) 'Resilience and stability of ecological systems' *Annual Review of Ecology and Systematics, 4*, pp 1–24

Hooper, S and Whitby, M C (1988) *Heather Moorland Management: an*

Economic Assessment Department of Agricultural Economics and Food Marketing, University of Newcastle upon Tyne

House of Commons Environment Committee (1996) *Rural England: the Rural White Paper* Third Report, Session 1995–96 HMSO, London

House of Lords (1991) *European Communities Committee* HMSO, London

Houston, F S (1986) 'The marketing concept: what it is and what it is not' *Journal of Marketing*, 50, pp 81–87

Hudson, P J (1986) 'The effect of a parasitic nematode on the breeding production of red grouse' *Journal of Animal Ecology*, 55, pp 85–92

Hunting Surveys and Consultants Limited (1986) *Monitoring Landscape Change* HMSO, London

Iacoponi, L, Brunori, G and Rovai, M (1995) 'Endogenous development and the agro-industrial district', in van der Ploeg, J D and van Dijk, G (eds), *Beyond Modernization: the Impact of Endogenous Rural Development* Van Gorcum, Assen, The Netherlands

Jones, B and Keating, M (1995) *The European Union and the Regions* Clarendon, Oxford

Josling, T E (1974) 'Agricultural policies in developed countries: a review' *Journal of Agricultural Economics*, 25 (3), pp 229–264

Josling, T E and Hamway, D (1972) 'Distribution of costs and benefits of farm policy', in (ed), *Burdens and Benefits of Farm Support Policies* TPRC, London

Joyce, J (1992) 'Aquaculture conflicts and the media – what associations can do' *World Aquaculture*, 23 (2), pp 14–15

Just, R E, Hueth, D L and Schmitz, A (1985) *Applied Welfare Economics and Public Policy* Prentice Hall, London

Kahneman, D and Knetsch, J L (1992) 'Valuing public goods: the purchase of moral satisfaction' *Journal of Environmental Economics and Management*, 22, pp 57–70

Kearns, G and Philo, C (1993) *Selling Places: the City as Cultural Capital, Past and Present* Pergamon, Oxford

Keeble, D, Tyler, P, Broom, G and Lewis, J (1992) *Business Success in the Countryside: the Performance of Rural Enterprise* HMSO: Department of the Environment, London

Kotler, P (1980) *Marketing Management: Analysis, Planning and Control* 4th edn, Prentice Hall International Inc, London

Krugman, P (1994) 'Complex landscapes in economic geography'

American Economic Review, 84 (2), pp 412–16

Labour Party (1994) *In Trust for Tomorrow*: Report of the Labour Party Policy Commission on the Environment. Labour Party, London

Laffont, J and Tirole, J (1993) *A Theory of Incentives in Procurement and Regulation* MIT Press, London

Lancaster, K J (1966) 'A new approach to consumer theory' *Journal of Political Economy*, 74, pp 132–157

Laverton, S (1962) *The Profitable Use of Farm Chemicals* Oxford University Press, London

Lloyd, E M H (1955a) '"Proper Remuneration" for Farmers: I Subsidies and Efficiency.' *The Times*, pp 9

Lloyd, E M H (1955b) '"Proper Remuneration" for Farmers: II Subsidies and Incomes' *The Times*, pp 9

Lowe, P and Bodiguel, M (eds) (1990) *Rural Studies in Britain and France* Belhaven, London

Lowe, P and Buller, H (1990) 'The Historical and Cultural Contexts', in Lowe, P and Bodiguel, M (eds), *Rural Studies in Britain and France* Belhaven, London

Lowe, P, Cox, G, Goodman, D, Munton, R and Winter, M (1990) 'Technological Change, farm management and pollution regulation: the example of Britain' in Lowe, P, Marsden, T and Whatmore, S (eds) *Technological Change and the Rural Environment*, Fulton, London, pp. 53–80

Lowe, P, Murdoch, J and Ward, N (1995) 'Networks in rural development: beyond exogenous and endogenous models', in van der Ploeg, J D and van Dijk, G (eds), *Beyond Modernisation: the Impact of Endogenous Rural Development* Van Gorcum, Assen, The Netherlands

Lowenthal, D (1991) 'British national identity and the English landscape' *Rural History*, 2, pp 205–230

MacKenzie, D and Wajcman, J (1985) *The Social Shaping of Technology*, Open University Press, Milton Keynes

MacLaren, D (1992) 'The political economy of agricultural policy reform in the EU and Australia' *Journal of Agricultural Economics*, 43 (3), pp 424–439

MAFF (1990) 'Review of older agricultural pesticides making good progress' *Press Release No. 349/90*

MAFF (1995) *Press Release 122/95*

MAFF/IB (1996) *The Government's Expenditure Plans 1996–97 to 1998–*

99 Cm 1903 Ministry of Agriculture, Fisheries and Food and Intervention Board

Marquand (1988) *The Unprincipled Society: New Demands and Old Politics* Cape, London

Marsden, T, Murdoch, J, Lowe, P, Munton, R and Flynn, A (1993) *Constructing the Countryside* UCL Press, London

Marsh, J (1982) *Back to the Land: the Pastoral Impulse in Victorian Britain from 1880–1914* Quartet Books, London

Matless, D (1994) 'Doing the English Village, 1945–90: an essay in imaginative geography', in Cloke, P, et al (eds), *Writing the Rural* Paul Chapman, London

McCann, N (1989) *The Story of the National Agricultural Advisory Service: a Mainspring of Agricultural Revival, 1946–1971* Providence Press, Ely

McCarthy, J and Perreault, W (1984) *Basic Marketing: a Managerial Approach* Richard D Irwin, Homewood, Illinois

McInerney, J P (1986) 'Agricultural policy at the crossroads', in Gilg, A W (ed), *Countryside Planning Yearbook Vol. 7* Geo Books, London

McInerney, J and Turner, M (1991) *Patterns, Performance and Prospects in Farm Diversification* University of Exeter, Exeter

Midmore, P, Ray, C and Tregear, A (1994) *The South Pembrokeshire LEADER Project: an Evaluation* Welsh Institute of Rural Studies, the University of Wales, Aberystwyth

Mingay, G (1990) 'British rural history: themes in agricultural history and rural social history', in Lowe, P and Bodiguel, M (eds), *Rural Studies in Britain and France* Belhaven Press, London

Mingay, G E (1987) *The Transformation of Britain, 1830–1939* Paladin, Grafton Books, London

Ministry of Works and Planning (1942) *Report of the Committee on Land Utilisation in Rural Areas* Cmnd. 6378 HMSO, London

Moxey, A P, White, B, Sanderson, R A and Rushton, S P (1995) 'An approach to linking an ecological vegetation model to an agricultural economic model' *Journal of Agricultural Economics*, 46, pp 381–397

Murdoch, J and Marsden, T (1994) *Reconstituting Rurality* VCL, London

National Audit Office (1994) *Protecting and Managing Sites of Special Scientific Interest in England* HMSO, London

National Farmers' Union (1994) *Food from the Countryside* NFU, London

National Research Council (1993) *Pesticides in the Diets of Infants and Children* National Academy Press, Washington

Nature Conservancy Council (1990) *Scientific and Policy Initiative: Heather Regeneration in England and Wales* NCC, Peterborough

National Rivers Authority (1995) *Pesticides and the Aquatic Environment*, Water Quality Series 26, National Rivers Authority, Bristol

Nelson, R R and Soete, L L G (1988) 'Policy conclusions', in Dosi, G, Freeman, C, Nelson, R, Silverberg, G and Soete, L (eds), *Technical Change and Economic Theory* Pinter, London

Nelson, R R and Winter, S G (1982) *An Evolutionary Theory of Economic Change* Belknap Press of Harvard University Press, Cambridge, Mass

Newby, H (1979) *Green and Pleasant Land? Social Change in Rural England* Hutchinson, London

Newby, H (1982) 'Rural sociology and its relevance to the agricultural economist: a review' *Journal of Agricultural Economics*, 33, pp 125–165

Newby, H (1991) 'The economic and social context of farming and the countryside environment', in Miller, F A (ed), *Agricultural Policy and the Environment*, CAS Paper 24 Centre for Agricultural Strategy, Reading

North, D C (1990) *Institutions, Institutional Change and Economic Performance* Cambridge University Press, Cambridge

O'Donnell, R (1992) 'Policy requirements for regional balance in economic and monetary union', in Hannequart, P (ed), *Economic and Social Cohesion in Europe* Routledge, London

Ofwat (1993) *Paying for Quality: the Political Perspective* Office of Water Services, Birmingham

Ordnance Survey (1994) *United Kingdom: Protected Environment*, Ordnance Survey, Southampton

Parris, K (1994) *Environmental indicators for agricultural policy analysis* Paper to AES Conference, Exeter

Pearce, D W and Markandya, A (1989) *Environmental Policy Benefits: Monetary Valuation* OECD, Paris

Pearce, D W and Turner, R K (1990) *Economics of Natural Resources and the Environment* Harvester Wheatsheaf, London

Peters, T J and Waterman, R H (1982) *In Search of Excellence: Lessons from America's Best Run Companies* Harper and Row, New York

Rausser, G (1982) 'Political economic markets: PERTS and PESTS in food and agriculture' *American Journal of Agricultural Economics*, 64 (5), pp 821–833

Rawls, J (1971) *A Theory of Social Justice* Harvard University Press, Cambridge, Mass

Ray, C (1991) *The Economics of Self-Reliance – Cymru as a Case Study* Economic Research Paper 44, Department of Economics and Agricultural Economics, University of Wales, Aberystwyth

Ray, C (1996) *Local Rural Development in the Western Isles, Skye and Lochalsh and Brittany* Unpublished PhD thesis, Welsh Institute of Rural Studies, The University of Wales, Aberystwyth

Rayment, M (1995) *Nature Conservation, Employment and Local Economies* Royal Society for the Protection of Birds, Sandy

Rees, G (1984) 'Rural regions in national and international economies', in Bradley, T and Lowe, P (ed), *Locality and Rurality* Geo Books, Norwich

Renwick, A W (1992) *Income Inequality and the Distribution of the Costs and Benefits of Agricultural Support* PhD thesis, Newcastle upon Tyne

Ritson, C (1986) *Marketing and Agriculture: an Essay on the Scope of the Subject Matter of Agricultural Marketing* Discussion Paper 19 Department of Agricultural Economics and Food Marketing, University of Newcastle upon Tyne

Ritson, C (1993) *The Behaviour of the Farmed Salmon Market in Europe: a Review* Centre for Rural Economy Research Report, Department of Agricultural Economics and Food Marketing, University of Newcastle upon Tyne

Ritson, C (1996) 'Food marketing and agricultural marketing: the scope of the subject of agro-food marketing', in Padberg, D, Ritson, C and Albisu, L M (eds), *Agro Food Marketing* CAB International, Wallingford

Robinson, D (1980) 'The impact of herbicides on crop production', in Hurd, R, Biscoe, P and Dennis, C (eds), *Opportunities for Increasing Crop Yields* Pitman, London

Rodwell, J S (1991) *British Plant Communities Vol 2: Mires and Heaths,* Cambridge University Press, Cambridge

Rosen, S (1974) 'Hedonic prices and implicit markets: product differentiation in pure competition' *Journal of Political Economy,* 82, pp 34–55

Sattaur, O (1989) 'The threat of the well-bred salmon' *New Scientist,* April 29, pp 54–58

Saville, J (1957) *Rural Depopulation in England and Wales 1851–1951: Dartington Hall studies in rural sociology* Routledge & Kegan Paul, London

Scheinkman, J A and Woodford, M (1994) 'Self organised criticality and economic fluctuations' *American Economic Review*, 84 (2), pp 417–21

Schumacher, F (1973) *Small is Beautiful* Penguin, Harmondsworth

Schumpeter, J (1934) *The Theory of Economic Development* Harvard University Press, Cambridge, Mass

Schuurman, F J (1993) *Beyond the Impasse – New Directives in Development Theory* Zed Books, London

Scottish Office (1995) *Rural Scotland: People, Prosperity and Partnership* HMSO, Edinburgh

Self, P and Storing, P (1962) *The State and the Farmer* Allen & Unwin, London

Silverberg, G (1988) 'Modelling economic dynamics and technical change: mathematical approaches to self-organisation and evolution', in Dosi, G, Freeman, C, Nelson, R, Silverberg, G and Soete, L (eds), *Technical Change and Economic Theory* Pinter, London

Soderbaum, P (1987) 'Environmental management' *Journal of Economic Issues*, 21, pp 139–165

Tait, E J (1976) *Factors Affecting the Production and Use of Pesticides in the UK* PhD thesis, Cambridge University, Department of Land Economy

Tarling, R, Rhodes, J, North, J and Broom, G (1993) *The Economy of Rural England* Strategy Review Topic Paper 4 Rural Development Commission, London

Taylor, F D W (1955) 'United Kingdom: numbers in agriculture' *The Farm Economist*, 8 (4), pp 36–40

Topham, M R (1986) *Sheep Numbers and Heather Conservation in the Norh of England*, Discussion Paper 9, Department of Agricultural Economics and Food Marketing, The University of Newcastle upon Tyne

Traill, B (1988) 'The rural environment: what role for Europe?', in Whitby, M C and Ollerenshaw, J (eds), *Land Use and the European Environment* Belhaven, London

Tregear, A (1996) *Business, Ethics, and the Environment* Discussion Paper 2/96 Department of Agricultural Economics and Food Marketing, University of Newcastle upon Tyne

Tregear, A, McLeay, F and Moxey, A (1996) *Sustainable tourism: a marketing contribution* Paper presented to Sustainable Tourism, Ethics, Economics and the Environment, Newton Rigg College

UKDVS Consortium (1996) *UK Day Visits Survey 1994* Countryside Recreation Network, Cardiff

UK Government (1991) 'Pesticides in water – UK official comments on the EC Drinking Water Directive' *Pesticide Outlook*, 2 (2), pp 18–19

van den Doel, H (1979) *Democracy and Welfare Economics* Cambridge University Press, Cambridge

Venus, J (1994) *Monitoring Antur Teifi's Delivery of LEADER in the Teifi Valley – The Third Report* Centre for Continuing Education & Information Management, The University of Wales, Lampeter

Waldrop, M M (1992) *Complexity: the Emerging Science at the Edge of Order and Chaos* Viking, New York

Walford, N and Hockey, A (1991) *Social and Economic Restructuring in Rural Britain: a Methodology for Contextual Analysis* Countryside Change Initiative Working Paper 18 Department of Agricultural Economics and Food Marketing, University of Newcastle upon Tyne

Ward, N (1994) *Farming on the Treadmill: Agricultural Change and Pesticide Pollution* Unpublished PhD thesis, University College London

Ward, N (1995) 'Technological change and the regulation of pollution from agricultural pesticides', *Geoforum* 26, 19–33

Ward, N, Clark, J, Lowe, P and Seymour, S (1993) *Water Pollution from Agricultural Pesticides* Centre for Rural Economy Research Report, University of Newcastle upon Tyne

Ward, N and Munton, R (1992) 'Conceptualising agriculture–environment relations: combining political economy and socio-cultural approaches to pesticide pollution' *Sociologia Ruralis*, 32, pp 127–145

Ward, S (1994) 'The politics of mutual attraction: UK local government and the Europeanisation of environmental policy', in Gray, T (ed), *UK Environmental Policy in the 1990s* Macmillan, London

Welsh Office (1996) *A Working Countryside for Wales* HMSO, London

Westmacott, R and Worthington, T (1984) *Agricultural Landscapes: a Second Look* Countryside Commission, Cheltenham

Whitby, M C (1991) 'The changing nature of rural land use', in Hanley, N (ed), *Farming in the Countryside: an Economic Analysis of External Costs and Benefits* CAB International, Wallingford

Whitby, M C (1994) *Incentives for Countryside Management: the Case of Environmentally Sensitive Areas*, CAB International, Wallingford

Whitby, M C (1996) *The European Environment and CAP Reform: Polices and Prospects for Conservation*, CAB International, Wallingford

Whitby, M C and Lowe, P D (1994) 'The political and economic roots of environmental policy in agriculture', in Whitby, M C (ed), *Economic Incentives for Countryside Management* CAB International, Wallingford

Whitby, M C and Powe, N (1995) *Recent British Experience of Promoting Rural Development* Rural Realities, Proceedings of the 35th EAAE Seminar, Aberdeen

Whitby, M C and Ray, C (1996) *Rural Land Management Policy Instruments in the UK: a Comparative Inventory* Working Paper, Centre for Rural Economy, Department of Agricultural Economics and Food Marketing, the University of Newcastle upon Tyne

Whitby, M C and Saunders, C M (1996) 'Estimating the supply of conservation goods in Britain' *Land Economics* (to be published August 1996)

White, B and Wadsworth, R (1994) 'A bioeconomic model of heather moorland management and conservation' *Ecological Economics*, 9, pp 167–177

Wight, J B (1985) *The Territory/Function Dialectic: a Social Learning Paradigm of Regional Development Planning* Unpublished PhD thesis, Department of Geography, Aberdeen University

Williams, R (1990) 'Between country and city', in Pugh, S (ed), *Reading Landscape* Manchester University Press, Manchester

Willis, K G and Garrod, G D (1991) 'An individual travel-cost method of evaluating forest recreation' *Journal of Agricultural Economics*, 42, pp 33–42

Willis, K G and Garrod, G D (1993a) 'Valuing landscape: a contingent valuation approach' *Journal of Environmental Management*, 37, pp 1–22

Willis, K G and Garrod, G D (1993b) 'Not from experience: a comparison of experts' opinions and hedonic price estimates of the incremental value of property attributable to an environmental feature' *Journal of Property Research*, 10, pp 193–216

Wilson, G K (1977) *Special Interests and Policy Making* Wiley, London

World Commission on Environment and Development (1987) *Our Common Future* Oxford University Press, Oxford

Index